DISCOVERING CROCKETT'S GALLOWAY

VOLUME ONE

ADVENTURES IN
CROCKETT COUNTRY

Republishing the past

© C.Phillips 2015.

First Published in Great Britain, 2015.

ISBN 978-1-910601-013

Published by Ayton Publishing Ltd
Hillhead of Ardmiddle
Turriff
Aberdeenshire AB53 8AL

www.aytonpublishing.co.uk

All rights reserved. No part of this publication may be reproduced, stored or transmitted in any form or by any means, electronic, mechanical or photocopying, recording or otherwise without the express written permission of the publisher.

2

CONTENTS

I have never been alone in these hills

With thanks especially to George T. Wight, Ros Nolan,
Donny and Douglas Wilcox and Tom and Sheila Laird.
They have all, in various ways, helped me into the hills
and kept me from straying off the paths.

And of course thanks to SRC himself without whom I
would never have ventured forth but who constantly
reminds me that *to resolve is ever easier than to do.*

FOREWORD

It is often said that Galloway is Scotland's best kept secret. In my opinion, S.R.Crockett is Galloway's best kept secret. In this book I hope to unlock, at least in part, both secrets.

It may seem I am treading a well beaten path. While the Galloway hills may be a wild place, those who have visited them do tend to have written about them. I suspect I may be unique amongst those writing guides of the Galloway Hills in that I have not actually been there. From Glentrool car park I have never made it as far as the Gairland Burn. Though it might seem reckless or plain cheeky to write a guide of the Galloway hills in such circumstance, my inability to connect 'for real' with the Galloway hills is the whole reason this book came to be written.

I first came to Galloway twenty years ago. A large part of my life plan at that time was to get out into the natural landscape, but before I got as far as the Gairland Burn I was diagnosed with a chronic health condition that made it brutally clear I would never hill-walk again. From this dark place I found S.R.Crockett. The odd reference to his works in the guide book I had bought, in preparation of my own expeditions, sent me to the local library where I began what has now been a twenty year friendship. I have been held in the grip of a great romancer for nearly half my life now and his hold shows no sign of letting me go.

2014 saw the 100th anniversary of the death of S.R.Crockett and it was a busy year for me, marking the culmination of a debt repaid to a man I've never met. I took it upon myself to republish Crockett's Galloway writings in 32 volumes, to make them accessible to the modern reader. It was an adventure of its own – and like any such endeavour, had I known the difficulty of getting to the destination from the start point, I might not have begun. It was a Herculean task involving the copy-editing of some 3.5 million words. It was a steep learning curve and tested my skills and patience to the limit. After that I needed a holiday. Where better than Galloway and who better for company than Crockett?

The Galloway I set out in search of in the winter of 2014 – 15 is Crockett's Galloway. Indeed, until the area was rebranded as the Galloway Forest Park, it was not unusual for it to be referred to as 'Crockett country.' It includes hills and lochs, bogs and boulders and is a place of breath-taking scenery and even more breath-taking adventure. But Crockett country is also a place of the imagination.

Crockett was a fiction writer and more than that, a romancer, in the old Scots tradition. He takes the reality of the world he lived in and passes it through a magic prism, reflecting back what he sees as what might have been and allowing us all to share in a world which is somehow richer and more real than the one we see around us every day. And yet Crockett's romance is that of the ordinary hill-folk. For me Crockett is less about escapism and more about coming home. I feel at home in his company and in the company of his characters. And while I no longer live in the region, Crockett has taught me that for those who love it, you can leave Galloway but somehow it never really leaves you.

Cally Phillips, February 2015.

INTRODUCTION

What this is and what it isn't

There are guidebooks about Galloway in general and the Galloway Hills specifically. This book is not trying to replicate or compete with any of them. Each have their own strengths (and weaknesses) and their own goals. Many have gone before me, many with a far greater pedigree and a much greater right to write about the places explored in this book. And they have done a fine job of it. I have read many books about Galloway and listed those I found most engaging and useful at the back of this volume.

The uniqueness and direction of *'Discovering Crockett's Galloway,'* such as it is, is represented by the melding of Crockett's stories with the landscape he loved. Even there I'm not breaking new ground but following in his own footsteps. In his 1904 *'Raiderland,'* Crockett tried something new. He referred to it as *'a garrulous literary companion for Galloway lovers and Galloway travellers.'* With the benefit of a century of hindsight, and his complete works at my disposal, I hope I have been able to add something to his concept. But he laid my trail.

Any editor mediates a writer and in *'Discovering Crockett's Galloway'* I am mediating both Crockett and

11

Galloway for a 21st century readership. I hope through this series of books the modern reader will find (among other things) a way 'into' Crockett's writing as surely as they may find a way 'into' Galloway itself.

Fiction and reality

We may uncover the secret, but there is always going to be an air of mystery about Crockett's places, as there is about the man himself. We have reached the point in time where there is no direct connection. No one now living has met him in person. So we are always creating him; he will always be a fiction to us. The places in his stories, revealed in this book, are fictions, born out of the romance tradition, but they are based also on his own personal experience and observations. They are, as Stevenson noted, *'drowned in Galloway.'*

I set off into the hills in search of adventure, with no fixed path or goal. I imagined it would be lonely at times but I have never been alone in the company of Crockett, his characters, and a plethora of guides both real and imaginary. Along the way I discovered something quite unexpected about the connections between fiction and reality. I also learned that in some sense each one of us becomes part of someone else when we travel together. The best analogy I can offer for this is the quantum one. In some way, by reading Crockett you 'create' Crockett, just as surely as he is busy creating the characters you are reading. The reader and the writer meet in a deep way. This is the case whether you are simply reading fictional stories or whether you are engaged in the art of literary criticism. The observer positions the object. The reader in a sense 'makes' the writer. To read this book is to set out on a shared experience, even if you are alone in your armchair.

If it is facts you are after, the facts are that Crockett knew the Galloway hills well. He certainly roamed the Rhinns of Kells during his childhood and as research for *'The Raiders,' 'Mad Sir Uchtred'* and *'The Men of the Moss Hags,'* (his first novels to feature the Dungeon Hills extensively) he took guided trips into the heart of the Dungeon in the company, among others, of John McMillan, farmer of Glenhead of Trool.

While we are in the world of fact, I must point out that there are many vagaries of spelling to be found through this book. Place names are given different spellings in different contexts and most obviously the consistency of the appellation Mac is lacking. This is not from laziness on anyone's part, it is indicative of the mutability of language. For example the name MacMillan can be MacMillan, McMillan or M'Millan. There was no standardisation in Crockett's day and the M' indicates a closer tie, in the sense that the French use vous and tu.

13

I would caution the reader (or walker) when they think they have found a 'mistake' either in the book or the description, not to be too quick to jump to conclusions. Keep the spirit of adventure alive, look deeper and you will like as not find an explanation for the strangeness.

And who exactly was Samuel Rutherford Crockett?
If you know nothing of Crockett, there is a brief biography of his life at the back of this book. If you've heard of him only in the context of *'The Raiders,'* I'm here to tell you there is much, much more for you to discover. Reducing Crockett to author of *'The Raiders,'* is like stating that Shakespeare wrote *'Timon of Athens'* and expecting that to carry the weight of his genius. It is now possible to discover, or re-discover, much of Crockett's extensive catalogue and I hope that this book will offer an insight and inspire the reader to go and find out more about him for themselves.

Armchair adventurers
Most people (even those who read Crockett avidly) will not get into the Galloway Hills 'for real.' But that does not mean we have to be denied the experience. Crockett can take you into the hills. He can show you places and people you could not imagine on your own. If you allow him, he will lead you through history, adventure and

14

romance, breathless and panting over a landscape you may never even have set foot in.

Crockett has many strengths as a writer but the one most universally acknowledged is his mastery of the art of natural description. It is an absolute pleasure for those who love nature and the wild places to go on a trip with Crockett, whether that be from the armchair or by getting out there for real. This book is primarily designed for the armchair adventurer, the person who cannot, for whatever reason, pull on a pair of stout boots and head off into the Dungeon of Buchan, but who wants to have the experience nonetheless. It is to this end that the book does not follow the pattern of a conventional guidebook. Nor does it contain maps.

I could not draw you a good map of our adventures but I have listed both guides and maps which may help you if you want to explore further. If you are lucky, or brave enough to be able to embark on real trips into the hills, you can use this book along with a guidebook to plot your own 'real' adventure. In that case I would advise you to take, along with all the more obvious accoutrements and accessories of a hill walk, a well honed imagination. Because imagination is the key ingredient to finding Crockett's Galloway. I am looking forward to sharing these adventures with you, wherever we may be.

ADVENTURE ONE

THREE STEPS TO HEAVEN

1.RAIDERS AND ROMANCERS

'Galloway is a wide, wild place where the raw edges of creation have not been rubbed down.'

Our first adventure will take us on a journey in space and time. We'll start at Glentrool and end up at Loch Enoch, and there will be murder, mystery and suspense along the way.

We'll be following in the footsteps of Crockett himself, and we'll be keeping company with an assortment of guides and characters. Our travelling companions will include real and fictional guides from the past including Crockett's friend John McMillan who introduced him to many of the places in this adventure. You'll get to meet them as we go, and I hope that, like me, by the time we reach the end you'll think of them as friends.

We'll also be travelling in time from the 1680's to the 1890's and beyond. Anyone who has heard of Crockett has usually heard of *'The Raiders,'* but far fewer are aware that it is the middle story in a loose trilogy which comprises: *'The Raiders,'* its sequel, *'The Dark o' the Moon,'* and prequel, *'Silver Sand.'* On our journey from Glentrool to Loch Enoch we'll become familiar with stories and characters from the whole trilogy, as well as

19

other Crockett novels: *'The Men of the Moss Hags,'* and *'Rose of the Wilderness.'*

The Glentrool area is a good place to start a trip into the Galloway hills, whether you're doing it for real, or as we are, as armchair adventurers. You can park yourself at the Glentrool car park, or in your own armchair. You can have a beverage at the Visitor Centre or from your own kitchen; the choice is yours. You can furnish yourself with maps and the internet, or you can rely on your imagination to lead the way. But if you're ready to start, let's go.

LOCH TROOL TO LOCH VALLEY

'Trool is somehow of a newer creation, and the regularity of its pines tells us that it owes much to the hand of man.'

Crockett gives us a description of Loch Trool in the 19th century: *'Trool lies much like a Perthshire loch, set between the granite and the blue-stone—the whin being upon the southern and the granite upon the northern side. The firs, which clothe the slopes and cluster thick about the shores, give it a beautiful and even cultivated appearance. It has a look more akin to the dwellings of men, and that aggregation of individuals which we call the world.'*

Today you can walk or drive from the visitor centre at the Stroan Bridge end of Loch Trool along the length of the loch to a car park near Bruce's Stone. In *'The Raiders,'* Patrick Heron, May Maxwell and Silver Sand undertake this journey along the Loch on shelties: *'we were steadily moving along the edge of the Loch of Trool. The path was no more than a peat waggon track, and rough beyond the understanding, of southern folk.'*

The path is better than it used to be, and the modern traveller to Glentrool most likely uses a car or a bike. But even on foot it's an easier journey than it was for Crockett's characters.

21

Past Bruce's Stone, at the head of Glentrool, we come across The Buchan, a house currently available for hire to holiday-makers wanting an off grid experience. Here, real walkers go on to the left towards the Gairland Burn. We armchair adventurers can divert to the right instead, and visit Glenhead.

The armchair adventurer has the advantage of being able to travel both in time and space, without ever leaving their seat. And since we won't get tired in the same way as a 'real' walker, we can afford to take a diversion before we begin.

GLENHEAD

'Glenhead, a pleasant place for the wandering vagabond to set his foot upon and rest awhile.'

In the 1890's Glenhead was the home of John and Marion McMillan, with whom Crockett stayed on several sojourns into the Galloway hills. He first met them in August 1893 and they became lifelong friends. Crockett described their first meeting: *'Glenhead I saw for the first time in the broad glare of a mid-noon sun. All the valley swam in a hazy blue mist and the heat smote down from the white lift as through the glass of a hothouse.'*

While Glenhead is a bit out of the way for the real walker, we make our detour to Glenhead of Trool without even breaking sweat. Along the way we can revel, as Crockett did, in the view: *'The firs' shadows in the woods fringing the loch about Eschonquhan are deliciously cool as the swift cycle drives among them. We get but fleeting glimpses of the water till we come out on the rocky cliff shelf, which we follow all the way to the farmhouse of Buchan.'*

Leaving the Buchan, he continues: *'The road gradients along Troolside are steep as the roof of a house. From more than one point on the road the loch lies beneath us so close that it seems as if we could toss a biscuit upon* its placid breast. *The deep narrow glen may be flooded with intense and almost Italian sunshine. But the water lies cool, solid, and intensely indigo at the bottom. Far up the defile we can see Glenhead, lying snug among its trees, with the sleeping giants of the central hills set thick about it. Nor it is not long till, passing rushing burns and heathery slopes on our way, we reach it.'*

Crockett introduces us to a Glenhead full of life and love, as it was over a century ago: *'Heartsome content within, placid stillness without as we ride up—a broad straw hat lying in a friendly way upon the path—the clamour of children's voices somewhere down by the meadow—a couple of dogs that welcome us with a chorus of belated barking—this is Glenhead, a pleasant place for the wandering vagabond to set his foot upon and rest awhile. Then after a time, out of the coolness of the narrow latticed sitting-room (where there is such a collection of good books as makes us think of the nights of winter when the storms rage about the hill-cinctured farm), we step, lightly following, with many expectations, the slow, calm, steady shepherd's stride of our friend—the master of all these fastnesses—as he paces upwards to guide us over his beloved hills.'*

Glenhead (also known as Bongill) had been tenanted by the McMillan family for centuries and served as a base for Crockett on several trips into the hills with

24

John McMillan, undertaking research for *'The Raiders,'* and *'The Men of the Moss Hags.'* Several chapters of *'The Raiders'* were written at Glenhead in 1893, though the majority of the novel is believed to have been written at Laurieston before its final publication on March 10th 1894 by T.Fisher Unwin. The first edition sold out on the day of publication and a second edition was being advertised by 17th March!

Chapters of *'The Men of the Moss Hags'* were also written at Glenhead. It came out as a serialised story in *'Good Words'* magazine in 1895 before being published as a novel by Isbister & Co. Crockett wrote for several different publishers during his long career and many, if not most of his works, were written episodically for the periodical market before being published as novels. We'll find out more about this later in our journey.

Crockett also wrote non-fiction articles for magazines. In his 1894 article *'Galloway Fastnesses,'* in the magazine *'The Leisure Hour,'* he pays homage to John McMillan's knowledge of the local area, naming him 'the guide' and portrays a beautiful picture of the surrounding area: *'Waterfalls are gleaming in the clefts— 'jaws of water,' as the hill folks call them—the distant sound coming to us pleasant and cool, for we begin to desire great water-draughts, climbing upwards in the fervent heat. But our guide knows every spring of water*

*on the hillside, as well as every rock that has sheltered
fox or eagle. There, on the face of that cliff, is the
apparently very accessible eyrie where nested the last of
the Eagles of the southern uplands.*

*Year after year they built up there, protected by the
enlightened tenants of Glenhead, who did not grudge a
stray dead lamb, in order that the noble bird might dwell
in his ancient fastnesses and possess his soul—for surely
so noble a bird has a soul—in peace. As a reward for his
hospitality, our guide keeps a better understanding of that
great Isaian text, 'They shall mount up with wings as
eagles,' than he could obtain from any sermon or
commentary in the round world.*

*For has he not seen the great bird strike a grouse on
the wing, recover itself from the blow, then, stooping
earthwards, catch the dead bird before it had time to fall
to the ground? Also he has seen the pair floating far up in
the blue, twin specks against the supreme azure.*

*Generally only one of the young was reared to
eaglehood, though sometimes there might be two. But on
every occasion the old ones beat off their offspring as soon
as these could fly, and compelled their children to seek
pastures new. Some years ago, however—in the later
seventies—the eagles left Glenhead and removed to a
more inaccessible rock-crevice upon the rocky side of the
Back Hill o' Buchan. But not for long. Disturbed in his*

26

ancient seat, though his friends had done all in their power to protect him, he finally withdrew himself.

His mate was shot by some ignorant scoundrel prowling with a gun, somewhere over in the neighbourhood of Loch Doon. We have no doubt that the carcass is the proud possession of some local collector, to whom, as well as to the original 'gunning idiot,' we would gladly present, at our own expense, tight-fitting suits of tar and feather.'

Sadly, some things do not change with time. While he loved Glenhead, it is not portrayed as a rural idyll. Crockett knew Galloway too well for that. He points out: *'Yet I have been in Glenhead during those winter days when for six weeks the sun does not touch its highest chimney-top, so deep the little granite house sits under the giant hills about it—Bennanbrack, Curlywee, Lamachan, and its own Gairy shouldering up close behind it.'*

We'll come across many of these places in later adventures – there is so much to discover in Galloway, so many stories to tell. We have to pace ourselves.

Crockett clearly loved the peace and solitude of Glenhead but it was the people who meant most to him. His gratitude to John McMillan was profound, and in the preface to the 1895 *'The Men of the Moss Hags,'* he wrote: *'I am indebted to my friend, Mr. John McMillan of Glenhead in Galloway, who has not only given me in this,*

27

as in former works, the benefit of his unrivalled local knowledge, but has travelled with me many a weary foot over those moors and moss-hags, where the wanderers of another time had their abiding places. Let him accept this word of thanks. He is not likely to forget our stay together in the wilds of Cove Macaterick. Nor I our journey home.'

It is obvious that Crockett based some of his fictional adventures on the real ones he shared out on the hills with John McMillan. We can only speculate on which parts are true and which are fiction. But we can share in these adventures too. To spend time in the company of these men and women, real and fictional, all that's required of us is to read with imagination.

While Glenhead is unrecognisable today from the place Crockett describes, in the ten years between his article *'Galloway Fastnesses'* and his 1904 *'Raiderland,'* we see that time has not changed his feelings or ability to describe a place and people he held in his heart with great affection: *'Differing from all the other farms, at Glenhead everything is 'black-faced sheep.' Their ways, their care, their difficulties from season to season, their strange simplicity, their yet stranger outbreaks of unexpected wisdom—the latter chiefly among the ladies of the flock, those mothers in Israel, 'naw-breakers' by name, who charge some stubborn snow-wreath, and so lead out their juniors to safety, and new if scanty pastures.*

28

Especially in 'lambing-time' all here gives way to 'the yowes.' The ailments of a mere human are nothing to those of a ewe 'fa'en aval.' The mistress herself establishes hospitals and orphanages, and becomes at once house-surgeon, hospital dresser, and an entire staff of nurses.

Beneath the house are winding ribbons of meadow grass following the meanderings of a stream. Enclosed by a wall behind you will find a 'park' or two. A tennis-lawn of corn waves green in the hollow, a forenoon's work to cut for an able-bodied man. Beneath remote Clashdaan, away on the shores of Loch Dee, you will find another triangle of meadow grass, the produce carefully ricked and carried up beyond floodmark. Then behind these the farm rolls back mile after mile. The number of its acres none knows to a hundred or so, all hills of sheep—nothing but black-faced sheep, unless you may count a random fox marauding from Bennanbrack, or a rabbit cocking his white fud over a brae.

Heather and rock, loch and lochan, islet and bare granite peak! So it goes on mile after mile, growing ever more and more lonely and remote, till above Utmost Enoch you look out upon a land like that where never man comes

'Nor hath come, since the making of the world.'

This is the true Raiders' Country.'

Crockett prepares us for the adventure we are about to take, reminding us of the difficulty and distance involved: *'Yet even from Glenhead you must go six long Scots miles to set your eyes on Enoch and the Dungeon of Buchan, to look down the great chasm swimming with vapour, and see the three Lochs of the Dungeon lie like pale steel puddles far beneath, with the green and treacherous links of the Cooran winding past them through the morass.*

It is indeed a far cry! But on the way you will pass Cameron's Grave—not him of Ayr's Moss, the Lion of the Covenant, but a simpler wayfarer—packman or what not, gone astray in the storm and found dead by the shepherds in that still and lonely place.'

Sometimes, like all adventurers, he finds it hard to set out. He's so happy where he is: *'But I will tell further of these things when we take pilgrim staff and invade the last fastnesses of Hector Faa in the wake of Patrick Heron and May Mischief. It is of the farm that I would speak, and, in a single word, of the good folk who dwell therein.*

'Dwell,'—aye, there is the difference. At my other typical farms all is changed. Scarce stands the very stone and lime where it did.

But at Glenhead these my dear and worthy friends still hold the door open and cast the eyes of contented happiness upon the beautiful things about them. May their meal-ark be ever full to the brim—from their baulks may

30

the bacon flitch depend, and the ham of yet more delicious mutton. Oaten farles— I think of you and my teeth water— not cakes of Paradise so toothsome to men coming in sharpset off the muir. The God of the hills, to which you have so long time lifted your eyes, be your ward and your reward. John M'Millan and Marion his wife, I, unforgetting, send you this greeting across mountains and seas and the remorseless lapse of years.'

As we've seen, Glenhead was Crockett's base for some of his own adventures and it also finds a place in his fiction. So before we set out for the hills in earnest, let's see how it features in 'Men of the Moss Hags.' You'll remember of course that Glenhead was also known historically as Bongill.

The King's Men, in search of Covenanters, have heard of Macmillan and head off to find him: 'Douglas's refreshment had made him more easy to deal with.

'Nevertheless,' he continued, 'fettle on your blue bonnet and put us on the road to Bongill, at the loch-head. For there is a great Whigamore there of the name of Macmillan and he will no' get aff so easy. I warrant his Bible is well-thumbed!'

...Sandy Gillespie, canny man, tried to dissuade him from going to Bongill that night. Which only made Douglas the more determined, thinking there was something or some-body that he might light on there, and so get great

31

credit to himself...

...'And there's Bongill,' cried Sandy, suddenly stopping and dropping off his horse, 'an' guid e'en to ye!'

And with that the old fellow slid off among the brush-wood and copse, and we saw no more of him—which perhaps was as well for him...'

But by the time they arrive, the stable, so to speak, is bare and the Covenanters have taken to the hills. *'...When we went into the little house of Bongill, we found an open door both back and front. Peats were blazing on the hearth. Great dishes of porridge sat on a table. Chairs and stools were overturned, and Bibles and Testaments lay everywhere.*

'Curse the old dog. He has sung them a' to the hill,' cried Douglas. 'Have him out and shoot him.'...

...So the night being pit mirk and the hill unknown, we took up our abode at Bongill till the morning.'

Crockett is unusual in Scottish fiction, in that he wrote of Covenanters from a sympathetic perspective. During our adventure into the hills we'll encounter several of them. They hid in Galloway's caves and hills when they were 'put to the horn' (outlawed) by the crown during what became known as 'The Killing Times' of the late 17th century.

In the same way that the Highlands claims the Jacobites, you cannot separate the history of Galloway from the history of the Covenanters, and whatever your historic/political/religious leanings are, you should not try. One of the great joys of reading Crockett is learning about things which have been overlooked (some might say air-brushed) out of our general knowledge and cultural understanding of our Scottish past. Crockett is a romancer yes, but he grew up in Galloway, its history was his own history and he raided that history time and again for his adventure romances. We are the lucky benefactors of these raids.

While your heart may thrill most to the adventure of 'The Killing Times,' Glenhead gets another mention in Crockett's novel *'Rose of the Wilderness,'* set in the doucer years of the 19th century. Rose Gordon, the novel's heroine, tells of the remoteness of her family home and how her father had to rear her as a baby after the death of her mother: *'I had cow's milk fetched from the Macmillans' house at Bongill - a good ten miles. But father fell lame, and could not do the daily double journey, though he held out a long while.'*

One of the things Crockett reveals time and again in his fiction is that 'times change men.' But we do well to remember that time changes places too. What we see when we stand at Glenhead might seem rurally idyllic but life in the Galloway hills was never easy for those hardy folk who lived there. It still isn't.

Glenhead was tenanted for centuries, right through until the 1990's. It was then brought under the management of the Forestry Commission. Currently uninhabited, sadly neglected and essentially derelict, we can only hope it is saved from demolition and brought back into functional use.

Whether it is once more restored to a family home, a working tenanted farm or re-purposed as something considered more appropriate to modern needs, it is a building of cultural and historical significance and deserves a better future than its recent past. It currently serves to remind us of the fragility of rural life and the rural past. I hope that one day soon its hearth will again burn brightly, though I'm not hugely optimistic. There are so many places like this which have vanished into history and become no more real than fiction. But we have to leave Glenhead now. Time to strike out.

GLENTROOL

'The Glen of Trool was dark and narrow as we went down into it along the waterside, and the loch itself lay black as night at the bottom of its precipices. It might have been the mouth of the pit of blackness itself.'

Leaving Glenhead behind, as we set out into the Galloway Hills from Glentrool, we are following in the footsteps of cattle reivers both real and fictional. I promised you that we'd share our journey with characters real and fictional, so let's travel for a while in the company of Sammle Tamson and Patrick Heron from *'The Raiders.'*

Sammle has no doubt about the easiest route into the hills: *'The cattle reivers would certainly, he said, take the easiest road, and slowly find a track by the Loch Dee and Loch Trool, past Glenhead, and up the narrow defile of the Gairland Burn, into that tangle of lochs and mountains under the brow of Merrick, which formed their robbers' fastness. There would be better grazing by the loch shores than anywhere else, though indeed the Faas never wanted for fodder so long as there were hay crops on the Cree water or corn in the Glenkens. It was easy work taking down a bevy of horses and bringing up a supply—easier than cutting and winning the meadow hay upon their own sparse waterside.'*

There are various routes into the Galloway hills and the reivers' way is only easy in terms of relativity, but it's the way we're following for now. We'll take other options in later adventures. Please be warned that even on this easy option there's a more than average chance of getting wet feet.

The first challenge we face is the Gairland Burn. The route is a familiar one not only to fictional guides. Writing in his *'Galloway Hills'* from the 1930's, McCormick follows a route along the side of the Gairland Burn. Other guides find their own distinct paths into the hills but all that I've met take us along the left side of the Gairland Burn, crossing it at a little island. Today, there is a style to cross and a wall to follow which eventually leads across a bracken covered slope and ends up running parallel to the Gairland Burn. A hundred yards further on and we arrive at Loch Valley. A mere hundred yards? How much adventure can we have? The answer is - plenty.

Today the Burn itself may not look much of a barrier, but let Patrick Heron share his experience of it in wilder mode in an episode called 'The Breaking of the Barrier.' He is with the Maxwells, who intend revenge upon the Raiders who kidnapped May Maxwell, the heroine of *'The Raiders'* and stole their belongings. Even from the armchair, you may need to take a moment to feel prepared for what follows! *'We were soon deep among the hills, and yet not a shot had been fired at us. Not a dry red bracken had waved. The rime lay close and thick, and the brown heather kept the feet quiet. Only a scabbard rang now and then on a jutting point of granite, or a nail in some brogan screamed stridently against a stone, harsh and slippery with frost. No whaup or peewit cried. Only on a rock high on the Clints of the Nether Hill of Buchan, a black corbie croaked his dismal anticipative song.*

It was not cheering, all this, yet I felt some real elevation to think that we were soon to come to grips.

We were just at the corner of the burn where, under a great black face of rock it is hemmed in a deep defile, when our scouts on the hillside set up a great crying, the cause of which we could not at the time understand.

'Come up!' they cried. 'The water's broken lowse!'

Our herd guide and I took the hill at once, and so did many who were acquainted with the wild lochs and precipices about us, and with the nature of the wilder men whose lives were forfeit to the law.

Suddenly we heard before and above us a tremendous roaring noise, as though the bowels of creation were gushing out in some great convulsion. The hills gave back the echoes on every side. I found myself climbing the brae with some considerable verve and activity till I was fairly among the higher rocks...

...The great roaring noise still continued. Indeed the whole of the foregoing since I took the hill passed in a brief tale of seconds. Suddenly we that were up on the side of the Gairy saw a wondrous sight. A great wall of water, glassy black, tinged at the top with brown and crowned with a surging crest of white with many dancing overlapping folds, sped down the glen. Our array was pent in the narrow passage—all those, that is, who had not taken the hill at the first alarm. As the wave came down upon them there was the wildest confusion. Men threw away their guns and took blindly to the hillside, running upward like rabbits that have been feeding in a bottom of old grass. From where we stood the water seemed to travel with great deliberation, but nevertheless not a few of our men were caught in the wash of it and spun downwards like corks in the inrush of the Solway tide.

The black, white-crested wave being passed, the great flood ran red again in a moment, with only a creamy froth over it, and we could hear the boulders grinding and plunging at the bottom of the burn.

Then upon us, scattered as we were in confusion over the brae face, there broke a storm of bullets from behind the rocks higher up the Gairy. It was the first sign of the enemy we had found, and we resented it

38

exceedingly.

A strange sense of the unfairness of the proceeding took hold of me. We had come prepared to give battle and to deliver an assault; but we wanted to do it in our own way and on our own terms. We felt that it was most perfidious (indeed unfair and scoundrelly) thus to scatter us over a great area of ground, and then have at us when we were least prepared.

But Will Maxwell had some of the spirit of a general. Standing on a rock, he sounded his pipe, calling all down from the bare hillside, where each man was a mark for the guns of the outlaws into the closer cover of the burnside, thick sown with boulders. The flood was still running, but was evidently past its strength. The great roaring sped farther and farther down the valley. We gathered off the hill, running like foxes about the stones, and taking advantage of the chance cover as we went. Bullets spatted uncomfortably among the rocks, but the fire of the hill men was not good, and the light was becoming uncertain, so that very few of our men were wounded.

As soon as he had us all collected in the valley, our captain began moving in loose skirmishing formation along the side of the burn towards the loch. The outlaws above us also kept parallel with our march, shots cracked, and on the hillside there was a noise of cheering. But we held on our way, and so far no one was seriously hurt, which *showed that the aim of the enemy had been bad. But we knew not if our own were much better.'*

This pulse racing description reveals the skill of the romancer; taking reality and moulding it into an exciting fiction. Because the story is based on a true event, albeit one which happened a lot later. A timber dam and sluice was built across Loch Valley by a sporting tenant in the 19th century, but after heavy rain the dam burst, sending water and a huge boulder rushing down the valley. Crockett is, after all, himself a raider and he raids from history to suit his own purposes. Time, we should recall, is relative. In fact and fiction.

Anyone walking along the Gairland Burn today is sure of a much quieter time, whatever the season. But using your imagination, which some find easier from the armchair, just look up the steep sided gully and think back to more adventurous times. Recall Crockett's description and you can just about hear the water – and the men shouting. We are transported to the land of reivers. And we quickly discover it's a wild place even on a calm day.

We should remember as we walk, that the Galloway Hills of days gone by were a home not just to shepherds and tenant farmers or a retreat for Covenanters. They were also the abode of gypsies and smugglers as well as the reivers we've already encountered. Like Covenanting, smuggling is inextricably tied up with Galloway. It was not just an activity confined to the coast (although we'll see plenty of that in Volume 2 of *'Discovering Crockett's Galloway.'*)

While the hills are some distance from the coast, contraband has to be transported and the Galloway hills provided a route relatively safe from the tax men. Crockett wrote about smuggling many times, charting its history across the centuries. Indeed it's a trade which nearly everyone seemed to take some part in throughout the history of Galloway, right up to Crockett's own day. Unlikely as it sounds, even ministers and dominies were often implicated.

So, having cleared the Gairland Burn, let's pause a while to take stock before we arrive at Loch Valley. It's a mere hundred yards ahead but that gives us plenty of time to listen to the somewhat pedantic Nathan Crogo, fictional editor/narrator of *'Silver Sand,'* as he tells us of his own complicity in the Gentle Trade: *'I have hitherto said little about myself, and with reason. For he who is the true author of this book has mostly been permitted to speak and shall be again. But, seeing that on the first page, I re-vindicated the responsibility for everything that appears betwixt cover and cover, it is meet that I should inform the world concerning myself—at least in so far that the reader may know in whom he is trusting.*

I set it not down to praise myself up, living the life of a recluse and having no need of testimonials, but I may say—nay, it behoves me to put on record, that one who has had so long the confidence of Sir Andrew Agnew and his son James, a session clerk for nigh upon forty years, is, and must be, a man well kenned for sobriety and discretion.

I was not, and I am not now, any party man, and I admit that many look 'cross their noses' at me because I took whatever Tests, Oaths, Affirmations, and such like just as they were demanded of me. What a man of official trust is compelled to do by 'the major force' is not his doing, but the King's. I could not have brought up the bairns of Leswalt and Port Patrick unless I had been supple with my tongue and pen. I could not have continued session clerk under Bishop Sydserf and saved many score of honest folk from persecution. I could not have clerked at the courts both military and civil, made out warrants, and then sent on warnings ahead so that when they arrived, the dragoons might find a toom nest and a bird flown, if I had not done as the great apostle of the Gentiles bade, and made myself all things to all men.

In all this I acted wisely and prudently, not only for myself (which mattered little) but above all, for my neighbours.

For one thing I could go about at all hours, and so

42

saved many a man from facing a firing party. I had only to give a cry in to the curate at the manse on some pretext of a theological difficulty to be solved, or a book to be lent or returned. There I got my information, and so, a little later, did the threatened family.

Furthermore, I was friends with the lads on the muirs who made the potheen, the secret of which had been brought back as a precious gift by the godly exiles who had been sent to Ireland—as indeed was only just, for these good men, expelled from their parishes in the black year 1662, spent a great part of their lives preaching and praying in Ireland, without fee or reward, save and except the knowledge of how to make the potheen.

So as I say I knew the bulk of these free distillers of the hills and northern moors as far as Pinwherry and the Gairland. Also I made it my business to stand well with the revenue men whom King Charles of unhappy memory sent among us. (They were mostly called 'Plunder Jacks,' 'Bore-a-Hole Jenkins,' and other more opprobrious names, and were generally much despised by the people). Indeed they were glad enough to talk to one like myself, who made them free of my larder and my pleasant conversation. So I not only got early notice of their intended seizures, but was kept well supplied with cognac and French wines taken from the smugglers. So I was enabled to do without danger to myself a great many good *turns to vast numbers of poor folk who would otherwise had been despoiled, not only of the fruits of their labours, but of the little drop of comfort which, with a squeeze of lemon, sent them cantily and soberly to their beds, at peace with their neighbours and, I hope, with their Maker.'*

Nathan Crogo reminds us about the role seemingly insignificant people take in history, while in the process illustrating Crockett's great skill in placing ordinary people at the heart of his romances. With his talk of *'party men* and *major forces,'* we are left under no illusion that a *'suppleness of tongue'* is a thing of value and necessity in Galloway of old.

'Silver Sand' was Crockett's last novel, and in Nathan Crogo we might see Crockett himself lurking as narrator. Crockett loved to play with narrative voice and Nathan's style is redolent with Crockett's trademark self-deprecating 'Scots' humour. He is wordy, he is long-winded, but he's entertaining all the same. Crockett is a writer of depth. In his company you experience the dancing of water on the shimmering surface of a burn, but he can also take you to the depths of Loch Enoch – and beyond. All you need is an open mind and a good imagination.

If nothing else, Nathan's admission serves to remind us that even the most douce of folk have hidden depths. And that's a thing worth applying to the landscape of the Galloway Hills as well. Whatever the weather, you need to watch your step. The Gairland Burn may be inconsequential as you pass it, but there is much more water to come, and it is not always restricted by the banks of the hill lochs. It is everywhere. Time to press on.

LOCH VALLEY

'It takes a Napoleon of engineering to fool with Loch Valley.'

At this stage we hook up with another guide from the 1930's. In his *'The Merrick and Neighbouring Hills,'* John McBain, a man who always strikes me as more interested in facts and figures than fiction, tells us that Loch Valley's water is pure and clear: *'its shores are composed of boulders embedded in a sub-stratum of white sand and gravel.'* He also records that *'it is the only upland loch that has trees growing on its margin,'* which he numbers at around a hundred. While this sets something of a picture and while McBain is a reliable enough guide, especially for those who exclusively walk the path of reality, somehow for me he lacks the romance of Crockett.

See what you think as Crockett sets the scene for us in his non-fiction *'Galloway Fastnesses'* piece: *'Loch Valley and Loch Neldricken form, with the twin lochs of Glenhead, a water system of their own, connected with Glen Trool by the rapid torrential burn called the Gairlin, that flashes downward through the narrow ravine which we leave behind us to our left as we go upward.*

At the beginning of the burn, where it escapes from Loch Valley, are to be seen the remains of a weir which

46

was erected in order to raise artificially the level of the loch, submerging in the process most of the shining beaches of silver granite sand. But the loch was too strong for the puny works of man. One fine day, warm and sunny, our guide tells us that he was working with his sheep high up on the hill, when the roar and rattle of great stones carried along by the water brought him down the 'screes' at a run. Loch Valley had broken loose. The weir was no more, and the Gairlin burn was coming down in a ten-foot breast, creamy foam cresting it like an ocean wave. Down the glen it went like a miniature Johnstown disaster, while the boulders crashed and ground together with the rush of the water. When Loch Valley was again seen, it had resumed its pristine aspect—that which it had worn since the viscous granite paste finished oozing out in sheets from the great cracks in the Silurian rocks, and the glaciers had done their work of grinding down its spurs and outliers. It takes a Napoleon of engineering to fool with Loch Valley.'

You'll notice that once more Crockett gives us a version of the story of 'The Bursting of the Dam.' Crockett frequently adds a sense of romance even to his non-fiction descriptions, but let loose in the realms of fiction in *'The Raiders,'* through the character of Patrick Heron, he excels himself, offering us something much more than we could ever see in stark reality: *'When we*

47

came to the southern side of Loch Valley, whence the Gairland Burn issues, we saw a strange and surprising sight. There was a deep trench, the upper part of which had been cut through recently by the hands of man, for the rubbish lay all about where the spades had been at work. The ends of a weir across the outlet of the loch were yet to be seen jutting into the rushing waters. This had evidently been constructed with considerable care and certainly with immense labour. But now it was cut clean through, and we could see where their sappers had first set their picks; the power of the flood had done the rest. So great had been the force of the water that the passage was clean cut as with a knife down to the bed rock. The deep knoll of sand and jingling stones, which lies like a barrier across the mouth of the loch, had been severed as one cuts sweet-milk cheese, and the black waters were yet pouring out from under the arch of ice that spanned the loch as out of a cave in some frozen Tartarus.

But as we looked over the black and glistering expanse of hollow ice which swept away to our left, bright cracks began to play like forked lightning across its whole surface. The water had been sucked from beneath it, and it held up only by its own weight. The hills echoed the deep-voiced roaring as the cracks and rendings ran across and across. Gradually the play of this flashing and thundering turmoil centred at a point beneath our eyes,

48

and fair in the middle of the loch. An intensely black spot began to yawn there, from which the white, roaring cracks rayed out like the spokes of a wheel from the hub. On the edge of the loch we stood as it were on the rim of a whirlpool, for the ice sloped down from our feet every way into the black centre. Had any one set foot upon the verge of it they had been carried down to the yawning hole, for the entire ice of the loch was giving way as the roof of a great cavern slopes and sways before it falls in.

Then with a crash that shook the ground the ice cave fell in upon the water in a thousand pieces, sending the white foam mixed with dark lumps of ice high into the air, while underneath the broken fragments tumbled and crunched against one another like bergs in a heavy sea (such as I have heard the whalers tell of). Then little by little, groaning and wheezing, the turmoil settled down; and Loch Valley, with its shivered covering of broken ice, went to sleep ten feet beneath its level of the morning.

Hardly elsewhere in Scotland had such a thing been possible; but the outlaws took advantage of the higher barrier of sand and shingle which had so long dammed back the waters of the deep rock-bound lake. It was a true stroke of generalship, and showed us that we had others than ignorant red-handed Marshalls and bloody Macatericks to deal with. It was so well thought on that it did not seem like the rough-and-ready knife-and-bullet *method of the common catheran.*

And, indeed, nothing more calculated to shake one's nerve could well be conceived.'

However accurate guides like McBain may be, personally I would rather ascend to Loch Valley in the company of Crockett and his characters. Crockett can turn a walk into an adventure and it is adventure I am after, even from the armchair.

Loch Valley also features in *'Silver Sand,'* this time seen from the perspective of another young man, John Faa (aka Silver Sand). *'The Raiders'* and its sequel *'The Dark o' the Moon,'* show us Silver Sand as an old retainer. Central to *'Silver Sand'* are the adventures of his youth, including how he got his nick name.

Before we move on from Loch Valley, let's join him on his way back from delivering food to men in hiding during 'the Killing Times.'

As a child, Crockett's favourite game was Covenanters and King's Men, so it must have been a great pleasure for him as an adult to commit such deadly 'games' to paper. Stay awhile and watch as the young John Faa is intercepted and captured by the red coated King's Men: *'It was the greying of the afternoon when they came over the rig of the Loch Valley, following the white curves of the Gairland Burn. Silver Sand was on his way back from carrying provisions to a cave on the south-*

looking face of the Merrick where Barbour of the Brae and Semple of Rig were in special hiding. They were being sought for everywhere, because the death of the Curate of Carsephairn was (quite erroneously) laid to their charge.

Silver Sand was spied so near their cave mouth that he could not slip back without revealing their whereabouts. At the worst, he said to himself, I have a better chance than they. So he pushed straight on to where Morton was riding at the head of his troop, and saluted with his plumed hat sweeping the heather.

Morton, a rough tyke enough, shaggy as a Scaur Water collie, looked him up and down. He took in the details of the costume. The French clothes of the newest and finest material, braided by Tailor Byron after the pattern of my Lord's in which he went to London, might be a little out of date to a city eye, accustomed to the coffee-houses, but they were of a marvellous freshness on the side of the Merrick.

'Who may you be? Stand and give an account of yourself to His Majesty's officer.' Morton's voice was not quite so loud as usual. He was a little anxious to know with whom he had to do.

'My name is John Percy Faa,' said Silver Sand. 'I am here on the business of my people. I am an Earl of this kingdom of Scotland by the creation of James the First, and a cousin of his Grace the Duke of Northumberland,

51

whose name I bear.'

'I tell you, sir, you may be all you say, and yet you fall under my jurisdiction. Will you take the Test?'

'As often as you like,' said Silver Sand. 'I was bred of the King's religion.'

'A lie—a lie—!' cried a little foxy man running up from the rear of the column, fumbling all the while with his side wallet of notary's leather. 'I have his name, notification, and description. This is none other than John Faa the gipsy, attainted with the death of Ellerton and Kidney, art and part with the Prophet Peden, and the very man who snatched Sir Andrew Agnew out of our hands and set him on the high seas!''

John Faa is both a gypsy and chief of an ancient dynasty. As a character he reflects the duality in the very psyche of Scotland. Many Scots writers have focussed on duality as a theme and Crockett explores this time and again in his fiction. He is always keen to remind us that there are other ways than those fed to us by our leaders. For Crockett (and his characters), honour and loyalty, trust and royalty are big issues; but they are also personal issues which each man (and woman) must wrestle with individually.

Rarely are things what they first seem in a Crockett novel. Throughout the Raiders Trilogy there is much mystery and much of it revolves around the character of

Silver Sand. Trust is difficult to maintain in the face of the mysterious, and both Patrick Heron and his son Maxwell have equal cause to trust and mistrust Silver Sand in their stories. But it is in the novel which bears his name where we find out most about the man.

As a character he owes much to the legendary figure of Aiken Drum and to Nicholson and Hogg's versions of the Brownie of Bodsbeck. While reminiscent of these, still Crockett's creation of John Faa/Silver Sand is all his own. He adds something to the archetype, giving us an individuality in the character of Silver Sand which allows us much pause for thought – and it has to be said – much enjoyment.

But we can't hang round Loch Valley all day. It's time to move on. With Crockett, we can take a look around to make sure we are not in danger from either rushing water or blood-thirsty King's men in hot pursuit. This is what we see: *'Behind us, as we rise upwards into the realms of blue, are the heights of Lamachan and Bennanbrack. Past the side of Curleywee it is possible to look into the great chasm of air in which, unseen and far beneath us, lies Loch Dee.'*

We'll come to these places and their adventures in due course, but for now just enjoy them for a brief moment in the distance. Crockett is ready to guide us on our way: *'We gain the top of the high boulder-strewn ridge.*

53

Fantastic shapes, carved out of the gleaming grey granite, are all about. Those on the ridges against the sky look for all the world like polar-bears with their long lean noses thrust forward to scent the seals on the floes or the salmon running up the Arctic rapids to spawn. To our right, above Loch Valley, is a boulder which is so poised that it constitutes a 'logan' or rocking-stone. It is so delicately set as to be moved by the blowing of the wind.

From this point we keep to the right, passing the huge moraine which guards the end of the loch and effectually prevents a still greater flood than that which our master shepherd witnessed. These mounds are full of what are called in the neighbourhood 'jingling stones.' Without doubt they consist of sand and shingle, so riddled with great boulders that the crevices within are constantly being filled up and forming anew as the sand shifts and sifts among the stones. As we proceed the sun is shining over the shoulder of the Merrick, and we are bound to hasten, for there is yet far to go.'

Crockett reminds us that the ground is uneven and treacherous, and it's often wet; stout footwear is a prerequisite for any trip into the Galloway Hills at any time of year. Burns (also called 'lanes' in Galloway) and boulders are everywhere – most usually running or standing between where you are and where you want to go!

54

As we skirt the west shore of Loch Valley with Crockett we move north-eastwards through boggy ground and come to an old sheepfold by Mid Burn: *'We have crossed the Midburn near the old sheep rees, and it is lucky for us if we have managed the transit without wetting our feet. For the Midburn is an unruly stream and often comes raging down, uncontrollable as the Gairland itself. The sheep rees, where for defence the assailants of the raider Faas are said to have sheltered, are indeed 'solidly built of great granite stones like a fortress, based upon the unshaken ribs of the hills.''*

A sheep-ree is a sheltering place for sheep, out on the hills. And sometimes it shelters more than sheep. It is pressed into service a couple of times in *'The Raiders.'* The first is when Silver Sand carries an injured Patrick down from the hills: *'Silver Sand pointed it out.*

'Had the worst come to the worst,' he said, 'we micht hae focht that place again' a dozen Macatericks.'

We saw it only dimly through the starlight, so we could not remark the great stones of which it was built, set firm and solid upon a breastwork of the ancientest rocks of the world. But my heart was no more for fighting. There was a smell of blood in my nostrils, and the broad of that poor fellow's back stuck yonder in the sea-chest, lay heavy on my mind. I could not rid myself of it.

Then away we went again, Silver Sand, though both

twisted and slender, almost carrying me in his arms, and May Maxwell, saying the while no word, but helping even more than he. We were soon at the spur of Loch Valley, and heard the crunching of the granite sand along its margin underfoot. It was precious to the feet after the miles of heather.

The Loch chafed behind us, crisping white on the shore. It seemed to run an incredible way eastward, clapping against the ledges of its rocky basin, while the little waves seemed to applaud our haste. And, indeed, we strove to deserve those soft-palmed plaudits...'

The second time Patrick comes to the Midburn sheep-ree he is *'mustered into Will Maxwell's company,'* though his heart still seems somewhat reluctant to fight. He goes along to take on the Raiders on a *'cold, dim, raw day with a thick yellow haze in the air and grim grip of the black frost underfoot...'*

Arriving at the sheep-ree, they use it as a shelter before the fight... *'as the darkness settled deeper, we drew down to the old sheep rees by the Midburn, which are solidly built of great granite stones like a fortress, based upon the unshaken ribs of the hills.*

There was room for us all here. By nature the place was strongly protected—on the one side by the roaring and dangerous Midburn, and on the other it is fenced in by a morass.'

However, *we* do not have time to stop or shelter here. We are pushing further into the hills, towards The Murder Hole on the second step of our big adventure.

2.THE MYSTERY OF THE MURDER HOLE

'A space of crag and rock, and then, tortuously disposed in a rocky basin, with frowning heights rising about it on all sides.'

Leaving Loch Valley behind, our next goal is the Murder Hole. Or to be more precise, Crockett's Murder Hole. If you employ McBain as guide at this stage you'll find he is most insistent that the real Murder Hole is north, near Shalloch-on-Minnoch. He does however accept that this Murder Hole, sited you'll note in Ayrshire, no longer exists, while Crockett's fictional one, in Galloway, is now a fixture on OS maps. This has been something of a bone of contention, especially between Ayrshiremen and Gallovidians, over the years. You have to remember that whichever guide you select has his own way of seeing the world, which both affects the paths he chooses and the stories he tells. Distinguishing fact from fiction is rarely as simple as McBain would like.

Indeed while McBain is disparaging about Crockett's Murder Hole, which he calls *'the fairy ring,'* he does reluctantly give it a whole chapter in his *Merrick* book.

Hearing McBain talk about Crockett one gets the feeling the former is somewhat disapproving of the whole concept of fictionalising: *'Mr Crockett had a real prototype which he made subservient to a tragic episode in his narrative, and when I said that it was fictitious, I meant that it was fanciful only so far as its reputation is concerned. For we may safely conclude that no murder ever was committed in or near it.'*

When I hear McBain talk about Crockett it puts me in mind of nothing so much as a quote from Shakespeare's *'Romeo and Juliet'* - *'do you bite you thumb at me sir?'* His grievance seems to miss the whole point of fiction. I cannot take it too seriously. It seems not a little churlish. I want to tell him to lighten up. But he's a man of his time after all. He has his own agenda; his own version of reality. I'd just suggest that for the armchair adventurer it matters not a jot whether the Murder Hole is 'real.' What's important is the romance.

Crockett is not unique in his telling of the story. He borrowed it from earlier myth and legend, as many great writers do, and turned it to his own advantage. It is most likely Crockett got the story from John Nicholson's version in his *'Historical and Traditional Tales Connected with the South of Scotland,'* published in 1843. Crockett was undoubtedly familiar with this work and it includes other versions of stories and characters he adopted, for example Aiken Drum who, as we've already seen, is part of the make-up of Silver Sand. Nicholson also mentions Sawney Bean. Crockett 'borrows' from this more than once – when we meet 'Granny Eggface' later on you might care to remember the legend of Sawney Bean the cannibal. Crockett uses this character in earnest in his Ayrshire based novel *'The Grey Man'* and again, in parody, in *'A Galloway Herd.'*

I suggest that if we don't let the facts get in the way of a good story, we'll enjoy our journey towards The Murder Hole that much more.

Our other guide from the 1930's, McCormick, is more entertaining than McBain on the subject. While I find that McBain always stands a little bit aloof, McCormick allows more of himself into his writing. He clearly loves the hills and writes: *'I always feel God's presence very close to me when walking amongst these grand evidences of his Handiwork. Crockett has woven his fine story 'The Raiders' around the neighbourhood... changed the peaceful 'wall-ee' in the end of Loch Neldricken into the murder hole of romance.'*

Leaving from Glenhead, as we did, McCormick sets out one misty day on a journey similar to ours in his *Galloway* book. If you want the company of a more modern guide, Paddy Dillon will give you the directions in his classic *'Walking the Galloway Hills,'* and Dane Love will give you an up to date take on the topography and history in his recently published *'The Galloway*

61

Highlands.'

I've made the journey from Glenhead to The Murder Hole from my armchair many times in the company of all these guides and I get something different from being in the company of each of them. But personally, Crockett is my companion of choice. Some things cannot be conveyed by measurements and geological or topographical 'facts.' I want story. I crave fiction. And Crockett gives me the murder, mystery and suspense that leaves me breathless, without causing me physical pain! For me, Crockett is the true armchair adventurer's companion.

Whoever you choose to go into the hills with, remember that there are many journeys to be had even travelling along the same path. And more so when we leave the safety of paths and head out into the wilderness of the hills. It's for each of us to choose our guides and travelling companions. Adventure is an individual and individualised experience.

Remember too that we are all part of a larger whole. We are all of our time, and we all have our own concerns. Crockett was writing in the 1890's. McBain and McCormick were writing in the 1930's. Paddy Dillon wrote at the end of the 20th century and Dane Love offers a 21st century 'update.'

This book itself is just a waymarker, offering the

benefit of a certain degree of hindsight, but partisan all the same. But perhaps uniquely among the guides, this book allows the merging of what we might call fact and fiction without getting hot under the collar. And hopefully that will enable you to enjoy the best of all worlds past and present.

For now, I think I've spent enough time reflecting on the thought that our culture is both mediated and constructed from a variety of time perspectives. That's deep water. Look up and see the dancing of the sun on the loch. It's time to move on. My best advice at this stage of the journey is: give in to the adventure romance and you will find the places you are looking for without having to pore over the OS map over long.

'Neldricken and Valley are wide-spreading mountain lakes, lying deep among the hills which spread nearly twenty miles in every direction. The sides of the glens are seared with the downward rush of many waters. Waterspouts are common on these great hills. It is no uncommon thing for the level of a moorland burn to be raised six or ten feet in the course of a few minutes.'

All our guides seem to accept, with varying degrees of reluctance, that perhaps the most exciting thing about Loch Neldricken is the (fictitious) Murder Hole, and next to that, Crockett's fictional description of Patrick Heron's escapades on the frozen Loch in *'The Raiders.'*

Forgetting his plighted word to May Maxwell, Patrick offers to act decoy for the men who are facing the gypsy-raiders, with guns trained on them. He straps on his ice-runners and takes us on a fast-paced, and dangerous birl around the Loch. It's worth noting that ice-skates had been in use in Holland from the 14th century. Patrick says that his father brought them over after his time there during the Covenanting era in the late 17th century. That is during the narrative time frame of *'Silver Sand'* and *'The Men of the Moss Hags.'*

'The Raiders' itself is set loosely at the beginning of

the 18th century. The metal skates we know today did not come to Scotland until the mid 19th century, so Crockett's description of Patrick's 'iron' skates, refers to an earlier version which did exist in Holland from the 16th century but were not as advanced as the ones used either in Crockett's day or today.

The skates may not be the same but the excitement of skating itself is perhaps greater in *'The Raiders'* than anything we can experience today. Oh, and in case you're planning a trip to the Galloway Hills in winter, can I suggest you leave the ice-running on Loch Neldricken to Patrick Heron.

Brace yourself and let Crockett take you out on the ice: *'But all the lads of the raid cried out upon me, and said that I was the bravest of the brave, and other things which please a young man. So I took my ice-runners in my hand—which, as I have said, my father had brought from Holland. Kennedy Maxwell and four others, all proper young men with well-grown beards on their faces, whom for this cause I often envied, came to see me safely off, for I proposed first to circle Loch Neldricken on the ice, that I might be sure there were no enemies lurking about it. This I did, not because I thought that the outlaw men would encamp there, but that these young men, especially Colin Screel and Kennedy Maxwell, who had formerly despised me, might see me start off alone into the night. Such a thick-skull was I, and so void of common understanding! For I ever loved to be admired and to be exclaimed upon for doing that from which others held back. And this same quaint kind of cowardice, for I had little real courage, has often carried me through with credit. I am of the faction of the old soldier who said, when complimented on his bravery in battle, 'We are all black afraid, only—we do not all show it!'*

So I had enough sense to keep my fears to myself at that time. Now it does not matter, for I am a man of middle years, and such is the power of reputation that I cannot do away with this repute myself, so that even this plain confession of weakness will not be believed; which is perhaps, after all, the reason why I make it here. So apt is man at deceiving others—and himself.'

Note that the middle-aged Patrick breaks his own narrative to reflect upon the actions of his youth. This is one of Crockett's more familiar (and endearing) narrative styles, and works to great effect to remind us of the follies of youth.

Patrick continues: *'But sally forth I did, binding my ice-runners of curved iron to my feet at the little inlet where the Midburn issues—too strong and fierce ever to freeze, save only at the edges where the frost and spray hung in fringes, reaching down cold fingers to clasp the rapid waters.*

Away to the left stretched Loch Neldricken, the midmost of the three lochs of that wild high region — Valley, Neldricken and topmost Enoch. I set foot gingerly on the smooth black ice, with hardly even a sprinkling of snow upon it, for the winds had swept away the little feathery fall, and the surface was smooth as glass beneath my feet. Each of the young men shook me silently by the hand. I suppose they thought me at once brave and mad, for I had lost no cattle and had a sweetheart at home to make a bride of. Yet there was I, setting off into the black night in the face of dangers unknown—dangers to which the close-packed well-fenced camp in the sheep ree was as one's own fireside.

I struck out from the edge with great strokes, moving my hands with each sway of my body as my father had taught me. In a moment the four lads sank behind me and I was alone on the black ice; yet I had that feeling of high defiance which all swift motion gives. The ice whirled behind. Following the southern edge, I was between the narrows in a minute. Here a jutting promontory of land—a mere tongue of sand and boulder—cut the loch almost in two. There was a fire kindled on the south shore nearest our camp, and on the opposite side as I sped by I seemed to see two men standing with muskets in their hands; but so dark was it that of this I could not be sure. If they saw me (which with the fire on the shore opposite to them and

67

the passage through which I went not more than twenty yards wide, they could hardly fail to do) they must have thought me the evil one himself, flitting by as it were on the wings of the wind.

I sped away with the irons on my feet, cutting crisply through the thin-sprinkled snow, the immanent mass of the Black Gairy casting a gloomy shadow overhead. An odd flake or two of snow came into my face as I bent low to look sideways up the hill. I went slowly, moving only my body and hardly making a sound, as the night parted before and closed behind me.

It took but little time to make the circuit of the loch and come back to the narrows; but as I passed I put on speed, for I knew that it was dead earnest this time. The watchers would now be on the alert and might very properly bethink themselves that the devil did not use iron runners, but wings like the bat. So I bent low and scudded through the strait with the dying fire on one side and the land closing in to trip me upon the other. I was just in the middle and running my best, when a couple of shots went off, and the bullets tore past behind me screaming like plovers whistling down the wind.'

Now we come face to face with the mysterious Murder Hole. For us it's the first time, for Patrick the second. He knows what there is to fear. But we... we should approach with caution.   Let Crockett lead the

68

way. He appreciates that it's too good a place not to fictionalise: '*strangest of all the strange things about Loch Neldricken, is that circle of dull, oily-looking water surrounded with tall reeds towards its north-western shore, which has been named 'The Murder Hole.'*'

Other guides may underplay its significance but make no mistake, in the company of a romancer, it's a place to be wary of. Prepare yourself.

'With open mouth it lay ever waiting like an insatiable beast for its tribute of human life; it never gave up a body committed to its depths, or broke a murderer's trust.'

Since we don't have Patrick's ice runners, the safest way to get to the Murder Hole is to go upstream with Crockett on the track by Mid Burn, arriving at the reedy southern end of Loch Neldricken and taking a boggy path on the western shore we come to a little bay. McCormick describes this as the *'wall e'e'* to the west of Loch Neldricken.

Crockett describes its appearance in reality in *'Raiderland'*: *'On the edge of Loch Neldricken lies a mass of green and matted reeds— brilliantly emerald, with the deceitful brilliancy of a 'quakin' qua,' or shaking bog, of bottomless black mud. In the centre of this green bed is a perfectly-defined circle of intensely black water, as exact as though cut with a compass. It is the Murder Hole, of gloomy memory. Here, says the man of the hill, is a very strong spring which does not freeze in the hardest winters, yet is avoided by man and beast. It is certain that if this gloomy Avernus were given the gift of narration it would tell of lost men on the hills, forwandered and drowned in its dark depths.'*

McBain remains to be convinced that it never freezes, but this seems to miss the point. Undeterred, Crockett takes his descriptive powers to another level when he adds fiction to the mix. In *'The Raiders'* we find the Murder Hole a spine-chilling place: *'The Murder Hole—foul and notorious was its name. There had long been the tradition of such a place in the stories that went about the countryside, and made our flesh creep as we told tales by the fire in the winter forenights. I had never been a believer in such like, accounting it foolish clatter; but now it seemed likely that I should learn something very definite concerning it.'*

Patrick Heron and May Maxwell first encounter the Murder Hole on their escape from The House of Craignairny (a place we have yet to visit). He says: *'Now we were on a platform on the north side of Loch Neldricken, but close down by the waterside. There was a strange thing beneath us. It was a part of this easternmost end of the loch, level as a green where they play bowls, and in daylight of the same smooth colour, but in the midst a black round eye of water, oily and murky, as though it were without a bottom, and the water a little arched in the middle—a most unwholesome place to look upon.*

As she knelt over me May Maxwell pointed it out to me, with the knife which was in her hand.

71

'That is their Murder Hole,' she said, 'but if we are to lie there we shall not lie there without company.'

The lights of the pursuers were dancing now among the heather, and their cries came from here and there, scattered and broken.'

May Maxwell thus reveals herself as the feisty heroine we can come to expect from Crockett. While Patrick sets out to rescue her, when it comes down to it, she is every bit as responsible for rescuing him. It's surely a match made in heaven?

You'll remember we last left Patrick beside the Murder Hole on his own. Hold onto your hats. Here's the end of his story: *'I was so excited with my escape and proud of my daring that I shouted as I flew; but I had better have held my tongue, for a moment after I saw that the force of my impulse was taking me out of the region of sprinkled ice among a low forest of dense green reeds. As swift as thought I turned, but my impetus was too great. I was carried among them, and there, not twenty yards before me, like a hideous black demon's eye looking up at me, lay the unplumbed depths of the Murder Hole, in which for the second time I came nigh to being my own victim. I remembered the tales told of it. It never froze; it was never whitened with snow. With open mouth it lay ever waiting like an insatiable beast for its tribute of human life; it never gave up a body committed to its*

72

depths, or broke a murderer's trust.

The thin ice swayed beneath me, but did not crack—which was the worse sign, for it was brittle and weakened by the reeds. The lip of the horrid place seemed to shoot out at me, and the reeds opened to show me the way. I had let myself down on all fours as I came among the rushes; now I laid hold of them as I swept along, and so came to a standstill but a little way from that black verge. Here I hardly dared to move, till, by slow degrees, pulling myself forward and pushing backward, I got once more upon safe ice; then I made directly for the shore, for the Murder Hole was more dreadful to me than a tribe of Faas armed to the teeth

In a few moments I had unshipped my runners, gained the heather, and was making the best of my way over the Ewe Rig towards the great barrier of Craig Neldricken, behind which Loch Enoch lay.'

We'll be taking that route ourselves soon enough. However, while you're getting your breath back, I should tell you that several other of Crockett's characters have dealings with The Murder Hole. While we're here, we may as well experience their adventures too.

'*The Dark o' the Moon,*' is set a generation later, and Maxwell Heron, Patrick and May's son, is warned about The Murder Hole at the start of his own adventure. Hector Faa, the gypsy who has kidnapped Maxwell, warns him thus: *'Have you no fear to be where you are? Has no father told you—have ye never heard tell of the House of Craignairny, of the Murder Hole in Lochricken, of the Brig, over the Black Water, where the outlaws broke their way through, and sent your coward kin whirling down to the Airds pool?'*

It is made as crystal clear as spring water to Maxwell that if he refuses to marry Joyce Faa (Hector's daughter) there is only one alternative. Silver Sand (Hector Faa's brother) explains it in words of one syllable: *"My brother does not offer you any alternative—save that.'*

He pointed to where, over the shoulder of the Rig of Enoch, we could just see the lean, leaden oval of the unplumbed Murder Hole cutting the autumnal russet of its fringing reeds.

'That is your alternative,' he repeated, with a certain grim solemnity."

The young Maxwell considers his alternatives. He loves Joyce but refuses to marry under duress. He's a man of principle after all: *'She was my alternative to the Murder Hole of Loch Neldricken. I must marry her—or die! And at that point I stopped. No, I would show them. I would not do that which I most desired, at the word of command from any bog-trotting desperado that ever drove stolen cattle and poached other men's mutton.'*

On this decision so much of the novel's romantic

narrative turns, and we'll find out much more about it in our second adventure.

'The Dark o' the Moon,' is much less well known than 'The Raiders,' which I find both a shame and rather incredible, since it's every bit as excellent a tale. You do have to take the imaginative pinch of salt when reading the sequel, because there is no way that Maxwell could have grown up in the intervening years between the end of 'The Raiders' and the beginning of 'The Dark o' the Moon,' but the modern reader has a much more accepting notion of dramatic licence than previous generations, who found fault with 'The Dark o' the Moon' specifically because the timings were inaccurate.

For the modern armchair adventurer I suggest that we should stop watching the clock and the calendar, worrying no more about the compression of time than we do about the positioning in 'reality' of the Murder Hole. That way, we'll get swept along in the romance, which, after all, is what we want from adventure.

'The Dark o' the Moon' was written some seven years after 'The Raiders' and it was not a planned sequel, although Crockett had considered the title for his first novel, but was worried people would not understand the reference. Seven years later he didn't have to worry; he knew his readers would trust him to guide them through their adventures. The real event around which the plot is set, the Levellers Rebellion of 1724, was too much gold-dust for Crockett to resist, so he compressed time and placed his familiar characters into this little known but very interesting historic scene.

In his fiction Crockett offers us history mediated by adventure and romance. Today we don't have issues with the notion of the relativity of time. Or with the concept that we create our own reality in fiction (and some would say in reality!) To enjoy Crockett's writing to the fullest you need to learn to 'go with the flow.' Read the story for the story to begin with. There are many more levels to engage with his work, but until you get to know him better, some of his hidden depths may elude you. If you have adventure and romance in your soul, Crockett will not disappoint you. If you are a strict facts and figures type like McBain, you may not fare so well on a journey with Crockett.

We make our own choices, as we all relate individually to a story. Instead of worrying about how Maxwell Heron grows up so fast and Marion Tamson stays young for a remarkably long time, I had the following thought. Patrick Heron wrote his own story *'The Raiders'* in his maturity, looking back. Could it be possible (in the world of the fiction) that this is what he was doing when his son Maxwell was languishing unrescued in the Shiel of the Dungeon?

76

That possibility is just an example of letting yourself go in the world of the fiction. It's a personal thought which I simply offer in order to show that we can play with fiction and create our own possibilities from the text. But this can only happen if we rise above a desire to criticize perceived inaccuracy. And if we trust the author as our guide. Fiction is not reality after all. And in fiction everything is possible.

There's one more story from the Murder Hole. One more experience before we move on to our ultimate goal of Loch Enoch. This time it's a scene from *'Rose of the Wilderness.'* The novel is set to the east of the Dungeon Range in the mid 19th century. We'll visit the place in our last adventure. But for now, we're about to meet an urchin who is known simply as 'Stoor.' This nickname, which means a pile or cloud of windblown dust, is the reason he threatens to drown himself in the Murder Hole.

When you hear his story, perhaps you'll feel some sympathy with his stated insignificance. He's not being melodramatic, he is deadly serious as only a child can be. You have to remember that in the 19th century illegitimacy carried a huge stigma. Stoor finds it shameful to be without a name. So, before we finally leave the Murder Hole, let's take our time to hear him out. Let's give some validation to his character.

Just make sure you don't sit down too close to the

77

edge of the Murder Hole while we listen as Muckle Tamson, a man perhaps too big for *his* name, tells Rose Gordon about Stoor. Be warned, they're talking in Gallovidian dialect. You may need to attune your ear:

"But after a' it wasna wi' Tammy that the trouble began. Tammy was as pleased as Punch. Na, believe me, an' ye will—it was Stoor. He said first that if I married Selina, and that loon Tammy had a richt to my name, he wad gang and howk up Chugbridge and— bring him to the waddin'!

'A bonny like thing that wad hae been!

'But I telled him that, first and foremost, he couldna find Chugbridge, him bein' thirty or forty feet deep in black peat glaur by this time. And then what did the young deil's brat up and say?'

I shook my head, but did not interrupt.

'That he wad gang and droon himsel' in the Links o' the Cooran or in the Murder Hole. He wasna gaun to hae Tammy swelling aboot the hills wi' a handle to his name, and him be caaed plain 'Stoor'.

'Never could I hae thocht there was that kind o' auld desperate gipsy bluid in the callant!

'But, certes me, he was camsteery and ill to deal wi'. And the third nicht he got up, quaite as pussy gaun veesitin' the mice. I hadna been in my bed mair nor half an hour, when I awakened wi' a presumption on me—no,

78

Miss Rose, that's no the word—'

'Presentiment?' I suggested.

'Aye, that's mair like it. English is an awesome language for whaup-nebbit, pheasant-tailed words. Weel, then, Miss Rose, as ye say, I awaked wi' a pregumption on me.'

This I let pass, for indeed the word was a good one, both in sound and sense—from the Scots point of view, that is.

'That Stoor—deil pyke his banes—had ta'en the road, and even noo he wad be half road to the Murder Hole. Ye ken that's the auld warlock-haunted bit near the lochs whaur the Faas, the Marshalls and ither raider folk pat awa' their prisoners lang syne, when they could get nae mair ransom oot o' them!

'Certes, I was on my feet in three ticks o' the clock. My hands took haud on Mistress Nan's loupin'-pole and, faith, it saved Stoor's life.

'He's a fearsome callant, yon—no to meddle wi' — ony mair than me when I was young. I'm guessin' that the faither o' him maun hae been 'a warmer'.'

'Claes? Breeks? Na, Miss Rose, there was nae time for ony cleadin' save the sark that was on my back when I raise frae oot my bed. If I had waited to pit on a coat and tie, or to black my shoon—faith, it's Stoor that wad hae been at the bottom o' the Murder Hole!

79

'Ye maun mind, Miss Rose, that the gleds and peewits on the Dungeon are nae sae particular as the folk on Princes Street in Edinburgh Toon. Na, na, it was Tamson in his sark that nicht—or naething!

'Certes, but Tamson didna touch the heather often atween the Dungeon and Neldrichen, and yince he left the maist feck o' the skin o' his taes stickin' in a craig. But he whurled on, loupin' like the black deil comin' through Athlone, as the Irishers say.

'Only ye see he was a white deil—no to say angel— what wi' his sark and—but there, if Tamson doesna mind, his descriptive poo'er will be rinnin' awa' wi' him.

'Sufficient is it to say that he fand Stoor on the edge o' the Murder Hole. The foolish laddie had tied a great muckle stane to his feet, and was ready for the jump. Mair nor that, he had started to crawl on a' fowers, or rather on threes, for his feet, being tied thegither, made but yin!

'Aye, through the fleein' carry o' cluds, that ran in wisps across the mune, Tamson saw Stoor. He grippit him. And oh, Miss Rose, I was that glad to see him that I nearly clouted him dumb and blind. Faith, I'm thinking I learned him what it was to frichten Tamson. But he never grat! Na, no him!

'He only said, 'Find me a name, or if ye dinna, I'll droon mysel' yet, that I wull! Never will I hae that Tammy caain' himself Tamson and castin' it up to me that I am

80

named 'Stoor' like a dowg! Oh, cuff me if you like, Muckle Tamson, but I'll rin awa' and droon mysel' just the same!'

Terrible queer things, boys! Here was Stoor, had been content for near on to saxteen years juist to be caaed 'Stoor'—no a syllabab mair. And a' because Tammy was to carry Tamson after his name, the silly loon maun rin aff to droon himsel'!

'I'll no hae him castin' it up to me,' he said, 'so there, ye are warned, Muckle Tamson!'

'So I says to him, 'Stoor, I'm no a man o' great combustion—oh, bother, I forget the word, but I minded it then, it meaned juist sense—but it was a fine word, and garred Stoor gape wi' fair astonishment. 'Stoor, lad,' says I, 'haud on for five minutes and then ye can droon yoursel' as often as ye like and Tamson will stand by and gie ye a pork doon wi' his loupin'-pole, to save ye needless suffering as it were!'

'But as for Stoor, he said naething mair. Me sayin' that, sort o' calmed him down. For he kenned that Tamson wad do what Tamson said.

'Then I sat on the edge o' the Murder Hole and thocht. Did ye ever try to think when the life of a fellow-craitur depended on it—you sittin' on a travelled stane in your sark, wi' your feet a' scarted wi' comin' across the Clints o' the Buss at a hunder mile an hour! Hoots, what am I sayin'—of coorse, Miss Rose, the like o' that is no to

81

be thocht o' for a lassie. But, at ony rate, that was what Tamson had to do.

'And the wund was in the North; Tamson was aboot as caller as a laird when he meets on wi' yin o' his tenants that hasna paid his rent for three or four terms! There's places in the Arctic whaur they say whusky freezes (Lord, talk o' your peppermints, what a sweetmeat that wad mak' to tak' to the kirk wi' ye!). Weel, I'm tellin' ye—sittin' on the edge o' the Murder Hole wi' the North wind gusting doon oot o' the Hass o' Enoch, wad hae frozen a barrel o' whusky as big as that they drooned the man in. Ye'll hae read aboot it in the history buiks, nae doot—him that was pitten to death in a muckle cask of Glen-leevit, and, bein' a Wast Country man, died wi' thae memorable words on his lips, 'This is no sae bad, but Lang John's the stuff!'

'Howsomever I saved Stoor, though I nearly becam' a block of ice doin' it, there bein' neither Glenleevit nor yet Lang John handy, mair's the peety. I said to the laddie, keepin' my airm firm roond him, and in his lug the promise o' a broken heid if he steered. That's a funny thing, too. Here was Stoor, the gipsy laddie, determined on droonin' himsel', and yet sitting as quaite as a moose for fear o' a broken heid or a 'wapp' on the chafts frae Muckle Tamson.

'But I talked sense to him—oh, sense was nae name for't.

'Stoor, says I, 'here's me—I never had ony ither

name in my life but Tamson. Or if I had, I hae clean forgotten it. Though I mind folk caain' me 'That young Deevil Tamson.' If ever I had anither name, sic as Robert, I wad gie ye that and welcome. Ye micht caa yoursel' 'Stoor MacRobert,' but I suppose 'Stoor MacDeevil' wadna serve ye— onyway, no juist sae weel?'

'Stoor shook his heid. There's nae contentin' some folk, ye see, so I had to bethink me again. Ech, how, Miss Rose, it was weary wark! I wad raither hae ploo'ed the Merrick, though plooin', to a herd, is eediot wark onyway ye tak' it. But it's nocht to thinkin' on a name for a lad that wants to droon himsel'.

'And Stoor didna help. He just sat and sullened, wi' his knuckles in his e'en holes, and the wind aff the North playin' 'jook-my-joe' atween my sark and my back-bane! I could hae thocht it oot a deal mair comfortable in my bed. But it wasna to be, so I drave on wi' the thinkin'!

'See, here, Stoor,' says I, 'I hae it this time! The folk that drooned ither folk in this Murder Hole were named Faa—for the maist pairt, that is, or sae I hae heard. A man wrote a lee-buik aboot it, and the rate thae raider-fowk o' his nippit aboot the country wi' their nowt-beasts was something remarkable. Noo, Stoor, ye hae tried to do the like, and had it no been for Tamson's lang legs, ye wad fairly hae drooned yoursel' in this same Murder Hole. What hae ye, then, to say against the name o' Faa, that

83

was yince sae great—lords and earls o' Little Egypt, as I hae read!'

'I will hae nae gipsy name—hear ye that, Tamson?' muttered Stoor between his knuckles.

'Ye ungratefu' wee messan!' I cried, 'and Tamson sittin' here like a short-shrouded ghaist waitin' for Gawbriel to blaw his trump—a' on account o' you!'

'I will hae nane o't,' says Stoor again, dogged as auld Wull Batchelor, 'I'll droon first!'

'He made a move in the direction of the Murder Hole, but Tamson's richt hand made anither movement— contrarywise, as yin might say. And then Stoor sat him doon, and grat and grat, juist because he wasna allooed to droon himsel'! As if Tamson was paid over-time to freeze his marrow, and hae a' the puddocks in the Murder Hole crawlin' ower his bare feet juist to gie a gipsy wastril like Stoor the pleasure o' droonin' himsel' ! He micht hae kenned better, haythen as he was!

'Then I had a thocht—oh, a fine grand idee, worthy o' a minister. Says I to Stoor, 'Stoor, lad, I never was ony the waur o' haein' only yae name mysel', but since ye are set on it.'

'Ye hae twa names,' Stoor sobbed, 'doesna a' the world caa' ye Muckle Tamson?'

'There—I had it! It was a grand idee, I tell you.

'Stoor,' says I, 'twa names ye shall hae, and if

84

Tommy is to be caa'ed Tamson seein' I'm to mairry his mither.'

'It's a peety,' moaned Stoor, 'that I hae nae mither for ye to mairry. Ye could hae had her and welcome. And then I wad hae showed Maister Tommy wha wad hae had the first pick o' names! But puir Stoor has nae luck!'

'What for are ye a' sae set on being caa'ed after me?' says I. 'A' my life I was never a man to make or mell wi' the baptism' o' laddie bairns? What's a' your fret noo?'

'Because ye are Muckle Tamson and that strong!' says Stoor.'

You'll be relieved to know that Muckle Tamson manages to talk Stoor out of drowning himself and in the process gives him a name. To find out how you need to read *'Rose of the Wilderness'* in its entirety.

The issue of names and 'faitherless bairns' was a familiar one to Crockett, since he himself was illegitimate. But unlike Stoor, Crockett was accepted whole-heartedly by his maternal grandparents and had a comfortable life within a loving family. However, he often wrote from the perspective of characters who were stigmatised by illegitimacy, most notably in *'Kit Kennedy.'* That, however, is outwith the scope of our current adventure, so we'll move swiftly on.

Despite no one actually getting thrown into the Murder Hole in Crockett's stories, I think you'll agree

85

we've enjoyed more than enough excitement on the shores of Loch Neldricken. Crockett's Murder Hole certainly serves to remind us that fiction creates its own reality and that if you are keen on discovering Crockett's Galloway you need to keep your imagination alive at all times.

But it's time to move on. In the final stage of this adventure we are heading for Loch Enoch. As Crockett says: *'Loch Enoch is the goal of our desire. For nights past we have dreamed of its lonely fastnesses.'* But between Loch Neldricken and Loch Enoch, we have to negotiate Loch Arron. Or is it Loch Arrow? Thereby hangs another point of contention, or just another tale.

LOCH ARRON OR LOCH ARROW?

'We passed a little tarn among the rocks which has for name Loch Arrow, and then on again among the heather'

Arron or Arrow? Which is it? Don't spend too much time scratching your head. It can be either. Crockett certainly refers to it as both. And we've already seen that it's not necessary for the armchair adventurer to be overly concerned with such detail. But the dilemma gives me an opportunity to say something more about places' names, and names on maps.

Of course you can stick slavishly to the Ordnance Survey, but if you do so, don't for a minute think they have all the answers, or that they'll help you get where you're headed – especially if you're travelling with a fiction writer.

Crockett's stock in trade is adventure. So prepare for the unexpected. Accept that even the Ordnance Survey can get it wrong, or if not wrong, that things change over time. We'll see time and again in our adventures that an overstrict reliance on fact will do nothing except hinder our progress. Of course place names have a value, but in the same way that Stoor's identity should not be fully embodied in his name, or lack of one, so we have to accept (and nowhere more so than in Galloway) the dictum one name, many places. A prime example is Bennan. I would heartily recommend that if you arrange to meet someone in the Galloway hills you don't suggest to meet at the top of Bennan. There are several hills called Bennan in the immediate region. As we go through our adventures together, we're going to come across all kinds of places that could be, or should be, or aren't where we might have thought them. Hence the need for a guide you can trust as well as a map. Trust Crockett. He changes names, he plays with names, he fictionalises names but he has his own reasons for doing so.

It's not a present concern though, since you *can* find Loch Arron on the modern Ordnance Survey map. And Crockett calls it this in *'Raiderland'*: *'From Neldricken, the Rig of Enoch is seen to hang above us like a mural fortification. Little Loch Arron we leave away to the left. It is little more than a mountain tarn. For now all our thoughts are intent on Enoch—it is at once the most remote of Galloway lochs and the strangest.'*

But in *'The Raiders,'* he calls it Loch Arrow. Does he live to confuse? No. In the case of Arron/Arrow, both names are correct because both have been used historically. It reminds us that whatever name a map may use, local people will call something what they like. And the two may vary not just in spelling (indeed consistency of spelling should be noted as quite a modern concern). You need to get acclimatised to this flexibility now because we'll come across this dilemma later in our adventures in the Dungeon of Buchan.

For what it's worth my advice is that we simply accept and respect that it doesn't matter what you call a place; what matters is the place itself. And here is the place, as we find it with Patrick and May in *'The Raiders'*: *'We came to the bed of a little burn that trickled down the steep sides of the Clints of Neldricken. I went first, feeling with my 'kent,' striking from side to side like a blind man because of the darkness.*

Sometimes as we scrambled down I would catch her by the waist and run with her many yards before I set her down, then on again as though I had carried a feather. So we ran our wild race, and I think gained on our pursuers.

Lanterns began to dance on the slopes above us— that frowning many buttressed table-land, the outlaw's fortress, which we were leaving. Only the booming of the dogs came nearer. We ran on downwards and still down. We seemed to leave the ground beneath us. We passed a little tarn among the rocks which has for name Loch Arrow, and then on again among the heather.'

The escaping couple don't have time to stop and wonder about the name, they are in too much of a hurry.

Later in *'The Raiders,'* during his second sojourn

89

into the hills, Patrick says: *'Instantly, as on the night of the blowing of the silver whistle, I was answered from either hand; my summons had aroused a whole colony. Only towards Loch Arrow, lying straight in front of me, there was not a single sound. So I called again more persistently and, as it were, querulously; and immediately set off running headlong upward in the direction of Loch Arrow, which I judged to be my best chance of safety.*

More than once I had to crouch among the rocks to let a man run past me, so efficacious and imperative had my second call been. It was a blessing that almost everywhere over all that country there is a capable hiding-place within each half-dozen yards; else had I been ten times a dead man.

I skirted Loch Arrow without putting on my ice-runners, because it is little more than a mountain tarn, and I knew that if there were any guards in the direction I was travelling they would be up at the Nicks of Neldricken, or at the Slock of the Dungeon—the passes which are the usual roads to the tableland of Enoch. Without a moment's hesitation, therefore, I set my feet upon the rugged Clints, hoary with rime and slippery with frost.'

So, Arron or Arrow, the name doesn't matter. Whatever name we give it, along with Patrick and May we have now negotiated our way around the 'little tarn' of a

Loch. So we're all set for the final step of our adventure. On to Loch Enoch. We are nearly there.

3.THE SILVER SANDS OF LOCH ENOCH

'Loch Enoch is the goal of our desire. For nights past we have dreamed of its lonely fastnesses. Now they are immediately before us. Enoch is literally a lake in cloudland.'

Anyone who has been to Loch Enoch will tell you it has plenty to recommend it. It is well worthy of being the end of an adventure. It is rarely visited and yet is a beautiful place (given the right weather conditions!) Crockett praises it in *'Raiderland'*: *'Enoch is held up to the firmament as upon a dandling palm of granite rock by Nature.'*

In his non-fiction writing, Crockett revels in the pure nature of Loch Enoch. Comparing it to Loch Trool he writes: *'Loch Enoch, on the other hand, is plainly and wholly of God, sculptured by His tempests, its rocks planed down to the quick by the ancientest glaciers of 'The Galloway Cauldron.''*

Of course other guides can take you to Loch Enoch. McBain, McCormick and latterly Dane Love all give good descriptions of the place. But Crockett adds something both in his factual and in his fictional descriptions. The others show you the place, but Crockett takes us to the very heart of the place.

93

So, because it's the end of our first adventure, and because it's a place that was so significant to Crockett, I hope you won't mind that we spend a fair bit of time enjoying the scenery.

Crockett offers us a chance to place Enoch in context of the surroundings: '...as we thread our way upward towards the plateau on which Loch Enoch lies. We are so high now that we can see backward over the whole region of Trool and the Loch Valley basin. Behind us, on the extreme south, connected with the ridge of the Merrick, is Buchan Hill, the farmhouse of which lies low down by the side of Loch Trool. Across a wilderness of tangled ridge-boulder and morass is the Long Hill of the Dungeon, depressed to the south into the 'Wolf's Slock' —or throat. Now our Loch Enoch fortress is almost stormed. Step by step we have been rising above the rugged desolations of the spurs of the Merrick.'

We feel that we are in company of Crockett and John McMillan when Crockett reports McMillan as saying: "I will show you a new world.' He strides on, a very sturdy Columbus. The new world comes upon us, and one of great marvel it is. At first the haze somewhat hides it—so high are we that we seem to be on the roof of the Southern Creation—riding on the rigging of all things, as indeed we are. Half-a-dozen steps and 'There's Loch Enoch!' says Columbus, with a pretty taste in climax.'

94

McMillan himself documented in correspondence that Crockett was stuck with *'The Raiders'* until he saw Loch Enoch and then all became clear. Whatever the truth of this, the impressions Crockett recorded in his 1894 article *'Galloway Fastnesses,'* attest to the emotional response he had to this desolate and beautiful place: *'Strangest sight in all this Galloway of strange sights is Loch Enoch—so truly another world that we cannot wonder if the trouts of this uncanny water high among the hills decline to wear tails in the ordinary fashion of common and undistinguished trouts in lowland lakes, but carry them docked and rounded after a mode of their own.*

This still evening Enoch glows like a glittering silver-rimmed pearl looking out of the tangled grey and purple of its surrounding with the strength, tenderness, and meaning of a human eye.

Loch Enoch spreads out beneath us in an intricate tangle of bays and promontories. As we sit above the loch, the large island with the small loch within it is very prominent. The 'Loch-in-Loch' is of a deeper and more distinct blue than the general surface of Loch Enoch, perhaps owing to its green and white setting upon the grassy boulder-strewn island. Another island to the east also breaks the surface of the loch, and the bold jutting granite piers, deeply embayed, the gleaming silver sands, the far-reaching capes so bewilder the eye that it becomes difficult to distinguish island from mainland. It increases our pleasure when the guide says of the stray sheep, which look over the boulders with a shy and startled expression: 'These sheep do not often get sight of a man.' Probably no part of the Highlands is so free from the presence of mankind as these Southern uplands of Galloway, which were the very fastness and fortress of the Westland Whigs in the fierce days of the Killing.'

Our guide McBain wakes up at this point. He's interested in trout in Loch Enoch. He's also interested in Loch Enoch, giving it a couple of chapters in his *Merrick* book, which fill in some background detail for those who like that sort of thing. Once again, I think he's more interested in fish than fiction. The closest he gets to lyricism is describing it as: *'an expanse of water that may be described as all limbs and no body, as an octopus that insinuates its tentacles into every depression that the water can reach.'* And McBain's greatest interest is in measuring the depth of the Loch. It takes all sorts to make a world.

Whatever your reason for going there, the journey to Loch Enoch is not easy but it rewards the effort. You might like to follow Crockett's advice in *'Raiderland'*: *'In making the journey to Enoch, fatiguing enough in any case, the beauty of hill and water is so amazing that the* traveller (if he takes my advice) will see as much as he can, draw, photograph, observe, and—read all about it in the next copy of 'The Raiders' which comes under his hand.'

We are lucky that Crockett himself did this, so that we can share his experiences in all three of the novels in the Raiders Trilogy. In *'The Raiders,'* Patrick Heron gives us his impressions of it: *'We stood towards the west along the margin of a loch that was lashing its waves on a rocky shore—a wild, tormented chaos of greyness.'*

Patrick finds Loch Enoch a wild and remote place, but as always this is just one impression on one day. Earlier in history the appeal of Loch Enoch on a sunnier day is recorded in *'Silver Sand': 'Juliana slipped from her pony at the sight of the blue lake set in its granite frame, with the dainty white beaches of silver sand, the like of which are not to be found in Scotland, and little green meads where the burns run down, gay and fresh, among the heather.*

She had not dreamed of finding anything so fair in this high wilderness of moor and mountain. So she went down to walk by the waterside, fearing (as all must who look upon Enoch from a distance) that such beauty must vanish into nothingness, as when one walks towards the end of a rainbow.'

Juliana Stanley is one of two heroines in *'Silver*

97

Sand' - Crockett never does anything by halves! - and as daughter of the gypsy leader, Jasper Stanley, she is as impressed by the landscape as the loon. It is key to the romance that John Faa and Juliana Stanley both come from ancient gypsy families because, in accordance with gypsy practices, she 'asks' Silver Sand to marry her.

Gypsies were quite prevalent in Galloway right up to the 19th century, but they were generally treated with suspicion. Crockett explains: *'Gipsies were not popular in Galloway, owing to the operations of the great raiding clans, the Mackittericks and the Valley Smiths, who had their headquarters in the wild country about Loch Enoch on the borders of Ayrshire and the Stewartry.'*

Crockett has an interest beyond the ordinary in gypsies and gypsy culture, and is always keen to show that there is more to the people and their way of life than we might first suppose. But that's for later down the track.

Following her proposal, Juliana and Silver Sand are 'handfasted' at Lochenochside. And when it comes to the end, it is at Loch Enoch that Juliana is buried. There are worse places from which to view eternity: *'They buried her in a sunny dale by the waterside of Enoch, just where a burn tinkles away half hidden among the heather. The snow was not all melted yet, but the spot was sheltered and the frost had not bitten deep. The*

98

sparkling white of fresh fallen snow marked all the precipices of the Merrick, and outlined the black arrogance of its Spear, to which, because of its steepness, no snow clung. The red-eyed smith had worked day and night to make from bog oak, iron and copper, a fitting coffin for his daughter, and Elspeth of the 'Star' had carried the babe home to nurse.'

Of course there are whole lives and stories in between the marriage and the burial, but you'll need to read *'Silver Sand'* in its entirety to find out everything.

In *'The Dark o' the Moon,'* Patrick's son Maxwell also finds himself at Loch Enoch and enjoys its romantic peacefulness while a captive of Hector Faa. Maxwell explains the role Silver Sand plays in getting him out of the house: *'I could see Silver Sand edging the conversation round to get us both out of the house. 'Would Meggat come out on the hills for a breath? It was years since she had trodden the white beaches of Loch Enoch. It would remind her of the days when he travelled the country with his donkey, and by selling 'sharpening' for the 'strakes' of the mowers, earned his name of Silver Sand.'*

'Na, na,' cried old Meggat, holding up her hands in horror of the suggestion; 'never on this side of Daith's river will the e'en o' Meggat Faa, that was born o' the Kers o' Blackshiels on the Border Side, seek to rest on the bluidy

shores o' Enoch, or on the Pit o' Sheep frae whilk was ta'en oot nae fewer than seventeen bodies o' strong men. Na, na; it's bad eneuch as it is, to ken that it lies awa' back there ahint the cliffs o' Buchan's Dungeon. But how you, John, that's a Faa born and the King o' a' the folk o' Egypt, can bide to look on that valley o' destruction is mair nor I can tell! But gang ye, gang ye blithely. Maybe ye will learn the second generation to mind what the first has forgotten, and, indeed, what nane but puir auld Meggat, that is as good as dead, ever gies a thocht to!''

Meggat might see Enoch as a 'bluidy' place, but the others experience it quite differently. For them it's a place of romance.

'So, thus despatched, the three of us went out again into the wide, wholesome morning, full of living breath and the crying of birds.'

Crockett, through the mouth of Maxwell Heron, reminds us that what you see often depends on when you see it: *'It is pleasant to be on Enoch-side when the sun shines—not so marvellous, indeed, as to see its surges through the driving snow-swirls as the short fierce afternoons of winter close in. Still, even so, and in the summer weather, there is ever a sense up there that somehow heaven is near, and the evil things of the earth remote. 'Not with change of sky changes the mind of man,' saith the ancient. But where Enoch is held up to the*

firmament as upon a dandling palm of granite rock by Nature, the Great Mother, the souls of men seem insensibly to grow larger and simpler, if not conspicuously wiser.

This is what we looked upon.

Beyond to the west, the massive buttresses of the Merrick descended to the water's edge in myriad scarp and counterscarp, bastion and piled earthwork, laid out by engineer greater than that French Mons. Vauban now so highly acclaimed.

Green snatches of turf, narrow selvage of granite-sand shining silver white, granite piers stretching out every way half across, with water enough alongside each to float a king's ship—fret and babble and lisp of live water all through this bright stirring autumn day—while above, continuous as the wavelets, the swoop and cry and blithesome clangor of muirfowl. Such was Loch Enoch as we saw it. And the sight has remained in my mind, from which so many things more important have utterly faded.'

Patrick Heron's experience of Loch Enoch in *'The Raiders'* is far less positive than that of his son. We'll let him have the final word: *'I gripped the icy clints of the granite rock tighter, and set my face to the thick-sown bank of stars above me, for the night had blown clear. Or perhaps, since the cliff was so high, I may have risen above the frosty mist. At any rate it was a place of deadly* cold, and my fingers became numb. Then they seemed to swell and thrill with heat so that I thought they were dropping off.

Presently I was on the topmost ledge of all, and crawling a few paces I looked down upon the desolate waste of Loch Enoch under the pale light of the stars. It is not possible that I should be able to tell what I saw, yet I shall try.

I saw a weird wide world, new and strange, not yet out of chaos—nor yet approven of God; but such a scene as there may be on the farther side of the moon, which no man hath seen nor can see. I thought with some woe and pity on the poor souls condemned, though it were by their own crimes, to sojourn there. I thought also that, had I been a dweller so far from ordinances and the cheerful faces of men, it might be that I had been no better than the outlaw men; and I blamed myself that I had been so slack and careless in my attendance on religion, promising (for the comfort of my soul as I lay thus breathing and looking) that when I should be back in Rathan, May and I should ride each day to church upon a good horse, she behind me upon a pillion—and the thought put marrow into me. But whether grace or propinquity was in my mind, who shall say? At any rate I bethought me that God could not destroy a youth of such excellent intentions.

But this is what I saw, as clearly as the light

102

permitted—a huge, conical hill in front, the Hill of the Star, glimmering snow-sprinkled, as it rose above the desolations of Loch Enoch and the depths of Buchan's Dungeon, To the right the great steeps of the Merrick, bounding upward to heaven like the lowest steps of Jacob's ladder. Loch Enoch beneath, very black, set in a grey whiteness of sparse snow and sheeted granite. Then I saw in the midst of all the Island of Outlaws, and on it, methought, a glimmering light.

So I set me to crawl downward. I went now as though I had left fear behind me sticking to the frosty Clints of Neldricken. The space between me and the loch was hardly a bowshot, and I found myself putting on my runners on the edge of the ice behind a great logan-stone, or ever my heart had time to beat faster. Then I was not at all afraid, thinking that on the ice so black and polished I could distance all pursuers, for none had that art in Galloway save myself.'

You've guessed it. It's time to strap on our skates once more as Patrick takes to the ice of the frozen Loch Enoch. This time the danger is less from underneath the water and more from the surrounding hills: *'The ice sloped away from the edge, and there was a little quiver within me as I slid downwards, lest I should be slipping into such another chasm as I had seen open for me at the Murder Hole of Loch Neldricken. But only the great flat met*

103

me, and I struck out softly. It was beautiful ice, smoother than I had ever seen, having frozen early, and by the first intention, as it were, being close up under the sky—with a skin on it like fine bottle glass.

But withal so clear and still was now the air that, do as I would, I could not hinder the ringing of my ice-runners, and the whole loch twanged like a fiddle-string when one hooks it with the forefinger and then lets go. Yet as I swept along, swinging my arms nearly to the ice, and taking the sweeping strides of the Low Countrymen, I had a sense of pride that nothing in Galloway could come near me for speed.

So sure was I, that with a sweep like an albatross (as I told myself) I circled about to the island whereon was the dying fire. As near as I could observe it the light was in a kind of turf-covered shelter—not a clay-built house with windows like that in which I had spent a night of terror on the slopes of Craignairny. There were men crouching around the fire, all looking out to the loch, from which no doubt there came the strange ringing of my ice-runners, the like of which was never heard there before. Suddenly these men seemed to take alarm, and like a brood of partridges dispersing when one sets random foot among them, they sped every way into the cover. I laughed within myself. But I laughed not long, for as I went I had that sense of being hunted, which comes so quickly and is so unnerving. I heard not, saw not my pursuer. I knew not whether the thing were man or beast, ghost or devil. But I was being followed, and that swiftly, silently. There was that behind me— I knew not what— something that my nature feared, perhaps just because it knew not what. In wild terror I clenched my hands and flew. My runners cut the smooth ice in long, crisp whistlings. The black shores sped backward. On my track I heard ever the patter of feet galloping as a horse gallops, yet noiselessly, as though shod in velvet. As I turned at the eastern end of the loch something grey and fierce and horribly bristling sprang past open-mouthed, straining to take me; but overshooting the mark with the impulse of extreme speed, the beast shot past with all four feet hissing taut on the glistening ice, yet looking back with fangs gleaming white.

So to and fro there was the rushing on the glassy ice of Enoch—the beast that hunted me gaining ever on the straight, and I at the turnings. After a time or two I regained my composure in some degree. It was a boy's game this, and I had played it before on the ice, though not with such a fearsome playmate; nor yet with savage men scrambling and watching among the stones at the edge, dirks in their hands and murder in their hearts.

But I clearly saw that I had only the advantage so long as I could keep up my speed. Did I slacken or trip but

105

once, the fangs were at my throat.

Likewise, though the nights were long, the morning must come at last, and then I would be but a poor hare waiting for the shot of the huntsmen, driven by the hounds to die. Yet this I did not mind so much, had there only been some one there to tell May Maxwell and the people of my country how I took my fate.

But very suddenly the end came, even as I darted between two isles that stand out of the middle of the loch—my runner scraped the edge of a long ridge of granite, and I pitched over on my face. In a moment I felt the horrible breath of the beast on my face, as it came rushing after and drove headlong upon me.

I had my knife out in a moment, and struck wildly again and again at nothing till my arm was seized as in a vice.'

We leave Patrick on the ice, but once more in hot water. He does seem to attract adventure, doesn't he?

As does Loch Enoch. Because, as with the Murder Hole, Crockett cannot quite leave Loch Enoch as the exclusive province of the Herons, Maxwells and Faas. A century later it features again in *'Rose of the Wilderness.'* We've already met some of the characters from this novel, but it's time to meet Will Gillespie, who goes mad when his love for Rose Gordon is rebuffed. In his deranged state he kills some sheep, and threatens to kill people.

The action incurs the wrath of many, none more so than our familiar friend Muckle Tamson. Will takes to the hills, pursued by Muckle Tamson and some local shepherds. The chase is on: *'He broke away and escaped out of their hands. When they thought they had him most securely cornered between the Long Loch and the Dungeon face which rises above steeply as a precipice, yet he went up it as a sailor climbs a mast, and disappeared amid the mists that girdle the trackless granite wastes of Enoch..*

... And the shepherds filed out silently from the first service in the barn of the Dungeon, saying 'Amen' in their hearts; while above, on the cliffs of Enoch, poor Will, tracked like a wolf, rent by the evil spirit within him, cursing the day he was born, watched the scattering of those who had worshipped God, as it were, in His newly-consecrated house of the Dungeon.

But already Muckle Tamson, leaping-pole in hand, was creeping among the scattered rocks and six-foot heather, nearer and nearer to the unconscious sentinel.'

The need for a 'leaping pole' will be explained in a later adventure. Meanwhile let's get back to the action: *'For Tamson held by the Elder Law, the law of Moses and of all law-givers before the coming of the carpenter's son—of tooth and claw and give and take.*

'I'll learn Wull Gillespie,' he growled, 'to let oor sheep

alane, the cowardly hound. Gin he had wanted plain fechtin', wadna Muckle Tamson hae gied him his belly full o't ony day o' the week? Forgiveness! says Absalom Kenmore! Ow aye, Tamson will forgie him when he has 'melled' him till he doesna ken his richt hand frae his left."

Will Gillespie is caught and placed in the recently built Crichton Lunatic Asylum for his pains. The Crichton is now a University campus. You see - time changes places as well as people.

Madness is something that finds its way into quite a few of Crockett's novels and you can learn a lot about 19th century attitudes to mental illness in his writing. In Will Gillespie we find echoes of Mad Sir Uchtred, from an earlier novel. We'll encounter him in the hills all in good time. We can't be everywhere at once. One thing at a time. And we've not yet had our fill of Loch Enoch. There are still mysteries to be unravelled.

SILVER SAND

'Silver Sand can fill his bags o' the fine, white granite piles on Loch Enoch shore, watched by a dozen of the bloody Macatericks and the wilder Marshalls, an' no yin o' them a hair the wiser.'

So much for the Loch itself. What of the so called silver sand? The observant amongst you will already have picked up on the references to the *'granite sand'* that is used for sharpening scythes, but now it's time to look at the connection between the silver sand of Loch Enoch and the character who takes his name from it.

McBain instructs us, as we would expect, that the silver sand is: *'white detritus of the contiguous granite... the sand is of all grades of fineness, from coarse gravel to grains nearly as fine as sea sand.'* He notes that it used to be a common expedition to go to Loch Enoch to bring back a bag but: *'since the advent of mowers and reapers and ready-made emery appliances... these days no man ever thinks of visiting Loch Enoch for a load of sand.'*

He suggests that: *'it must have been a hard day's work for a strong man to make Loch Enoch from Loch Trool or Loch Doon to bring away as much as he could carry.'*

So much for the facts. What about the story? On Rathan Island in *'The Raiders'* Patrick first learns about the silver sand of Loch Enoch from the man himself: *'Silver Sand came and told me tales, teaching me all the lore of the woods, and strange old sayings among the gypsies that made me wonder where he had learned them; but that he seemed to be well learned in everything. He had set up his tent again, and, though I paid him all his tale of guineas, he went back to his trade of selling the scythe sand, all made out of the hardest white grit of the granite where it is ground down and sifted by the rain and the wearing of the rocks on the edges of the lochs in the granite districts.*

Three kinds of sand he brought me to see, but not being a scytheman I could not tell the difference.

Then, very willingly, Silver Sand instructed me.

'This,' he said, running his hand through the fine, white, sandlike meal that he had in one bag, 'is the sand which I gather from the edge of the little Loch of Skerrow near to Mossdale that Sammle Tamson kens so weel. This is the commonest kind, yet good for coarse work, such as mowing ordinary grass, or the weeds and girse about a field's edges. This sort also is the cheapest; but this,' he said, showing me another very fine sand, 'is the sand from Loch Valley, which, when last we passed, I had not time to show you.' (It was not indeed likely.) 'It is fine, and sticks smoothly on the strake, and is used for corn on the braes, and for short hay that is easy won.

110

'But this,' he said, taking up a smaller bag as if it had been the fine gold,' is the sand from Loch Enoch itself. It is the best, the keenest, and lies closest to the blade of the scythe. It is used for the mowing of meadow hay, which is hard to win, because it has to be cut about the Lammas time, when the floods come. Then it is sore work to mow for a long summer's day, and the great swing of the scythe is indeed needed. At that time of year you can hear the 'strake, strake' of the mower in the shade as he puts an edge on his tool, and nothing else is used for this purpose through all Galloway, Carrick, and the Upper Ward of Lanerickshire than the Loch Enoch sand—that is, when they can get it.'

He passed it over to me in a canvas bag. It was certainly very beautiful, and I let it trickle through my fingers.'

One of the joys of travelling with Crockett is how much we can learn about the old ways of life of the ordinary folk. Where else would you find out about scythe sand? Crockett's fiction is riven through with this sort of detail and even though he is a romancer, one can trust his descriptions of the day to day, because he was writing from his own observations and experiences.

If you do make it out of the armchair and visit the sands of Loch Enoch, pick up a handful, and think of Silver Sand and his skill at sharpening scythes.

JOHN FAA, KING OF GYPSIES

'He was John Faa, gipsy chief and man of the world. To me he was a gorgeous pomegranate flower, flaming scarlet in a world of modest daisies and douce pot-plants'

We've found the origin of the sand, but the reason for the name still eludes us. Our journey is therefore still unfinished. But we are coming closer to an end.

We need to appreciate that the character of Silver Sand and the setting of Loch Enoch are inextricably intertwined in Crockett's fiction. But more than that, Silver Sand is the character who ties Crockett's first and last novels together. As much as he is central to Crockett's first published novel *'The Raiders,'* whose full title is *'The Raiders, being some passages in the life of John Faa, Lord and Earl of Little Egypt'* published in 1894, so he is the title character of the last novel Crockett wrote, in 1914.

Silver Sand in one sense frames all the rest of Crockett's fiction. The world has moved onwards over the decades in between 1894 and 1914 but at the last Crockett takes us back in time to learn more about his character's youth.

Yet Silver Sand is not a standard heroic figure. We noted earlier that Crockett was a 'raider' of stories and we have also noted that Silver Sand is based in part on Hogg's *'Brownie of Bodsbeck'* who is in turn a version of the legendary Aiken Drum.

Of fearsome appearance, Silver Sand can easily *'play the bogle'* and scare the lasses. He generally travels with his wolfhound Quharrie, who on a dark night, and even on a not so dark night, can convince the unwary that he is a hell-hound.

This tells us something about Silver Sand but it doesn't tell us who he *is*. We should remember that no one, character or person, remains fixed through their entire life. They change with age, and they are viewed differently by different people at different times. Silver Sand is no exception.

While Patrick Heron describes him in *'The Raiders,'* as: *'Silver Sand was a slenderish man, of middle height, stooped in the shoulders, and with exceedingly long arms, which he carried swinging at his sides as if they belonged to somebody else who had hung them there to drip. These arms were somehow malformed, but as no one had seen Silver Sand without his coat, no one had found out exactly what was wrong. Also he was not chancy to ask a question of. It was curious, however, to see him grasp everything from a spoon to a plough-handle or a long scythe for meadow hay, with the palm downwards.'*

As a young man he appears quite differently to

Juliana Stanley: *'all men seemed awkward and rude beside him. He was somehow attuned with this wild stillness, to the blue loch, the green granite-fringed islands, and the far spread glittering beaches.'*

How did this handsome young gypsy become a disfigured old retainer? To discover what happened to his arms we need to go back to *'Silver Sand.'* A character we will meet properly later on, rejoicing in the name of The Red Killer, can tell us more: *'There flashed on his mind the word which alone is more terrible than murder— torture.*

They were torturing some one in there, man or woman —but almost certainly man—the man he was seeking— John Faa, his lord and chief—upon whom his heart was set as a mother's on a favourite and unfortunate son.

The Red Killer flung himself flat on the rocky platform which led to the back entrance of the cavern. He wormed himself forward with a swift, keen action, like that of a snake. He poured his lithe body delicately about the obstacles, as if he had been a slowly moving fluid.

The moaning continued, hastening the advance of the Killer, and tightening every muscle of his body to be ready for the spring. He turned the corner, or rather his unwigged head did, for only his close-cropped poll emerging from the rocks could be seen. Two men were

114

bending over a third, who was stretched bound upon the little apron of rock and turf in front of the cave. Their backs were towards him, and they were twisting a pair of sticks about which a cord was wrapped.

'Tell us where the money is, John Faa,' said one, whose voice stung the Killer like the tooth of a serpent. 'Tell us, and we promise you shall be put aboard a vessel bound for France.'

'I know you will kill me,' answered a voice which could hardly be known for the firm ringing tones of Silver Sand, so hoarse and low they sounded. 'But it is no use to ask. The money of Egypt is far out of your reach, and of all such cowards and traitors!''

We can only assume that it is the torture Silver Sand suffers here which is responsible for his malformed arms.

Noting that times change men and that we are all different, at different times to different people, reminds us of another of Crockett's favourite themes – duality. Few characters in Crockett's fiction embody this duality more than Silver Sand.

As a young man Juliana Stanley tells us: *'Gipsy* *born and gently bred, he had two sides to his nature, and one or the other of them was certain to bring him into trouble. This had happened now, and with the eternal reticence of the sons of the Black Blood, he had been silent*

115

when half-a-dozen words might have cleared all. His own fault! Of course, but then he was not you or I. He was John Faa, gipsy chief and man of the world. To me he was a gorgeous pomegranate flower, flaming scarlet in a world of modest daisies and douce pot-plants.'

And his dual nature is further explained and explored. He was: *'a gypsy king, but he was also a well educated, much travelled, experienced man of the world, with talents and reading, prudence and sagacity quite beyond his years. Yet all these did not aid him to control the leaping blood within him, nor how to be one man not two.'*

'One man not two.' Crockett uses Silver Sand/John Faa to individualise a much greater duality. Among many other things, Silver Sand represents a dilemma faced by many Scots in the 17th century, both sides of the Union of Crowns. This dilemma is played out as historical adventure romance in many of Crockett's novels, particularly those which focus on the Covenanting times. Some of us like to think that a divided Scotland is a modern construction, a contemporary reality, but Crockett reminds us that divisions and duality are almost hard-wired into the character of the Scot.

And as already mentioned, he shows that Gypsies come from lineage at least as royal and often more

116

honest, than the British monarchy. Crockett makes this radical but perhaps subtle suggestion several times in his novels, most obviously in stories where he lampoons the House of Hanover. This might come as something of a surprise to those who have supped only on the standard fare of Jacobites and Covenanters, or Whigs and Tories. Crockett has a keen political awareness which is easily overlooked by the modern reader. I told you he had hidden depths. It's for us to find them. No point looking at Loch Enoch on a sunny day and denying that it ever snows there.

If the young Silver Sand is intriguing as a character, the older man still carries a mystery. Patrick Heron describes him: *'To begin with, there seemed nothing uncanny about Silver Sand more than about my clogs with their soles of birk. But after you knew him a while, one strange and unaccountable characteristic after another emerged and set you to thinking. We shall take the plain things first...'*

Silver Sand was a long-time friend of Patrick's father John (who dies at the beginning of *'The Raiders'* leaving Patrick with a large dose of good advice and a slightly smaller portion of land.) And it is as Silver Sand that Patrick first knows John Faa. He sees him as little more than a gypsy traveller: *'...Silver Sand made no secret of his calling and livelihood. He had a donkey and a*

117

dog, both wonderful beasts of their kind—the donkey, the largest and choicest of its breed—the dog, the greatest and fiercest of his—a wolf-hound of the race only kept by the hill gypsies, not many removes in blood from their hereditary enemy. This fierce brute padded softly by his master's side as he in his turn walked by the side of the donkey, not one of the three raising a head or apparently looking either to the right or to the left...

...Afterwards Silver Sand introduced me to Quharrie— that terrible dog—making him tender me a great paw in a manner absurdly solemn, which made me kin and blood-brother to him all the days of my life. And I have received many a gift which I have found less useful, as you shall hear.

In these troubled times to be a third with Silver Sand and Quharrie, was better than to be the Pope's nephew. So in this curious way began my friendship with Silver Sand.'

You may remember of the many things Patrick learns in *'The Raiders,'* not the least of them is that Silver Sand is both more of a man and more of a friend than he ever imagined. Together with Quharrie, he rescues Patrick and May: *'So we were lying side by side when suddenly Silver Sand came and found us. So near were we, that the dead bloodhounds had blown their bloody froth upon us in their gasping. Silver Sand brought*

118

water from Loch Neldricken to throw on May's face.

'Not from the Murder Hole,' I cried in terror, 'from the burn.'

So he went again and brought it and she awoke.

'What was the terrible beast?' she said, clutching me.

'It was no greater beast than I,' said Silver Sand, 'my twisted arms are turned the wrong way about for some good purpose. 'Twas but a matter o' a hair coat, a little phosphorus, and Quharrie."

You are aware of Crockett as a 'raider' of stories and mention of Quharrie may stir distant memories of another story - *'The Hound of the Baskervilles.'* Conan Doyle was a contemporary of Crockett's and the use of phosphorescence is common to both stories - but it's worth remembering that Silver Sand and Quharrie are the earlier fictional creations, first appearing in 1894; whereas the *'Hound of the Baskervilles'* wasn't published till 1902. Writers are all magpies. All draw from the works of others. And at least as many times as we see Crockett raiding from others, we can find others raiding from his work.

Great fictional characters never die, they just time-shift. Conan Doyle, under pressure from his public, brought his hero Sherlock Holmes back from the dead, but Crockett took another path. At the end of the *'The Dark o' the Moon,'* the brothers Hector and John Faa go

119

out in a blaze of glory, I always think of akin to that other outlaw pairing Butch and Sundance. Yet Silver Sand cannot be dispensed with that easily. He's woven into Crockett's creative psyche, but when Crockett 'brings him back,' in 1914 he takes us all back in time to reveal some of the mystery and explain some of the duality.

And now, since we've finally reached the end of our first adventure, it's time to reveal this big, unanswered question: How did Silver Sand get his name? The answer lies in the opening of *'Silver Sand.'*

There has been some trouble in Wigtown and the young John Faa meets Sir Andrew Agnew, Sherriff of Wigtown. It's a bit out of our hill settings but I think we can allow ourselves that little diversion to reveal the denouement. John Faa says: *"I am at your service. Command me.'*

'I daresay you are,' cried the man of the leather shoe latchets, 'but you are also on my ground.'

The young man shrugged his shoulders as if it were no use arguing stupidities.

'I fear, Sir Andrew, that you have not read your title-deeds,' he said. 'Your man of business (if you had one worth his salt), would have told you that when King James of the Baggy Breeches conveyed Ryan Moor to your ancestor he excepted Leswalt Dale and the Burnside of Knock-an-mays in favour of his loveit, John Faa, Lord and

120

Earl of Little Egypt.'

'I have heard of such like,' quoth bluff Sir Andrew, 'but suppose it were so, what has that to do with you?'

'Because I am John Faa, and my granddad's own choice. You are of an ancient family and royally connected on the distaff side. But I am royal—so, as they say hereabouts, 'Mochrum before Monreith,' an earl before a baronet!'

'Pech, lad, but how will you justify that?' cried Sir Andrew.

'As for my title-deeds and parchments,' retorted Faa, 'the Lyon King-at-Arms must be your informant. I do not carry my titles of nobility in my tail pocket. As for the rest, there is a sword at your side and another at mine, and I am ready to justify any and all of my pretensions. Or it may be that you, being a man loving to do as the people do, would prefer the simple arbitrament of the bare hands.'

Sir Andrew burst into a fit of laughter which resounded all about the dell.

'Ah no, my lord,' he said, 'the clean metal maybe, I'll no say. I have some skill in fence learned from canny William Forbes, but the knuckles—mind, I saw you streek that English loon as quick as twice two is four, so you and I will not play at that game, no, my lord!'

He spoke with a certain mockery in his voice which

121

was very evident to the young man, and which aroused an anger at the bottom of his heart that he should be so mocked and lightlied.

'Sheriff,' he said, 'if I pay you the respect due to your rank, I do not claim from you, save in private, the respect due to mine, I am aware that there is a difference between a gipsy, even of the blood royal, and the tenth hereditary Sheriff of Galloway.'

'I beg your pardon, Master John Faa,' said the Sheriff, 'but your figure like a willow by the burnside, and your comely youthful countenance, have played the deuce with my good manners. I would give much to have you for my doer—my helper, to aid me at home with my papers, and to ride at the head of my posse against evil doers.'

The young man seemed to bethink himself a while.

'There is a word to be advanced both for and against,' he said. 'It is true I have had a suitable and sufficient education abroad, aided and perfected after my return in matters classical by diligent private study, and not forgotten while in Claverhouse's company. Now I would gladly be your man and help you in all things, only let it be understood that at all times you treat me as a gentleman and not as a dependent.'

'Agreed!' cried hearty Sir Andrew. 'I know well who will be the master. You shall be as one of mine own house, I promise you—like young French or my nephew of

Garthland—can I say more?'

'There needs no more, Sir Andrew, save that I must not be known by my own name of Faa, which has been somewhat too often put to the horn at the cross of Edinburgh by the King's orders, and may be again.'

'Faith, as to that,' said the Sheriff, 'so have we all one time and another. But I am not a man to strain either at gnat or camel; why not call you Silver Sand, which is a good name and one well earned in your business of carrying sythe-sand down from the straths of the mountain lochs where no other dares venture—no, not I myself, the Sheriff with thirty men in armour clinking behind me. So Silver Sand be it then. And we shall take our way home to Lochnaw, for my lady and Lillias will be sore put to it to think what has become of me.'

... 'Sir Andrew,' said Silver Sand, 'I wager that you and I by laying our heads together can turn most corners of this crooked way by which we are sent athwart the world. A gipsy is not born with any conscience, and if I had suchlike it must have been gotten from my mother who was not of the blood of Egypt,'

Sir Andrew looked puzzled, as if a remembrance he could not locate pricked him.

But the young man only smiled and whistled a well-known tune—the Ballad of John Faa.

'The gypsies cam' to Cassillis yett, And oh, but they

123

sang sweetly, They sang sae sweet and sae complete.
That doon cam' our fair lady!'

'So you are the son!' said Sir Andrew, suddenly
enlightened. 'I knew there was more about you than plain
gipsy. Laddie, ye gar me forget my wife and bairns—and
what's mair extraordinary, my dinner o' fine black-faced
mutton. Ye have either the honeyed speech of the
enchanter or the forked tongue of the serpent that deceivit
Eve—aye, even as the daddie o' ye coost the glamour ower
the leddy o' the castle when her guid man was frae hame.'

This is not the end of Silver Sand of course. We'll
fall into his company many more times during our
adventures in the hills. So, while it might be pleasant to
stay here for quite a spell, especially when the weather is
fine, there are plenty of other places to go and people to
meet, and we must move on. Being so high up, we can
see many of the places we're going from here. Looking
over to the north-east we see Mullwharchar which in
Gaelic is 'The Hill of the Huntsman's Horn,' but Crockett
calls it 'The Hill of the Star.'

Crockett describes the area thus: 'On the east side
of Loch Enoch the Dungeon Hill rises grandly, a thunder-
splintered ridge of boulders and pinnacles, on whose
slopes we see strewn the very bones of creation. Nature
has got down here to her pristine elements, and so old is
the country, that we seem to see the whole turmoil of 'taps

124

and tourocks'—very much as they were when the last of the Galloway glaciers melted slowly away and left the long ice-vexed land at rest under the blow of the winds and the open heaven.

Right in front of us the Star Hill, called also Mulwharchar, lifts itself up into the clear depths of the evening sky—a great cone rounded like a hayrick. At its foot we can see the two exits of Loch Enoch—the true and the false. Our guide points out to us that the Ordnance Survey map makes a mistake with regard to the outlet of Loch Enoch, showing an exit by the Pulscraig Burn at the north-east corner towards Loch Doon—when as a matter of fact there is not a drop of water issuing in that direction, all the water passing by the northwest corner towards Loch Macaterick.

Beyond the levels of desolate, granite-bound, silver-sanded Loch Enoch lies a tumbled wilderness of hills. To the left of the Star is the plateau of the Rig of Millmore, a wide and weary waste, gleaming everywhere with grey tarns and shining 'Lochans.' Beyond these again are the Kirreoch hills, and the pale blue ridges of Shalloch-on-Minnoch. Every name is interesting here, every local appellation has some reason annexed to it, so that the study of the Ordnance map—even though the official nomenclature enshrines many mistakes— is weighted with much suggestion. But no name or description can give

125

an idea of Loch Enoch itself, lifted up (as it were) close against the sky—nearly 1700 feet above the sea —with the giant Merrick on one side, the weird Dungeon on the other, and beyond only the grey wilderness stretching mysteriously out into the twilight of the north.'

Let's just allow ourselves one last look around, and remind ourselves that if we want to 'find' Silver Sand, this is probably the place to look for him. Listen to the voices of those long gone: *'As for Silver Sand he never was comfortable inside a room for more than half an hour together. The wide lift was his house, and sun or shine, rain or fair, made little difference to him.*

The tales he told about the wild country by the springs of Dee set me all agog to go there, and I often asked him to take me with him.

'Ah, Pathrick, my lad, it's no for me to be leading you there, and you with neither father nor mother. It's a wild country and the decent folk in it are few. Wi' man, I dinna even take Neddy into the thick of it. 'No farder than the Hoose o' the Hill for Neddy,' says he, 'and thank you kindly.' But Quharrie and me's another matter. Where Quharrie and his master canna gang, the Thief himsel' daurna ride. For Silver Sand can fill his bags o' the fine, white granite piles on Loch Enoch shore, watched by a dozen of the bloody Macatericks and the wilder Marshalls, an' no yin o' them a hair the wiser.' And this was no idle

boast, as you shall hear ere the story ends.'

Now, as Crockett says: *'It is with feelings of regret that we take leave of Loch Enoch, and, skirting its edge, make our way eastward to the Dungeon Hill...'* to continue with our next adventures.

ADVENTURE TWO

THE HEART OF THE DUNGEON

4.THE DUNGEON OF BUCHAN

'Now the Dungeon of Buchan is a wide place, and many men can be safely accommodated there, not to be found even if a regiment should come searching them—that is, not without someone to guide them.'

Our first adventure which took us from Glentrool to Loch Enoch, while exciting, was relatively easy to follow and relatively easy to find. This next adventure changes things. We are going into the heart of the hills where it's easy to get lost. And once you've lost your bearings, anything can happen.

I'll start with another warning. The places we are headed for are less easy to pinpoint on a map. Some of them may not exist and may never have existed, so it is important to dust down your imagination and have it to the fore as we progress. It'll serve you at least as well, if not better, than all the guidebooks in the world where we are going.

If you've read *'The Raiders'* you will already be excited about the prospect of venturing to the Wolf's Slock and Craignairny. But for me, the most exciting place in all of Crockett's fiction is The Shiel of the Dungeon of Buchan. This is a key location in *'The Dark o' the Moon,'* Crockett's sequel to *'The Raiders.'* It's both

131

evocative and elusive and remains the place in the world I would most like to get out of my armchair and see for real. And yet, the likelihood is it never existed.

Our three goals for this adventure are: the Wolf's Slock, Craignairny and the Shiel. So it's time to strap on our imaginations like crampons, and head out into the heart of the Dungeon of Buchan.

Over the years many people have searched for Crockett's places in these hills and been unable to 'place' them. Guides have offered a variety of possibilities and some have even blamed Crockett for a lack of veracity in his description. I think this is unfounded criticism. And as we'll discover in this adventure, other guides and even the OS map are not always reliable or consistent. As I said, where we're going you need to take imagination along with you as well as a map. And you need to trust Crockett as a guide, while remembering that he is a writer of fiction.

The relationship between fact and fiction is an interesting one in itself. We should never lose sight of the fact that Crockett was fictionalising a real place. He was a great observer, of people and of places, and for me the relationship and interplay between fact and fiction in his work is one of its greatest strengths.

The Dungeon of Buchan is a pot which boils both in reality and in Crockett's imagination. It's a melting pot for all kinds of experiences. And we are headed for its heart. You can approach the Dungeon of Buchan from all points of the compass, and Crockett approaches it from a number of directions in his fiction. In this adventure we're going to look at two of them: the southwest, via Lochs Enoch and Neldricken and the east, via The Nick of the Dungeon. In a later adventure we'll approach from the Northern Loch Doon area.

But where do we start on a journey into the unknown? It's important to note that the whole area we now call the Galloway Hills (between Merrick to the west and Cooran to the east, Loch Doon to the north and Glentrool to the south) was historically known as the Dungeon of Buchan. This is the 'wideness' Crockett refers to. In *'Raiderland,'* standing above Loch Enoch on Craignairny Ridge he says: *'Indeed, often as I have stood on this spot, I never remember to have looked into Buchan's Dungeon without seeing something brewing there. As soon as the sun begins to wester on the finest day of summer, with the first shadows, the cloud drifts and mist spume begin to weave a veil over the huge cauldron. The herds are used to call this phenomenon 'the boiling of the pot.''*

It's time to meet up again with Crockett, his characters and our other guides, and see where our journey takes us. Enough talking. It's time to go.

133

'The mountains I looked upon were wide and lowering, bossed with granite, and caverned with heather and peat-hags. Lochs, deep and solemn, cut across the glens and wider straths.'

Crockett knew the Galloway hills and knew them well. If we allow him to guide us, we'll never be short of history, adventure or romance. And after all, what more is there worth seeking for in life? So forget worries about 'is it really there?' and give yourself up to the adventure.

We're starting from the west, more or less where we left off at Loch Enoch. In reality the journey here from Glentrool would take three hours or more, but it involves less arduous climbing than the Eastern approach. Luckily for us, if we adventure from our armchair, we can save our breath for the view, which is certainly worth it.

We've already seen Crockett describe the Dungeon area from its western aspect, but now he offers us a perspective on the route ahead: *'We may peer down for a moment into the misty depths of the Dungeon of Buchan. A scramble among the screes, a climb among the boulders, and we are on the edge of the Wolf's Slock—the appropriately named wide throat up which so many marauding expeditions have come and gone. We crouch behind a rock and look downward, glad for a moment to get into shelter. For even in the clear warm August night the wind has a shrewd edge to it at these altitudes. Buchan's Dungeon swims beneath us, blue with misty vapour. We can see two of the three lochs of the Dungeon. It seems as if we could almost dive into the abyss, and swim gently downwards to that level plain, across which the Cooran Lane, the Sauch Burn, and the Shiel Burn are winding through 'fozy' mosses and dangerous sands.'*

The terrain is still familiar to us, lately come as we are from the pleasures of Loch Enochside, which we remember as a remarkable place: *'held up to the firmament as upon a dandling palm of granite rock by Nature.'*

But don't be lulled into a false sense of ease. Awareness of the mutability of the weather is wise for any adventurer, and certainly for those braving the Galloway hills. Our guide McCormick points out that: *'the appearance of these hills is ever changing and lifelike to shepherds.'* In *'A Day in Mountain Mist'* he records a trip into the hills under these conditions. He makes his way to Loch Enoch but then: *'I began to wonder how I was ever to get over the mountains to the Loch of the Dungeon as the mist had now completely shut out the nearer hills also from view. Over and over again, I*

135

consulted my Ordnance Survey sheet. The general outline of the loch on the map and the loch lying in front of me were not unlike one another.'

He admits to completely losing any sense of direction and this is easy to do in mist: 'The mist again came crawling up, and so swiftly had it enveloped everything that ere I had reached the end of the creek I could only see for a few yards around me. There seemed something treacherous and cruel about the mist and it stealthily enveloped me.'

McCormick is an experienced man of the hills (though one who takes too many risks for me to want him as a guide) and his description shows us just how dangerous it can be if you venture into the Galloway hills in poor weather.

McBain strikes me as more risk-averse than McCormick, as we might expect of a man motivated by facts and figures. He offers several warnings to those who might attempt to go into the hills. He even suggests it is an inappropriate activity for a man with a young family. He notes that to explore the Galloway Hills is to explore a 'rough, austere, chaotic domain,' and advises the traveller: 'to carry with him a map on as large a scale as possible.' But even he admits that this 'will not prevent him from losing his bearings and going astray until he has learned the lie of the land.'

In his *Merrick* book, he states that he has *'twice gone miserably astray'* in the Galloway hills. When even McBain admits to losing his way in these hills, we can begin to appreciate this is not an adventure to be undertaken lightly.

Mist and snow are the greatest challenges to those who venture out into the Galloway Hills. Yet these are the very conditions we will have to brave in the company of Crockett's characters. Crockett himself never allows us to forget the impact of weather. Indeed he almost revels in it. I know of no writer who captures winter and snowstorms better than Crockett.

In *'Silver Sand,'* during some seriously inclement weather, he writes: *'They reached the Dungeon of Buchan on a stubbornly bitter forenoon of blowing snow from the east, which came up out of the open jaws of the Wolf's Slock in a solid headlong push—like the fall of a wave on a deck, it swept the gorge from end to end.'*

However, our greatest challenge in finding the Wolf's Slock, the House of Craignairny and the Shiel of the Dungeon of Buchan is not the weather. The real challenge will become apparent as we progress. So please keep your wits about you and your imagination as close to hand as your water bottle.

The company of a good guide is always appreciated on an adventure and in *'Silver Sand,'* we have one who

137

knows the hills like the back of his hand: '*Silver Sand piloted his company into the heart of the wilderness, till he came to the bottom of the great precipice which is called the Spear of the Merrick. Then he led them behind a fallen rock where was a den of clean-laid sand and heather, wholly cleared of boulders. The hanging brows of the rock sheltered it...*

...Jasper Stanley and Silver Sand pushed on, leaving Juliana and the rest of the tribe behind. Silver Sand crossed many spouts of shifting rubble, with his eyes on the unstable material and on the inexpert feet of Jasper Stanley, who had never been in such a 'devil of a country,' and who wished himself back again safe in the seclusion of Moston Clough.

But there was no letting up of the speed. The man from the plains might pant and sweat, but the hill gipsy pushed on remorselessly over the lichen-covered rocks and across the dark-blue ridges about which the thin mist hung. Silver Sand and Jasper forded mountain brooks roaring down out of the wilderness of granite above. Silver Sand sprang across as if his feet were winged with the wind, while Jasper Stanley splashed and cursed in his rear. So they went till at last they came to a great parting among the hills from which they looked down upon Enoch, the loch of marvellous things, spread out with its islands, piers, and promontories, its bights of silver sand and glittering pebble reaches—all as if laid out by the hand of a cunning landscape gardener, and carefully tended every day.'

Faced with this description, we might feel leaden footed like Jasper Stanley. And as we go on, our response might be very similar to his: *'Stanley, the Lancashire blacksmith, was no little amazed, and the freshness and vigour of the air caused him to stride out, filling his huge chest with great sobbing intakes of breath, as he would have filled his bellows. All was strange to him. The brilliant colours of the water and shore, and the prodigious upspringing of the black and terrible ramparts of the Dungeon, lightning-scarred and seamed with tornado gullies, struck the man with amazement.*

But he stared and gaped when, without warning, Silver Sand led him to the Dungeon edge and, more than a thousand feet beneath him, he saw little lochs gleaming no bigger than so much water held in the palm of his hand, with streams that wimpled and meandered no thicker than a fine thread. This is the great cirque of the Dungeon of Buchan, the like of which is not in all Scotland, with the rocks falling away in purple precipices all about it, and only the one way out, which is shut by the bottomless green 'well-eyes' and sleechy quicksands of the ill-omened moss of Cooran.'

In this description Silver Sand approaches the

139

Dungeon from the Nicks of Neldricken. While we're here, up high with him, we might pause a while and look east to the *'ill-omened'* Cooran Lane. Because we're going to have to cross it later. From up here we can see Patrick Heron's approach which involves negotiating his way up the Nick of the Dungeon.

Let's pause awhile and allow McBain to earn his keep by telling us something about The Nick of the Dungeon, and 'nicks' in general. The word nick simply means a pass through a range of hills. It's like a gully. There are many of them marked on maps in the Galloway Hills and Crockett was familiar with the various nicks in the area. Strange then that he never mentions the Nick of the Dungeon even though it seems that Patrick himself climbs this.

Not so strange after all. There is quite a simple explanation if you are prepared to look for it. McBain proudly tells us: *'that name is not to be found on the maps and I never heard the pass so designated by the shepherds or given any other name by them. So far as I am concerned I invented the name.'* You see, all our guides have hidden depths. McBain, who generally seems to be a stickler for fact, has had a rush of blood to the head and invented something! So it's not surprising that Crockett doesn't mention the Nick of the Dungeon given that Patrick climbed it long before it was named by

McBain.

The point I'm trying to make here is that we might think twice about relying too exclusively on any guide, especially those who come 'after' the event. We may think the 20/20 vision of hindsight is a blessing, but I suggest it's every bit as much a curse. If we want to find Crockett's places, we need to be prepared to travel not only in space but back in time to the Galloway Hills as they were when he knew them at the end of the 19th century. This is the way to truly discover Crockett's Galloway. But I can't think of a greater adventure.

At this point then, a change of perspective is as good as a drink from a cool hill stream. I suggest we now approach the Dungeon from the East as Patrick Heron and Sammle Tamson do in *'The Raiders.'* Remember Sammle's 'easy' route?

Patrick and Sammle strike across country from Mossdale, which is a route I'd only recommend to armchair adventurers. While more direct than one from Glentrool, it's still by no means a walk in the park (not even the Galloway park!) But if it was easy, where would the adventure lie?

If you are going to attempt the eastern approach to the Dungeon of Buchan for real, it's best to get by vehicle to the Craigencallie car park. Then you can walk or mountain bike up the forest track, to the Backhill o'

Bush Bothy. On foot from Craigencaillie to the bothy is more than two hours walking, over an hour on a bike. Back Hill o' the Bush, which is somewhat derelict today, will feature in a later adventure.

Offering another view of the Dungeon, this time from Dungeon Hill, Crockett says: '...*Far across in the distance we can see the lonely steading of the Black Hill o' the Bush, and still farther off the great green whalebacks of Corscrine and others of the featureless Kells range, deepening into grey purple with a bloom upon them where the heather grows thickest, like the skin on a dusky peach.*'

However if we plan to get into the Dungeon from this direction, whether from the armchair or for real, we're going to have to navigate both the Silver Flowe and the Cooran Lane. Today the Silver Flowe is a Site of Special Scientific Interest, which means you have to skirt its pools to the north and you should not approach its lochs during the nesting season. In Crockett's day it was just a place where you might get drowned. So prepare to get your feet wet! And hurry up. Patrick and Sammle won't wait.

MOSSDALE

'In the brisk noon of a fine birling day in May, Sammle Tamson and I took to the hill. At first I misdoubted him and thought myself a better mountaineer than he. But I was soon to learn better.'

Sammle and Patrick start their trip into the hills from the relative civilisation of Mossdale. This is in the part of Galloway known as the Glenkens and it is Crockett's home territory. The Kells Range are tame in comparison to The Dungeon Range, though they have their own beauties and adventures. These can be enjoyed in other volumes of *'Discovering Crockett's Galloway'* and of course in his novels. But for now, there's no time to linger here as we set off from the Mossdale house of Sammle and Eppie Tamson with the young Patrick Heron in hot pursuit of the Raiders.

It's going to be a bumpy ride. But there will be some incredible views along the way. In Patrick's eagerness to rescue May Maxwell he takes the direct route across the hills, hoping that he'll get to the goal (the House of Craignairny) before the kidnappers themselves. He is determined to rescue May before she is married (willingly or unwillingly) to a gypsy.

Patrick explains the plan: *'It was therefore*

necessary for me to cross and take to the hills on the eastern side of the Dungeon, then make for the Wolf's Slock as fast as I could, and trust to Providence after that. At least, so said Sammle Tamson, evidently thinking that Providence would be no improvement upon himself as a guide among the hills of the Dungeon.'

Sammle offers himself as a guide and the route taken by the two men takes them onto the brow of a place familiar to and beloved by Crockett, Cairn Edward Hill: *'which rises bleak and grey above the rushing of the Black Water of Dee.'* From there they move onwards: *'we drew towards the verge of the Black Craig of Dee and saw beneath us the whole of the land backwards, with its lochs and lochans, clints and mosses, away to the little white house of Mossdale itself.'*

What follows is a chase over the heather every bit as exciting as those offered in Stevenson's *'Kidnapped'* or Buchan's *'The Thirty Nine Steps':* *'We had been out from the house at Mossdale more than two hours, when we came suddenly to the crest of the ridge and looked over the other side ere we were aware. As soon as Sammle got his first look he dropped like a shot.*

'Clap,' he said under his breath; 'for the love o' God, clap!'

I was beside him in an instant. Together we peered cautiously over the worn and water-pitted edge of the blue

144

whinstone rock, our bodies buried up to the chin in the heather.

Sammle pointed with his long whaup's nose.

'There,' he whispered, as though we were not a thousand feet in the air above the drove-road, 'd'ye see yon?'

This is what I saw. I saw the Links o' the Black Water o' Dee shining amid the dull yellows and greys of the grim mosses through which it slowly made its way. I saw the untenanted onstead of Clattering Shaws and the drove-road to the Cree Bridge wimpling across the heather. But what I mainly saw was a straggling line of black dots (as it were both upright and long) crawling irregularly over the moor by the waterside.

'There's the drove, and there's your Macatericks and Marshalls, an' I doot na a Faa or twa amang them,' said the goodman of Mossdale.'

As they make their way across the Kells Range, both men have plenty of time to think about the wisdom of the endeavour. And by the time they have climbed over Craignell and Darnaw, Sammle's confidence leaves him and he refuses to go further, as Patrick records: *'Presently we got upon what was one of the roughest parts of the country for heather and stones that I have ever seen. It is called, I hear, the Rig of Drumquhat, and I do not know who is laird of it; but one thing I know, that he*

145

has a barren heritage and routh of heather...

...We were now high above the misty basin of Loch Dee, which we saw shining blue away in the hazy south, with the burn running out of it into the Cooran Lane. We could see with the prospect glass the drovers letting the cattle stray wide, watched only by boys on the green meadows of the two Laggans by the loch side. A very great number of the poor beasts were standing in the water of the loch cooling their travel-weary feet and drinking deep draughts.

We were now on the smooth side of the furthest spur of Millyea, the last of the Kells Range, which pushed its wide shoulders on into the north, heave behind heave, like a school of pellocks in the Firth. I was astonished at their height and greenness, never having in my life seen a green hill before, and supposing that all mountains were as rugged and purple with heather or else as grey with boulder as our own Screel and Ben Gairn by the Balcary shore. But these I found were specially granted by a kind Providence to afford yirds and secret caves for our Solway smugglers.

It was always counted a Divine judgment on the people of the Glenkens that their hills are so smooth that the comings and goings of men and horses upon them can be seen afar, and the smoke of a still tracked for a summer day's journey...'

For me, Patrick's observations regarding the differences between the Kells Range and the Dungeon Range really illustrate Crockett's close observational powers and skill in natural description.

However, there's no time to wax lyrical about the view. If we want to get into the heart of the Dungeon, our immediate task is to get safely across both the Cooran Lane and the Silver Flowe. As Patrick says: '*...it was ordained that I should now be on the side of Millyea looking towards the great breastwork of the Dungeon of Buchan, behind which lay the outlaw country shrouded in dark and threatening mist...*' No time to back out now!

COORAN LANE and SILVER FLOWE

'It is not for any man to venture lightly at nightfall, or even in broad daylight, among the links of the Cooran, as it saunters its way through the silver flow of Buchan. The old royal fastness keeps its secret well.'

Right now perhaps we need to look at our feet, not at the sky. And we need to find some inner resolve. It's about to get really tough. Patrick knows that he's bitten off far more than he can chew, but he's determined to rescue May Maxwell. He reflects: *'...to resolve is ever easier than to do. Between me and the frowning ridges — now the colour of darkest indigo, with the mists clammily creeping up and down and making the rocks unwholesomely white, as if great slimy slugs had crawled over them—were the links of the Cooran winding slow, leaden, and dangerous. And there beyond them was the Silver Flowe of Buchan, where the little Marion had been drawn to her death either by the clinging sand or the dread arm of the water kelpie...'*

The knowledge that Sammle Tamson believes his daughter to have been drowned in the Silver Flowe should be enough to give us pause for thought, and to excuse his leaving Patrick in the lurch. Fortunately, time will prove him wrong. Marion was far too good a character to waste on drowning. She has much more of a part to play both in *'The Raiders'* and again in its sequel, *'The Dark o' the Moon.'*

The Cooran Lane is easily accessible from the shepherd's house at Black Laggan, but all our guides agree that getting across it is far from easy. And as we're about to risk our all to cross the Cooran Lane, I suggest it's about time we knew more about it. You will remember that 'lane' is a Gallovidian word for 'burn,' of course.

Our guide McBain describes the Cooran Lane as the principal headstream of the Kirkcudbrightshire Dee: *'The Cooran lane is the true upper reach of the River Dee. Notwithstanding the clearness of the water, the lane is so deep for long stretches that the bottom cannot be seen. ... the best walking in the valley is along the very edge of the stream, and as the path follows its windings it behoves the pedestrian to pick his steps with great wariness. A plunge into its depths would be a very undesirable experience.'*

Our other 1930's guide, McCormick, describes The Couran Lane, (note the variation of spelling) as: *'that land of purple heather, 'quakkin' quaa's and shining pools,'* and claims that the quakkin' quaa's could shake for twenty feet all around you.

But what is a 'quakkin' quaa?' and is the Silver

Flowe one? McBain to the rescue again. He tells us: *'perhaps every reader of this chapter does not know what a 'flow' is.* (note the spelling variance again!) *It is neither more nor less than a bog.'* He goes on to describe a variety of kinds of bogs, concluding that: *'The Silver Flow is the specific name given to a rather extensive bog, perhaps one of the most extensive in Scotland... I guess it to be about a third of a mile in area, and it lies on a low plateau... It is a true floating bog, and one who sought to cross it would do so at peril.'*

Patrick Heron has to cross it! And we're going with him. I doubt it will be any easier now we know exactly what it is:

'...As I went the ground became wetter and boggier. My foot sank often to the ankle, and I had to shift my weight suddenly with an effort, drawing my imprisoned foot out of the oozy, clinging sand with a great 'cloop,' as if I had begun to decant some mighty bottle. Green, unwholesome scum on the edges of black pools frothed about my brogues, which were soon wet through. Then came a link of silver flat where the sand was firm to the eye. My heart beat at the pleasant sight, but when I set foot on it a shivering flash like lightning flamed suddenly over it, and it gripped my feet like a vice. Had I not been shore bred, and that on Solway side, I had passed out of life even then. But I knew the trick of it, and threw myself

flat towards the nearest bank of grass, kicking my feet free horizontally, and so crawled an inch at a time back to the honest peat again. Then I found a great shepherd's stick lying on a link of the Cooran—a wide, black, unkindly-like water, seen under that gloomy sky, whatever it may appear in other circumstances. It had been placed there by some shepherd who had business on the other side, or mayhap had been cast up by that dangerous water after it had drowned the man who used it...'

You may remember I told you that a shepherd's stick is used to great effect by another Crockett character, Muckle Tamson in *'The Rose of the Wilderness,'* but right now we don't want to leave Patrick stranded between the Cooran Lane and the Silver Flowe. Muckle Tamson and his stick must wait their turn for a later adventure while we go back to Patrick's side: *'...Thus in time, by the grace of God, and by taking great pains, I crossed both the Silver Flowe of Buchan and the Links of the Cooran. It is ever the nature of Galloway to share the credit of any victory with Providence, but to charge it wholly with any disaster. 'Wasna that cleverly dune?' we say when we succeed. 'We maun juist submit,' we say when we fail—a comfortable theology, which is ever the one for the most feck of Galloway men, whom chiefly dourness and not fanaticism took to the hills when*

Lag came riding with his mandates and letters judicatory.'

We might want to allow ourselves some momentary relief having made our way across the Cooran and the Silver Flowe. But immediately, we are confronted, as Patrick is, with the full weight of the vista of the Dungeon of Buchan from the east. This is what he sees: *'The great clouds were topping the black and terrible ramparts opposite to me. Along the long cliff line, scarred and broken with the thunderbolt, the clouds lay piled, making the Merrick, the Star, the Dungeon, and the other hills of that centre boss of the hill country look twice their proper height. The darkness drew swiftly down like a curtain. The valley was filled with a steely blue smother. From the white clouds along the top of the Dungeon of Buchan fleecy streamers were blown upwards, and swift gusts spirted down. Behind, the thunder growled like a continuous roll of drums, and little lambent flames played like devils' smiles about the grim features of Breesha and the Snibe. Yonder were the frowning rocks of the Dungeon itself farthest to the north, and that great hollow-throated pass through which still a peep of sunshine mistily shot down, bore the grim name of the Wolf's Slock. Thither I must climb. Yet though there was no light in it, it was through it that I could best see the hell-brew of elements which was going on up there. Here on the side of the opposite brae did I lie face down on the grass and heather and look upward. The wind came in curious extremes—now in lown-warm puffs and gusts, and then again in sharp, cold bensles that froze the blood in one's veins.*

Then it was that for the first and last time, a kind of shuddering horror came over me, which now I shame to think upon. What right had I to be there? —I that might have sat safe and smiling on my Isle Rathan?...'

The adventure thus far is nothing compared to what is to come as Patrick finds his way into the Heart of the Dungeon. And in case you're tempted to think that Crockett is over dramatizing, our modern guide Paddy Dillon describes the view from the Back Hill o' Bush bothy thus: *'the forbiddingly rugged Dungeon Hills, which exhibit boilerplate slabs and soaring buttresses, which make the whole range seem unassailable.'* Just looking up to the Dungeon Range can be a daunting experience, but it's there we've got to go. Even if the elements are against us, this is the path we must take.

DUNGEON HILL

'Dungeon Hill rises grandly, a thunder-splintered ridge of boulders and pinnacles, on whose slopes we see strewn the very bones of creation.'

Let's allow ourselves to pause for a moment to get our bearings. We're now standing at the bottom of Dungeon Hill, which is one of the outstanding features of the Dungeon Range. My first guide to the Galloway Hills from twenty years ago, Paddy Dillon, describes it: *'all around Dungeon Hill is a desolate scene of bog and boulders, with great slabs of granite titling towards fearsome cliffs.'*

Our other modern guide Dane Love tells us that this granite hill is home to both mountain goat and blueberry. Don't let that fool you into thinking it's anything other than a harsh environment. Dungeon Hill is the peak of a range which it's possible (though not easy) to get to from all points on the compass. From where we stand it is immediately obvious why the Eastern aspect of the Dungeon of Buchan is predominantly the province of rock-climbers. The Dungeon and Craignaw Ranges are huge slabs of granite rock among which modern climbers have created their own lexicon (sadly none seem to take into account names from Crockett's stories) and doubtless about which the same rock-climbers have many stories to tell and adventures to recount. An internet search can yield descriptions and pictures galore.

Because, despite its harshness, the Dungeon Range has something to offer all who love the beauty of the wilderness. Let's stop for a moment and allow Crockett to show us it in panorama.

From the West, he describes it thus: *'On the east side of Loch Enoch the Dungeon Hill rises grandly, a thunder-splintered ridge of boulders and pinnacles, on whose slopes we see strewn the very bones of creation. Nature has got down here to her pristine elements, and so old is the country, that we seem to see the whole turmoil of 'taps and tourocks'—very much as they were when the last of the Galloway glaciers melted slowly away and left the long ice-vexed land at rest under the blow of the winds and the open heaven.'*

And from the top of Dungeon Hill looking down, as Silver Sand does, we see: *'Beneath, the links of the Black Water shone like frosted silver in the haze of heat. Yellow, brown, purple, and black the far-reaching peat-hags stretched about them. An eagle hung motionless above in the pearl-grey sky, and the smoke over the Dungeon of Buchan slowly melted into faint cloud mists against the uprising slaty blue of the mountains...'*

We are fortunate to be able to effortlessly take in

155

the view from all aspects. Did I say effortlessly? It's all about to get a lot harder.

Remember this is a wild country, inhabited by gypsies. We are about to pay them a visit at The House of Craignairny and the Shiel of the Dungeon of Buchan. But first we've got to tackle the Wolf's Slock. And believe me, that's no mean feat.

5.THE WOLF'S SLOCK

'A scramble among the trees, a climb among the boulders, and we are on the edge of the Wolf's Slock – the appropriately named wide throat, up which so many marauding expeditions have come and gone.'

There's a lot of confusion surrounding the Wolf's Slock. Even if we take out the obvious red herring of the one sited at Hoodens Hill further north (noted by Dane Love in *'Galloway Highlands'*) and the typo on certain OS maps where it's described as Wolf's Stock, it's still a matter of conjecture and debate amongst our guides both exactly where, and perhaps more importantly, exactly what the Wolf's Slock is.

It's an issue they get rather hot under the collar about. So prepare for tempers to flare on the subject. And if necessary, count to ten and remind yourself that it's Crockett's Wolf's Slock we're looking for if we want to find The House of Craignairny and the Shiel of the Dungeon.

We can at least start from the general agreement that the word 'Slock' is an Anglicised version of the Gaelic *sloc* which means pit, gutter, throat, gorge, ravine or defile.

For our purposes, the Wolf's Slock refers to a place

Crockett describes in *'Raiderland'* thus: *'Across a wilderness of tangled ridge-boulder and morass is the Long Hill of the Dungeon, depressed to the south into the 'Wolf's Slock' —or throat.'*

So for Crockett at least, the Wolf's Slock is a pass which sits at the end of the Dungeon Range. Seems easy enough. If only. It's a place you have to tread very carefully, and a place where you realise the importance of a reliable guide. Because everyone seems to have a different opinion about exactly where the Wolf's Slock is.

Perhaps it's time to remind ourselves that the adventure we are embarked on is fundamentally one of the imagination. We are in search of gypsies, smugglers and raiders after all. The Wolf's Slock is simply a means to an end, not a goal in and of itself. But it must be faced all the same.

We need to show the same adventurous spirit that Patrick Heron does when he knows he has to deal with the Wolf's Slock. He's afraid of its reputation but he's not going to let it stand in the way of achieving his goal. He has to tackle it in the dark. And tackle it he does. And where Patrick Heron goes, we go; even if in the cold light of our modern day it's not that easy to find. Especially from the armchair.

The problem at this stage of the adventure is not the lack of guides; it's the lack of consistency amongst

158

them. The more you read, the less likely you are to be able to find the place. We could spend a long time (and believe me I have) poring over maps and pictures and descriptions and still end up wondering 'exactly' where it is.

I won't admit that the Wolf's Slock has beaten me, but I cannot put my hand on my heart and guide you that way 'for real.' I'm not sure I would be able to even if I had ever been up in the hills myself. I know others who have got mightily lost in their attempt to locate it. One thing is certain, it is there to be found, but you need to make up your own mind which path you're going to take. And it all comes down to deciding which guide you trust to lead you.

In the spirit of helping you make up your own mind, here are the options. In 1916, a guide we've not yet met, C.H.Dick, in his work: *'Highways and Byways in Galloway and Carrick,'* calls into question Crockett's description of the Wolf's Slock in *'The Raiders.'* He says: *'the way to the Cauldron of the Dungeon lies along the rocky edge of Craignairny. If you pass here in spring, the hawk that nests in the clints below will come swooping towards you, screaming fiercely, veer away and come at you again and again until you disappear into the great gully opening on the east between the Dungeon and Craignaw. Crockett calls the gully the Wolf's Slock, but*

159

this is inaccurate. The name belongs properly to a narrow passage between two rocks at the head of it.'

There's some truth in what Dick says, though what he's describing is now known as the Nick of the Dungeon.

Patrick does climb up through the Nick of the Dungeon (although remember McBain only named it such some forty years later) and this is part of the chapter which goes under the chapter heading 'The Wolf's Slock.' And as we've already seen, Crockett does suggest that the Wolf's Slock is *'a wide throat'* whereas Dick calls it a *'narrow passage.'* So are they describing the same place?

McCormick tries to find a middle ground, noting that: *'the Wolf's Slock is really a passage between two rocks, but that name is now also applied to the natural granite pathway which leads to the three Lochs of the Dungeon.'* McCormick accepts that times change landscapes.

We should never forget that Crockett was writing in the 1890's, Dick in 1916 and McCormick in 1930's. There's no chance to get them all into the same place and thrash it out, even if they could. We may just have to live with the confusion. As we found with the Murder Hole, place names are not exclusive, and their flexibility can present problems when OS maps and local nomenclature

160

start to vary.

But this may not convince you. Or help you. How can we get somewhere if we don't know the route, I hear you ask, (perhaps just a little bit too tetchily.) Ah, what price a *reliable* guide?

How about McBain, you suggest? He's usually pretty accurate isn't he? I'm afraid McBain cannot help us much here, although he does offer many descriptions of the Wolf's Slock on his own trips into the hills. While he can help you build up a mind picture of the Wolf's Slock, he's not my guide of choice for *our* journey. He approaches it from a dizzying number of directions and pretty soon one is completely confused. Because unless you know where your start point is, and unless you know which direction you are facing, it becomes impossible to work out where in the world his Wolf's Slock is.

To illustrate my point, and in case you remain unconvinced, here are McBain's various descriptions from his *Merrick* book. First: *'I went along the upper shoulder of Dungeon Hill above the cliffs overlooking the Wolf's Slock and scrambled down into the Nick of the Dungeon.'*

This could be consistent with Crockett's description. Or not. On another occasion he takes a route into the Dungeon from Loch Neldricken and says: *'it lies in the deep, gloomy hollow which includes the open*

161

gorge called The Wolf's Slock.'

Note that for him it's an *'open gorge,'* not the *'narrow passage'* that Dick describes. Then again: *'In the Wolf's Slock on the west side of the Dungeon Hill, there is a granite boulder.'* Fine, but do you know how many granite boulders litter the Dungeon hills?

In another attempt at placing it he offers the description of: *'the sombre depths of the Wolf's Slock at the back of the Dungeon Hill'.* And then again: *'the Wolf's Slock ravine and great precipices of granite lay between me and the Nick.'*

So now it is a ravine with precipices. These descriptions may seem unfit for purpose, but remember they are part of McBain's adventures, not ours. However, amongst all the confusion, McBain does offer us some hope. One of his descriptions gives us a route which more or less accords with the one Patrick takes: *'If one makes one's way up the Nick of the Dungeon and at the top turns therefrom into the Wolf's Slock on the right one will see some of the grandest vertical granite cliffs in the district.'*

I told you that I thought it was the Nick of the Dungeon that started all the conflict. This is the closest I've managed to come to linking a real guide with our fictional story.

McCormick, who defends Crockett against Dick's

criticism, talks of: *'crossing the nick of the Wolf's Slock'* – heading to the crest of Craignaw. To qualify he adds: *'we crossed to the Dungeon'* which isn't wildly helpful. Nor is his: *'retracing our steps, so crossing the nick of the Wolf's Slock we headed for the crest of Craignaw.'* Like I said, I'm a bit too risk-averse to totally rely on McCormick – I think he's on a different path altogether at this point.

Maybe I could have just suggested that Dick's description is a red herring, like the Hooden's Slock. However, the plot, as they say, thickens. In some recent guide books (which shall remain nameless to spare blushes) there is a suggestion that the Wolf's Slock is actually somewhere up on Craignaw! This is surely taking McCormick's descriptions to the point of absurdity. One publication even has a picture which claims to be the Wolf's Slock 'on Craignaw.' How many adventurers has that confused? From the picture it's unclear whether what we are looking at is a picture of the Wolf's Slock, and the appellation 'Craignaw' is the error, or whether it's a picture of the feature known as 'the Seggy gut,' which *is* on Craignaw. I suspect the latter.

It's not giving up to admit that the Galloway Hills are riddled with contradictions. There are a few fixed points on which you can rely, peaks, named ridges and the like. But even these are seen differently by each person who views them. McCormick describes two of our more important fixed points: *'Craignaw and the Dungeon Hill which, from everlasting to everlasting, regard each other across the depths of the Nick of the Dungeon and frown down upon the two neighbouring lochs.'*

I wish I had his confidence in the everlasting. Instead I take some comfort from the fact that McBain readily admits the Wolf's Slock is a hard place to find and even worse in inclement weather: *'When the landmarks have disappeared you might find yourself in the Wolf's Slock on the opposite side of the range making for the Murder Hole and Loch Trool.'* And remember his earlier warning that the best map (or guide) *'will not prevent him from losing his bearings and going astray until he has learned the lie of the land.'*

The land I'm learning is Crockett's land. It is Crockett's Galloway we are discovering after all. And like the floating bog of the Silver Flowe, it's not something you can pin down to a fixed point on a map. Not always.

So while the weather can be a great challenge when going into the Galloway Hills, we do well to remember that the bewildering inconsistency of the names of places can be equally off-putting. Nicks, gorges, gullies, ravines, cols and cauldrons can just set your head spinning. Even if you trust McCormick and aim for an *'everlasting'* fixed point you'll discover that as well as the

164

Craignaw opposite Dungeon Hill, there's another one beyond Lamachan hill to the south. And as I pointed out much earlier, there are any number of Bennans.

We must face the fact that as a romancer, Crockett does pick up some places and move them. We must not expect him always to be in accord with the OS map or a guide from a later date. And we must not hold that against him. It's all part of the adventure.

While there is a lot of confusion about the Wolf's Slock, it's not solely, or even primarily Crockett who has caused the confusion. But we can perhaps understand then why generations of people wanting to re-create Patrick Heron's climb up the Wolf's Slock have gone home unhappy. We're experiencing enough confusion ourselves. Do you feel like you've been birled around the boulders in the Nick of the Dungeon? Well, I suppose at least now you'll know how Patrick Heron feels when we finally get to his adventure up the Wolf's Slock.

Believe me when I say that I have wondered from time to time whether the Wolf's Slock is a step too far for the armchair adventurer. I have wondered if perhaps you have to be there to fully appreciate it. But I think we've reached the point in the journey where we realise that there is no definitive guide. As far as I'm concerned it's every man for himself when it comes to finding the Wolf's Slock. There comes a time when you have to make your own decisions and live by them. That time is now.

Crockett's Wolf's Slock is out there to be found – you just have to take your imagination along with your map. For those who need to feel firm ground under their feet, this may be an uncomfortable journey. But it's all we have.

I'm going to trust Crockett. Because, above all, I intend to find the House of Craignairny and the Shiel of the Dungeon of Buchan. And I hope you'll come along however hard the next steps are. Throw down the map and rely on your imagination. Let Crockett lead the way. It's the only way we'll reach our goal.

All we have to hold onto is Crockett's description of the Wolf's Slock as the gully/pass/gorge/ravine at the southern end of the Long Hill of the Dungeon. That and its reputation. Which is all that Patrick has to go on. And after all, it's his adventure we're tagging along with. So it's time for us to stop looking up uncertainly, and join Patrick as we climb into the unknown.

Patrick first hears of the Wolf's Slock from miles away, as a vision inside the Cave of Adullum off the Solway Coast. Perhaps that in itself should give us an indication of the kind of place it is!

May Maxwell has been abducted from the cave by gypsies, including Hector Faa, and her dying father sees a vision: *"I see,' continued the old man, 'a time coming,* horses and men upon the green. I see the waving of their banners. The companies are marching to the tuck of drum. They are clattering up the Wolf's Slock. I see them go.'

'It is the second sight,' whispered Silver Sand. 'List to him. No horses can go up the Wolf's Slock."

Like all good adventures, the suspense builds further. As he sets out to rescue May, Patrick encounters Billy Marshall (the famous gypsy) who tells him: 'Ye'll hae a dark nicht o't in the Wolf's Slock. It'll be as dark up there as the inside o' that beast himsel'. But a' the better for you. Keep a guid heart and your breast to the brae.'

We need to accept that this is not a place to be taken lightly, or an easy place to find and it's certainly a place to be feared, but if we stay with Patrick it'll find us soon enough. Here goes: 'I went up the side of the Dungeon towards the Throat of the Wolf. It was indeed dourness and not courage which took me there. I had done no harm that I should be afraid of any Faa that lived. But all the same there was a small cold contracted feeling about the pit of my stomach, where ordinarily my courage lies. Other folks may tell that they feel bold as lions—at the heart—or have a mortal fear—at the heart. These are differently made from me, for it is low down, even in my stomach, that my courage lies, though it is oftenest rather the empty want of any that pinches.

The truth is I was most mortally afraid. To begin

167

with, I was wet through—not that I minded that much in itself, for so I was usually all day at the shore; but there the salt in the air, and the kindliness of the sea breeze, make it a comfortable wetness. Here, on the other hand, the wind off the hills had a cold nip about it, and seemed to freeze the very clothes on one's back. I felt also a sting of sleet on my face.

I clambered upwards through the great boulders and loose stones.'

At this point we can assume that Patrick is climbing up the Nick of the Dungeon, with loose rocks and boulders on either side:

'It was no jesting now. I could see only a hundred yards or so above me, but overhead the thunder was moaning and rattling, coming ever closer. There was a faint blue light, more unpleasant than darkness, high in the lift. Then little tongues of crawling cloud were shooting down as it seemed, to snatch at me, curling upward like the winkers of an old man's eye as they came near me. I hated them.

As often as they approached there was a soft hissing, and the rocks grew dim and misty blue. My hands pricked at the thin fine skin between the fingers that we call the webs. I had a strange prickling tightness about my brow, and my bonnet lifted. So for all my stubborn stoutness, I liked it not, and know not how I

168

went through with it. Were it to do again, I trow that I should instantly turn tail and make for Rathan's Isle, and Patrick Heron, his most defenced turret. But indeed I cannot tell how I went on. Certainly it was not out of courage.

What I liked least were the little spouts of stones that discharged themselves downward with a crash and a rattle. I know not why, for the waterspouts in the clouds had not broken. They came with a dry noise, like bones rattling into a vault, as once I heard them when they were clearing the Dullarg kirkyard to make room for new parishioners—a most unholy sound. I have wished many a time since that I had bided at home and not gone to hear it—as indeed my father had bidden me. So I was properly served.

Most of these spouts of stones fell on great tails that spread down the mountain steep, like rubble from a quarry toom (or dump, as they call it in the sea-coal district). Some of these I had to cross, and a most uncomfortable passage I made of it. Little sharp slate stones came down with a whizz, spinning like wheels, and passed quite close to the ear with a vicious clip; as the teeth of a dog snap when he bites and misses, yet means to do your business the next time (and you know he will)—a most vile feeling. One went past like a bullet of lead and clipped a piece of skin from my ear, which came

169

near to make me swear—a habit in which there is no profit, and which therefore I never use. But I ought rather to have said a prayer and given thanks, but that I did not either.

Then I came to one very wide spout, and my feet plunged into it quickly and eagerly, because I was wishful to get across with all speed, for, indeed, I liked not the place. But just when I was in the midst, the whole began to move slowly beneath my feet, with a feeling that sent my heart into my mouth, and made me faint and sick at once, for nothing is so discouraging as to lose faith in the solid earth underfoot. I stood a moment till I felt the whole side of the hill, as it were, moving downward. Then I minded me of the sand, and when I felt the push of the stones growing quicker, slithering all along of a piece, and heard the ominous rattling at the edges, I can take my oath that I said my prayers at the run. More, I flung myself out as flat on my belly as I could and dug fingers and toes, aye and face too, into the moving stone slide.'

Note how he changes 'voice' from first person to 'we' as he is caught up in the rockslide. He essentially becomes part of the whole terrifying natural movement. It's a clever stylistic move on Crockett's part: *'We went slowly and slowly, and for some years (so it seemed, and I took careful note of the time), I could not tell whether we were going faster to fall or slower to stop. But I prayed*

170

heartily as I had not done for months. I resolved that if I could only get out of this I should be quite a different man. I promised as many as sixteen promises that I would give up various sins (which indeed I had been meaning to do for a long time, and cared nothing about). Then when I was sure that the slide was going quicker, I added other sixteen sins that I really cared about. After that I called on Providence to do so to me and more also, if I did not give all these sins up (having no intention of ever coming that way again, if only this once I could win clear). Then suddenly in the midst of my promises and petitions I minded me of the great precipice which was below me, and how I had admired as I lay on the brae opposite, to see the spouts of white stones shoot over it and clatter against the rocks down, far down at the bottom. There were ravens, too, flitting heavily about the face of that cliff, and eagles balancing themselves above, and I cursed my imagination that saw these things all too clearly.

Would we never stop?

We must be near the top of the sheer fall by now—we were still moving, slowly and bit by bit it was true, but still moving. Would the thing never come to an end?

I began to long for the fall and wonder if it would hurt much. One thing came into my mind and stuck there strangely. I was glad I had called May Maxwell 'Impudent Besom,' but I regretted that I had not then and there

171

kissed her where she stood. It ran in my head that she might have liked it. And I should, certainly. But now it was too late.

We had stopped! No, we were moving on again. Stopped again! It was dark now for several years more, and I lay as one dead with my hands dug into the sharp-edged flaky gravel, my arms stiff-set in it to the armpits, my toes also covered, and all my soul and body on the strain, as one that is ready to be broken on the wheel and sets his teeth to bear the first wrench, praying only that it may be soon over.

How long I lay thus I know not, daring no breath or movement. Then with infinite softness and caution I began to move off, drawing out my arms inch by inch, and quivering with fear if a single slate stone the size of a crown piece clicked away downwards, or the gravel moved an inch to fill up my empty arm holes. I did not so much mind about dying, but the picture of that great corbie calling lustily to his mate, and plumping on the ground within two yards of me, sat chill in my marrow. Again I cursed my imagination—which, indeed, has been no friend to me, making me to endure not one but many deaths by anticipation.

For as I lay there I could see the black fiend alighting with an interrogative croak, cocking his rough head to the side. I could note him keeping his wings a little

172

off his sides ready for flight, the purple gloss on his black satin cloak, his beak sharp as a chisel. He waddled a foot nearer, gave a 'Craw ' to alarm me, if I would be alarmed, then hopped to my head, took a look round, and There was, I declare, a horrid pain in my eye as I lay on the loose slate heaps. Of a truth I thought for the moment that the corbie had struck it out. And that is but a specimen of the way my vile imagination served me.

I seemed altogether empty of all my interior and necessary parts, as I crawled and wriggled myself off that wide spout of rock. Now I would crawl a yard; then lie all so cold and empty within, that the stones felt warm and soft though they were cutting my hands, and the ice was glassing them where they had been wet.

Then in a moment more I was clear and sat on a solid knuckle of rock that shot up from the ribs of the mountain, which was more comfortable to me at that moment than the great armchair at Rathan that once was my father's and which now is mine, in which indeed I now sit and write.

I was trembling like a leaf. One moment I chittered with heat, and the next shivered with cold. I was drenched with perspiration, and then when I had time to look I saw that my hump of rock was quite on the edge of a deep gulf. The blue-white reek was surging up from beneath on some reverse current and boiling over the lip of

173

the cauldron. The reason I had not heard the stones falling over the edge of the slide, was that they fell so far that they returned no noise up here. There, too, was the raven, black against the darkness, sitting like the very devil I had dreamed of, cocking his eye at me from a neighbouring rock.

Whereupon such is the nature of man, or at least of me who count myself one (and, says my wife, like all Galloway men, no ordinary one), that my spirits rose swiftly. I taunted the raven with names. I threw stones at him. I pulled out my silver flask and pledged him, calling him 'old Mahoun'—at which he seemed much put out, for he rose abruptly, which he had not done for all the stone-throwing, and sailed away, crying as he went something that sounded like, 'Till another day!'

Whereupon I was again full of courage, and pressed upward into the belt of cloud. I was fairly within the Wolfs Slock now, and found it as dark as many a lamb has done that was more innocent than I. The iron pike of my staff shone with lambent light as it touched the rocks, and I had again the prickling feeling all over my body. But the tingling air somehow dried me, and thus probably kept me from taking my death of cold.'

We are now, if we're still beside Patrick, in the narrow gorge-like area even Dick accepts as the Wolf's Slock. And we're headed roughly north-east towards

Craignairny: 'And so upward ever I went. I rested none, because I had a kind of strength and a desire to see the thing through, which supported me mightily so long as it lasted.

I was in comparative quiet where I was, but the wind shrieked and 'reesled' among the teeth of the shattered rocks above. It yelled overhead as I got nearer to the top. Yet hardly a breath reached me, save and except those hissing down-drives of chill wind that were over again in a minute. I thought that I should do well even in the darkness if I got the bield of a rock, or the space between two that might act as a shelter from the rain. But suddenly I had news of that.

I came to the summit as quickly as one gets to the edge of a wall when a comrade gives a hoist up. The wind met me like a knife, and cut me as it were in two—the lower part of me being warm behind the wall of rock and the top half nearly devoid of feeling; also the rain drops drove level like bullets. I had on a coat that buttoned, a waistcoat with flaps, and other things beneath; but the rain drops played 'plap' on my naked skin, as though I had no more on me than a dame's cambric kerchief for holding scent to her nose in church. As for my face, I had to bend my neck and put the crown of my hat to the blast.

Yet I could not so stick all night like a fly to a wall, and though the discomfort was infinite, the fear I was in of *another stone spout was far greater. So without stopping to think, I set my elbows and then my hands upon the brink and pulled myself up. Arrived there, I could do nought for some minutes but lie prone among the rocks, gasping for breath like a trout on the bank.*

However, there was no advantage in that, but very much the reverse, for it was as chill up there as it is an hour before a March snowstorm. I got me on my feet and went stumbling forward, feeling all the time with my pike for the stones and hollows. Sometimes I fell over a lump of heather. Sometimes my foot skated on a slippery granite slab and down I came my length; yet strange to say I felt no harm thereby, either then nor afterwards, perhaps owing to the quivering excitement I was in.

Thus I went forward a great way, blindly and doggedly—so beaten deaf and dumb, dazed and stupid by the tempest, that I knew not whether I were living or dead—nor cared.'

Having reached the summit of Craignairny, Patrick thinks that he's reached the end of his journey, but it's only the start of the next one, containing its own terrors.

176

6.HOME SWEET HOME?

'...All at once my pike struck something that was neither stone nor peat bog. It seemed strange to me, striking through the prolonged strain of unaccustomed things, with the surprise of something familiar.'

This is our arrival at the House of Craignairny. Or one version of it. Here is Patrick's first impression: *'I struck again and yet again. It was like an outhouse or a door of wood. What good fortune, I thought! Some shepherd's shelter about a sheep ree, left from the nights of the recent lambing time, hardly yet over upon the hills.*

But I heard a noise and a pother within that was not of the storm. I struck again and louder. Like a flash a door opened, as it were in the side of the hill, and a great light blazed in my eyes, so that I could not see. A number of men sprang on me all at once, and dragged me in: The door was shut to, and there was a knife at my throat.

Then I prayed for the stone spout of the Wolf's Slock. I was out of the throat truly, but I was among the wolf's teeth here. I had scouted the corbie, but I was in the erne's claws—which neat expressions I did not think of at the time.'

I told you things were going to get harder.

177

THE HOUSE OF THE DUNGEON

'A house—or to be more correct and exact, a kind of lean-to of masonry against the rock, which here had been hollowed away inside, partly by nature and partly by the hand of man.'

We've just left Patrick Heron, with a knife to his throat, at the House of Craignairny in the early 1700's. But he'll have to stay there a moment. Our paths must briefly diverge. Because we are going back in time to the 1680's.

Where we encounter a 'clay house' in the company of Silver Sand. We reach it in dreadful weather which: *'plastered up the front windows of the Red Killer's house, and had already rendered exceedingly ill-tempered the temporary occupant thereof—Jasper, the head of the clan Stanley.'*

This is the House of the Dungeon. At that time it was home to The Red Killer (also known as Tim McKitterick). I suggest it is the precursor of the cot house of Craignairny inhabited by the McCatericks in *'The Raiders.'*

However and whenever you get there, it's a hard place to find and an inhospitable one once you do. This is how Jasper Stanley first sees it: *'There was no more than time for Jasper Stanley to stand farther back with a*

178

terrified halt and a dizziness of the head, before Silver Sand led him into a narrow twist or lirk in the rock. The cliff mounted high overhead, and Jasper cast an eye backward up the defile in case of the need of retreat. They were among many scattered rocks and boulders, set against each other like planks in a woodyard, and anon like slabs piled up in a bairn's play of keeping house. But Jasper felt that behind each of these lurked armed men, who might be friends, and again, who might be foes.

Then all suddenly they were fronted by a house—or to be more correct and exact, a kind of lean-to of masonry against the rock, which here had been hollowed away inside, partly by nature and partly by the hand of man.

The walls were thick and solid, of the undressed granite-stone of the country, but laid with mortar and carefully jointed. Jasper specially noted a door with a window on either hand protected by iron shutters of good blacksmith's work, and above three larger windows, barred only and admitting light to a covered walk or corridor from which the chambers opened out into the dusk of the rock-dwelling.

Silver Sand did not pause a moment, but stepped lightly to the door, laid his hand on the wooden latchet, and, with a cunning twirl, threw it open. A whitewashed hall full of arms and ammunition laid out in canisters and powder horns, was immediately in front of him. But the

179

place was empty with a wide resonant emptiness, and their feet sounded hollow as in some ocean cave. Silver Sand glanced into the rooms to right and left, but no one was within. He went straight to the staircase and mounted quickly enough, but by no means like one who hurries himself.

Evidently he knew how to find what he had come to seek and without pausing he opened the third door of the range which gave upon the corridor and stepped within. Jasper followed him, and there in the quietest room in the world, a sheep dog asleep on the mat beside him, his belt undone, his pistols laid on the end of the table to be out of the way, a squat little man with cropped hair was throwing dice all by himself, his right hand against his left, a red wig on his knees and a bottle of brandy at his elbow.'

The House of the Dungeon is more than a simple hut, set somewhere in the Dungeon Range. We can be certain of little more than that. While today it may seem improbable for a dwelling like this to have existed, we have to remember that many buildings from as recently as a hundred and fifty years ago are now little more than folk memory. It would certainly have taken some toil and skill to build and furnish such a place, but then the gypsies were used to ranging these hills.

We see this when Silver Sand brings his gypsy

180

bride Juliana Stanley (Jasper's daughter) there: 'A score of hardy little Galloway ponies were bringing up supplies to the house of the Dungeon of Buchan.

Several youngsters of the tribe straggled behind, getting what amusement they could out of the attempts of the English gipsies to control their small, spirited steeds among the accidental rock-scarps and boulder mounds of Loch Enoch side. Now and again one of the Stanleys would find himself thrown off, to their infinite delight. They danced about and yelled, stimulating the other shelties, so that they, in their turn should rid themselves of their cavaliers.

No harm was done and no bones broken, for the distance was nothing, and the heather soft. But the amount of swearing and chasing needed to establish order delighted the young McKittericks, who, fleet-footed as the hill deer, could easily run down and bring back the runaway ponies.

Often the young rascals would return lying full length on the shelties' backs, or with their faces to the tail, guiding with the heel, and riding as easily as if they were upon a horse carefully gentled and provided with saddle and bridle.

It was thus that they showed off their skill before the English, whom they looked upon as of an inferior blood to the Faas, Marshalls, Baillies, and McKittericks of these

181

ultimate hills.

Then all except Juliana, the only daughter of the red-eyed smith, turned along the edge of the Dungeon wall, and so upwards to the rock house where Chief McKitterick, called in his journeyings Killer Smith, was serenely throwing dice for groat pieces, his right pocket against his left.'

Tim 'Chief' McKitterick is known as The Red Killer, and also Killer Smith. The suggestion is that he's a blacksmith to trade, as indeed is Jasper Stanley. But don't confuse the two men. Juliana is described as 'the only daughter of the red-eyed smith.' The Red Killer Smith is another man entirely and I suspect the 'red' in his case refers not to his eyes but the colour of his hair.

Jasper Stanley is not as enamoured of the region as we remember Juliana being when she first encounters Loch Enoch, and he curses the place when an early snow in October leads him to suggest it is: *'fine, seasonable weather for the North Pole.'* However, he soon changes his mind when: *'the two grey asses came in, laden and content, with Silver Sand, grave as usual, and Juliania red-lipped and smiling – why skirmishing hail and volleying snow might fall and beat as they pleased upon the house of the Dungeon.'*

We know that Juliana falls in love with Loch Enoch, the Dungeon, and Silver Sand himself. He is

182

captured and tortured and she plays a part in his rescue. Yet, on their triumphant journey back to the Dungeon, having seen off the King's Men, Silver Sand has other worries about his hand-fasted wife, unable to understand her quietness. All is soon to be revealed:

'A joyous rout it was which brought the chief home to the House of the Dungeon, All across the wild frozen moor of Buchan, they had given free vent to their rejoicings. Only Juliana, riding by Silver Sand's side, was strangely silent.

'You are not hurt?' he enquired anxiously, 'surely you are not hurt?'

Always with a gentle smile she told him 'no.' She was only too happy to talk, she said. She had gone out white-faced and hopeless, ready to throw herself before the slayers of her man. She came back quiet and content. She had saved him. No bullet had touched her, and she was still riding the mare on which he had been tied so shamefully, his feet drawn tight with a cart rope beneath the beast's belly.

Yes, it was true, shots had been fired at her. She had heard the whistle of the bullets as she rode. But none had touched her...'

We already know how long the journey is from Glenhead up to the Dungeon. Imagine it on a cold winter's night: '... *The torches were lit at the Shieling of*

183

Glenhead, and the last of the journey had to be performed under hurried glimpses of a moon hidden among snow clouds, or, in the rifts of the black sky, the sudden radiance of a star.'

But gypsies are made of stern stuff and: 'Thus they came to the House of the Dungeon of Buchan, and there, at the entrance of the rocky gorge, (which might or might not be the Wolf's Slock!) they met the master of these solitudes, the Red Killer himself, newly lighted down from the long cross-country journey from the Gled's Nest on the Black Shore of Leswalt.'

The reason for Juliana's silence is now explained: 'And before midnight of that winter night, Silver Sand's first-born son lay within Juliana's folding arms, and between sleeping and waking, out of the great peace, she watched him by the flickering of the red peat fire, while without the snow made rage among the cliffs of the Dungeon.

Dazed and tremulous of soul Silver Sand sat by the window looking out into the night.'

Having risked her all to rescue her handfasted husband (a characteristic trait of many of Crockett's feisty heroines) Juliana dies in childbirth and as we already know, is buried by her beloved Loch Enochside.

But we must get back to Patrick at the House of Craignairny, some thirty years on.

184

THE HOUSE OF CRAIGNAIRNY

'A ridge that goes along from Dungeon Hill and on the eastern side overlooks Loch Enoch.'

We left Patrick, knife to his throat at The House of Craignairny. It's time to catch up with him again. The McKittericks have become McCatericks but they, if possible, are an even more desperate bunch of gypsies. None more so than the notorious matriarch known as 'Eggface'. They have a habit of despatching their victims in The Murder Hole, a good mile or so away from the House.

In case you are not familiar with the story of *'The Raiders'* you might be asking yourself why Patrick is here. It's simple. This is where he believes May Maxwell to have been taken by the Raiders. He is prepared to risk all for love. Are you? Then let's go into the House of Craignairny. He's just where we left him. Patrick is generally an honest man, but he has the foresight in his current dilemma to pretend he is a packman called Patrick Burgess. This is not destined to ensure his safety, as we're about to see: *'I lay back and stretched all my bones as though I were glad to be rid of them. But I now kept feeling my throat grow sorer than ever where Gil's knife had been. I was reeking all the time like a lime-*

kiln before the fire. The old woman came to stir the pot now and again. She kept eyeing me as I toasted first one foot and then the other, taking off my wet brogues to do it, and commenting on the cleanliness of the house at my leisure. I told them what a night it was outside, and how glad of heart I was to have a roof over my head.

"Deed,' said Granny Eggface,' it's no' a nicht to set a dog oot o' doors—let alane a lad like you. But you are far oot o' the road to Dalmellington, laddie. What took ye up the Wolf's Slock? Dalmellington disna lie on the top o' a hill that ever I heard!'

'I was striking a short cut for Loch Doon,' said I, for lying now came as easy as breathing. I toasted my feet at the fire, setting them on the hot hearthstone to dry. The pot boiled and fuffed out little puffs of steam, and gave forth a warm and comfortable smell, full of promise. I began to feel more at home.

Eggface went to the foot of a ladder that reached up to a room above—a mere garret it seemed to me, under the roof. 'Come doon, bairn,' she said in a more human tone than I had yet heard her use.

'Come now, we'll do yet. When a child comes in the devil flies out at the window!' said I within myself, as I heard a light foot on the stairs. But I forgot that he came in again.

A little girl of six came downstairs, looking terribly

186

*thin and pinched; yet a well-grown girl withal, and one
that would soon fill out with due nourishment.*

*The old woman set her to washing the tables and
laying wooden basins round the board. I counted them.
There was none set for me. This was not so good, for my
inside cried aloud for lining and cargo.*

*But I kept watching the child. She was, as I said,
pinched and haggard. Her eye was full and clear. Yet she
shrunk at the least sound, and only answered 'Yes' and
'No' when she was directly spoken to.'*

Patrick certainly gets more than he bargained for at
the House of Craignairny. He's come here to rescue May
Maxwell and he finds Marion Tamson. It is perhaps small
consolation that far from being drowned in the Silver
Flowe, she has been abducted by the McCatericks. But
it's time to eat: *'When the supper was served it was a
fragrant stew of all sorts of meat, boiled with vegetable to
a kind of pottage, very nutritious.*

*The men spoke among themselves in a language of
which I could make nothing, the old woman joining them
with a stray word.*

*The little girl and I sat apart. She dipped a tin skillet
in the pot and gave it to me with a whole partridge in it,
and much of the fragrant stew. I thought it was a good
opportunity to thank Eggface for her hospitality, and to
say that it was a blessing that there was such a house in*

187

so wild a place.

'Aye,' she said, dryly, 'it's fortunate in mair ways than yin. We often hae a veesitor for a nicht, but they seldom stay muckle langer. The air's tryin' to the health up by Loch Enoch and the Dungeon, ye see!'

'What kind of travellers come mostly?' I asked, as carelessly as I could.

'Oh, nearly every sort,' said Eggface. 'We had a stranger last nicht, nae farther gane, an', indeed, we hae hardly gotten redd up after him yet.''

In short order, Patrick comes across this stranger: 'I stood, with my brogues in my one hand and my rushlight in the other, and surveyed my narrow chamber. I turned down the bedclothes. They were clean sheets that had never been slept in but once or twice. But I turned down the sheet also, for I am particular in these matters. Something black and glutinous was clogged and hardened on the bed. I turned up the bed. The dark, red stuff had soaked through and dripped on the earthen floor. It was not yet dry, though some sand had been thrown upon it. I did not need to examine further as to the nature of the substance. I turned sick at heart, and gave myself up for lost. But it was necessary that I should make the best of things, even if I were to die. So next I lifted the lid of the great sea-chest.

Merciful Heaven! The back of a dead man, broad

188

and naked, took my eye. There were two open gashes on the right side, livid and ghastly. The rest of the man seemed to be cut up and piled within, as a winter bullock is pressed into a salt barrel ready for the brine.'

He barely has time to recover from the shock or contemplate his own fate when: 'I heard the noise of a woman sobbing above somewhere; not the child, but the slower, sharper sob of a woman.

Also somewhere about the house some one whetted at a knife.

As I arose to my feet a folded piece of paper fluttered down as from a crack in the black boards of the ceiling. I took it in my hand as I went shuffling bedward. There was writing upon it.

'For God's sake try the window. You are near your end by cruel men. The Murder Hole gapes wide. A friend writes this.'

Then there was written below in smaller characters—

'If by any chance you that read are Patrick Heron, I that write am May Maxwell. And be you who you may, God pity you!'

Now that he knows she is there, Patrick redoubles his efforts to rescue May. He climbs out of his window and then: 'I found myself in a narrow passage between the rock of the hillside and the wall of the cottage, which was all but built against the precipice.

Climbing up the rock I crept slowly along the thatch, feeling for an opening into the room whence the letter had fallen. With a throb of fear that was almost delirious, my hand suddenly encountered a hand stretched out in the darkness—a human hand which closed upon mine. It was as startling as though it had come up from the grave; but it was warm and small, and among ten millions I had sworn to it as the hand of May Maxwell, whom my heart called May Mischief.

I pulled the little hand up, but the little hand pulled me down. In a moment my ear was close to her lips. There was only a little skylight unglazed, like the window, but far too small to let any one through.

'Run for your life, Patrick! Oh, they are cruel! They show no mercy!' she said.

'Go I never shall without you,' said I. 'What! Leave you—you that I came to save?'

'You must,' she said. 'They will not kill me. And—and—I have a knife!'

'Give me that knife!' said I.

She leapt down like a feather and handed me up a great knife, which was almost like a sword set in a haft.

Readily I cut away the thatch till I felt the skylight about to fall on the floor. 'Catch it, May,' I said softly; and the next moment the iron frame gave way and fell into her

*lap, for in the darkness she was holding out her dress, as
I had told her.*

This also she laid down so that there was no noise.

*'But the little maid,' she said; 'she is in the next
room asleep?'*

*'Her they will not harm. We must get help,' I said
hastily, to get May away; for, to my shame, I thought only
of her.'*

Although you might hope so, we are not done with
the House of Craignairny. How could we leave Marion
there?

Patrick and Silver Sand return to rescue her in
some terrible weather. But that is part of a future
adventure. I'm sorry if you think I'm cruel leaving
Marion in danger, but no adventure is without some
jeopardy. And the Aughty Cave is an adventure of its
own. It forms part of the legendary Sixteen Drifty Days,
of which, believe me, you'll have more than enough soon
enough.

For now, all you need to know is that Patrick and
Silver Sand rescue Marion and they all get snowed in for
sixteen days. Finally on day seventeen when they emerge
from their snowbound captivity they discover this: *'on the
Dungeon Hill opposite, under the hanging brow of
Craignairny there was a great pit mark like a stone
quarry, in colour red and grey—the granite showing its*

191

unhealed edges, set about with the white snow. This landslip we had not seen before.'

They set out in the direction of the landslip: '*Then we went towards the House of Craignairny itself. But when we got there we found not the house, and we found not the landmarks. The great gash on the Dungeon brow, which we had seen from the Aughty, had been made by an inconceivable quantity of rock, which had fallen, crushing its way down the hillside and followed by a multitude of smaller stones mixed with snow. The lirk of the hill in which the ill-omened House of Death once stood, was covered fathoms deep in rock, as though the very mountain had hanged itself, Judas-like, so that all its bowels gushed out. Thus was the surprising judgment of God made plain and manifest. It was the roar of that great downthrow which we had heard when we were in the Aughty, and thought that the Star Hill was about to fall upon our heads.*

No man ever saw hilt or hair of Eggface or her sons, nor of any that had been seen in that ill house, save only the man that would have knifed me, whom I saw in the great Pit of Sheep under the lee of the Merrick. The place is now all overgrown with heather and the brown bent grass; but it is still plain to be seen, and the shepherds call it the Landfall of Craignairny. They say that no sheep will feed there to this day, but I know not the truth of that.'

And this is the reason why you will not find The House of Craignairny if you go to search for it today.

It is also fairly conclusive proof that our final goal, The Shiel of the Dungeon of Buchan, is not the same place as The House of Craignairny. Which is about all we can say for certain. Because we are now going completely off the map. And no guide but Crockett can help us, because it's doubtful The Shiel of the Dungeon of Buchan ever existed outside of his imagination.

THE SHIEL OF THE DUNGEON

'A strange place half natural cavern, the rest a rickle of rude masonry plastered like a swallow's nest on the face of the cliff among the wildest of southern hills'

For me, this is the most evocative place in all of Crockett's fiction. It's worth all the dangers and difficulties to get to, whether that be via the Murder Hole and Loch Enoch or up the Nick of the Dungeon and the Wolf's Slock. The search for the Shiel of the Dungeon of Buchan is the whole reason this book got started. It's in the heart of the Dungeon of Buchan and for me it *is* the heart of the Dungeon of Buchan. It is also the home of the Faas. And one of the key settings for Crockett's novel *'The Dark o' the Moon.'*

But my suspicions are that it exists only in the imagination – at least it has resisted all my attempts to find it for real, and so it's only as armchair adventurers that we can really appreciate it. Of course hardy folk may use the guidance contained here and try and 'place' it, but I suspect that will at best be supposition and 'might have been.' We are lucky though, because there are plenty of descriptions which allow us to visit it even from the comfort of the armchair.

We may not be able to pinpoint it on a map, but to

give you some idea of its whereabouts, Crockett tells us the Murder Hole: *'lies but a mile or two, as the crow flies, westward from the Shiel of the Dungeon.'*

Set in 1724, *'The Dark o' the Moon'* offers a series of challenges both to the armchair adventurer, and the general reader. While *'The Raiders'* is given no specific date, we can fairly accurately date it no earlier than 1711. Which presents a problem for those tied to dates. No problem for the imaginative. In the same way that we have to cast our guides aside, (no guide mentions this place), so we just have to cast aside our temporal worries about how Patrick's son could have been born and grown up in the mere decade since *'The Raiders.'*

If you can suspend disbelief; a thing I find particularly easy I'll admit; and if we allow ourselves to be drawn in to the world of the story, we are in for a treat. *'The Dark o' the Moon'* offers an adventure romance with many characters familiar to us from the earlier novel, but with others coming to the fore who were of less significance in the better known book.

Let's stop counting on our fingers and accept that we have moved on a generation. Patrick Heron is now a respectable middle-aged man, May Maxwell perhaps a slightly less respectable matron. Their son Maxwell is the ordinary hero of the novel and Marion Tamson plays a large and unexpected role in the adventure. Silver

Sand is now quite the old retainer, but still a man of mystery and his brother Hector Faa is now a force to be reckoned with.

Everyone reads a story differently and everyone enjoys different things. While Maxwell Heron is the hero, for me Hector Faa is the real star of the show. Silver Sand is reminiscent of Hogg's Brownie of Bodsbeck but Hector Faa is a villain cut from the same cloth as Long John Silver and Captain Hook. He draws from the former and pre-dates the latter. I don't mean to suggest he's a pantomime character, rather that he's a villain who thrills the reader, and who, while standing outside the normal rules of society, still abides by his own code. He has a charm and charisma and, while he exudes a sense of danger, I never really get a sense of menace.

He seems to me to be the embodiment of the Dungeon of Buchan. Both display a rugged beauty and challenge us to step outside of our comfort zone.

He is frequently referred to in *'The Raiders'* as Black Hector. But Patrick does acknowledge that he is a handsome man. I suppose if I'm totally honest, I see him as a version of Charlotte Bronte's Heathcliff, transported to the Galloway Hills. As with Silver Sand, we have descriptions of him from youth and age. In *'Silver Sand,'* we get our fullest description of him as a young man: *'a tall and insolent young man, dark and dangerous, with*

196

long hair and silver rings in his ears. He was well enough dressed, though in a strange style, with a doublet and hose all of velvet, silver buttoned and befrogged with many brandenbourgs.'

But in case you think he is just a dandy, he's later described as 'a dangerous loon.' By 'The Raiders,' Black Hector still knows how to dress looking: 'monsterously fine in a buff coat and a shirt with lace upon it both of which he had taken from the house of Richard Maxwell at the burning of Craigdarroch' and in 'The Dark o' the Moon,' he is a man with: 'a dark and many-scarred physiognomy, crowned with a thick thatch of hair, blue-black brindled freely with streaks of purest white, like sheep ribs scattered over the heather of a hill-side.'

He also is reported more than once as wearing 'a sardonic smile.' I have to confess, Hector Faa is my kind of a character. The heroic villain.

It is the charisma of Hector Faa, mixed with the sheer natural rugged beauty of the Dungeon of Buchan, which draws me back to 'the Shiel' time and again. From the outset Crockett sets it up as enticing: 'At the Shiel of the Dungeon of Buchan—a strange place half natural cavern, the rest a rickle of rude masonry plastered like a swallow's nest on the face of the cliff among the wildest of southern hills—this story begins. The Shiel of the Dungeon was indeed a fitting dwelling-place for Hector Faa and his

197

folk...'

We quickly see that this is a rough, unyielding place but it has a beauty too, even as Joyce Faa, Hector's daughter, has a beauty. We meet her early on: *'There was a lass looking out of the four-square aperture which served the Shiel of the Dungeon for a window. In bad weather this was closed with a painted board, and in times of danger a green bough or a sod from the hill-side screened it. But now it stood open, and, as the light of the evening sun slanted along the precipice front, the head of a young girl was set in it as a picture is set in a dark frame.'*

Joyce's home is described as a *'rock fortress'* where she dwells: *'the eaglet spying for the eagle's homecoming with the lamb in his talons.'* No surprise that the 'lamb' is one Maxwell Heron.

The views from The Shiel are truly remarkable. Joyce can see the sunset far to the West over Loch Moan but it is to the East her interest lies. Let's go with her. But mind your step, it's all too easy to lose your footing here: *'she ran and opened the low door of the Shieling, to which (on the outward side) heather and bog-myrtle had been nailed in sweet-scented sheaves to hide the outlaw's retreat.*

With a well-accustomed bend of her graceful head beneath the lintel, the girl found herself without. She stood

198

on a path perilous. Immediately below was the wide gulf of space, sinking away so sharply as to turn a stranger giddy; but Joyce Faa straightened herself and stood erect, with the grace and strength of a young birk-tree rooted in the clefts of the rock. She was, indeed, no stranger here. For three years she had stood and watched at this spot every night at this hour of sunset. Down the long valley of the three lochs she looked, and as she leaned eagerly forward the dark masses of her hair broke tempestuously from the single strand of ribbon that confined them, and fell over her shoulders, outlining them smoothly and largely as water does a rock in the linn.'

We have to imagine that she is standing somewhere near the summit of Dungeon Hill to see the three Lochs and we are told: *'Behind her, almost from her heels, fell away the great cauldron of the Dungeon of Buchan, wherein white ground-mists crawled and swelled, now hiding from sight and now revealing the three lakelets, the Round Inch, the Long Loch, and the Dry. There were also in the Dungeon gulf tonight certain eery cloud-swirls, that seemed to bubble and circle upward like the boiling of a pot. Yet all was still and silent at the Shiel, so that the faint streak of wood smoke from old Meggat's fire on the hearth rose straight up the cliff front, and was lost among the heather and rigged brushwood above. Down in the caldron itself, however, there was a veering, unequal*

199

wind, or, rather, strife of winds, teasing the mist into wisps white as lambs' wool and light as blown gossamer.'

One cannot read too much into this 'behind her.' It's hard, perhaps impossible to know exactly where she's standing from this description, but I think we can assume it's on the north side of Dungeon Hill.

Joyce is looking out for her father, Hector's return. And upon his return the adventure commences, although this is just one plotline – the other being tied up with the Levellers Rebellion.

Hector has abducted Maxwell Heron as an act of revenge (having been thwarted from marrying May Maxwell in *'The Raiders.'*) Maxwell is thus brought back to the Shiel, bound and stunned.

While for Joyce the Shiel is a homely place: *'When at her father's bidding Joyce Faa entered the little square living-room... she found it brightly lighted by a fire of green birk twigs'* (we are told these are stored in a nearby cave), it's less so for Maxwell.

He describes it as a: *'poor swallows nest of clay and wattles among the cliffs of the Dungeon.'*

We also discover that: *'Sleeping accommodations were scant at the best in the Shiel of the Dungeon, but within Hector Faa had arranged a number of cubicles, screened off from one another by hanging curtains of coarse stuff.'*

200

So Maxwell is laid to rest on a floor of: *'heather roots spread upon a broad bench of beaten earth,'* and in such an unlikely place the romance of the novel commences.

Hector is determined that Maxwell will marry his daughter Joyce, and tries to scare him into it: *'Do you mean to kill me?' said Maxwell Heron, in a quiet manner— the way of a child that knows no reason to be afraid.*

'Kill you!' cried Hector Faa; 'that were over eager an exit! Somewhat slower shall be the gypsy's revenge! First we will drain your father's money-bags. He shall pay for your body—ear by ear, tooth by tooth, finger by finger. He shall sell his land to raise ransom. For your sake he shall die landless—fiefless; stripped even as the gypsy outlaw of the hill is stripped!'

'There is a proverb,' said Maxwell Heron, called 'Mickle land—little wit!' If you strip me of my land perhaps in time I shall get some wit—which, indeed my mother says I greatly lack.'

It was now the gypsy's turn to be disconcerted by the youth's assured calm.

'Have you no fear to be where you are? Has no father told you—have ye never heard tell of the House of Craignairny, of the Murder Hole in Lochricken, of the Brig, over the Black Water, where the outlaws broke their way through, and sent your coward kin whirling down to the

201

Airds pool?'

'I have heard of these things,' said the young man; 'but I never yet heard either a Heron or a Maxwell called a coward kin.'

Hector has long nursed a grievance and explains why he now inhabits the Shiel: *'Hector Faa and his folk dwell like corbies in the clefts of a rock because of these two – Patrick Heron of Rathan, your father and William Maxwell of Craigdarroch, your mother's brother. Since I cannot reach them, on your head it shall be. As they have dealt with me, so I shall deal with you.'*

Hector has little patience, especially with Maxwell, who in turn seems to show little fear and certainly no respect for his captor. Things threaten to turn fatal, but Joyce intervenes and Hector makes her responsible for preventing his escape. This will later backfire on him.

The description of the Shiel says that its: *'rough rocky walls were half concealed by hangings and pitiful little attempts at ornament – rough slabs of coloured stone from the hills and scraps of carpet,'* but it has a roaring fire and a few surprises, as when Joyce: *'opened a little door and revealed a score or so of books in a small square 'aumry' let into the wall of the Shiel.'* It may not be everyone's ideal home but Maxwell could be in worse places.

Which is lucky because, far from Maxwell's first

202

protestation that his father will already be out looking for him, he later reveals that: '*Patrick Heron and his wife did not say much about my absence, and that to those who knew them was the truest gauge of what they thought. The negotiations for my ransom were conducted through Silver Sand, and that wise counsellor had advised no overt movement against the outlaw of the Dungeon in the mean time. He was convinced that my liberation could be effected better without bloodshed. The county was quieter than it had been twenty years ago, when the country rose against the hill gypsies. Hector, driven to extremities, was a more desperate outlaw than any of those who had sojourned about the Dark House of Craignairny, and if his scouts brought him word of the advance of any armed party against him, it was ten to one that he would cut my throat out of hand, and forthwith remove himself out of the country.*

Besides, Silver Sand expressed to my mother his confidence that I would certainly be well looked after by Joyce and Meggat, the two women who dwelt with Hector Faa in the Shieling of the Dungeon.'

You'll remember from earlier on that Hector's revenge was to marry Maxwell to his daughter Joyce. He sees this as a fitting way to make amends for Patrick Heron intervening in his own plans to marry May Maxwell. But Maxwell Heron has a stubborn streak and

203

is determined he will not be forced into marriage, even once he's fallen in love with Joyce.

His stay at The Shiel lasts considerably longer than he anticipated. As the weeks pass on: *'I remained with Joyce and Meggat Faa upon the rocky side of the Dungeon of Buchan. The real negotiations for my release were not carried on among the hills, but at some of the low-country haunts frequented by Hector Faa and known to his brother Silver Sand.'*

Maxwell reflects that: *'in the Shiel of the Dungeon I dwelt with my friend Joyce Faa, not wholly happy, yet by no means ill-content. It was already autumn, and that and no other is the crown of the Scottish year. The front of October, so be it brings with it a week or two of still, gracious weather, is the very height of living. Oh! These early crisp mornings up there at the Dungeon, when the hoarfrost lay for the better part of an hour grey on the heather, and then was lifted away with such an elation of golden sunbeams set aslant from over the edge of the world, and such brisk whirrings of muirbirds (which I went out to shoot for the larder, Joyce following after, like a young roe among the mountains), such inexpressible freshness of the clean high air, such nearness of the sky – which nevertheless, when you lay on your back and looked upward at it became instantly infinitely removed. Will such good days come again? I wot not. We have* grown old.

For one cannot run the wheels back upon the tracks of life, nor again be two-and-twenty, and out on the hills with a maid whose hand meets yours by instinct at each steepy turn of the brae.'

I have to say, I can think of worse places to be a prisoner and no better place to be free. Over time Maxwell warms to the place. Even though he's a prisoner, Maxwell and Joyce are able to wander the sides of Loch Enoch (as we've already seen) but any real escape would be difficult, not only because of the danger of the terrain, but because of the consequences for Joyce: 'All the same, it was undeniably pleasant in the Shiel of the Dungeon. If Joyce Faa and I were not lovers, there were few boundaries to our friendship for each other. Having once accepted my parole, she and I wandered freely upon the tops of the wild mountains of slate and granite. Joyce it was who showed me how to climb the face of the great Craiglee precipice by paths that seemed no more deeply cut on the granite than if they had been scored with a slate-pencil.

Often we went hand in hand. For in necessary places she would give me hers, with none of the silly young maidish coquetry I had seen my sister and other pretty girls practise—ay, even upon each other, as it were, to keep their hands in...'

205

Maxwell continues: *'...I found Joyce Faa grave beyond her years, often content to be silent with me for half a day, with nothing all about us but God's high airs, the wide swooping courses and clanging choruses of the birds, and our two hearts that beat as one (in no mere lovers' sense) plunging and loud as we mounted upward, anon flagging deliciously as we flung ourselves down side by side on the heather. This was our comradeship day by day, and afterwards we slept soundly in our several curtained bunks in the Shieling as snugly as in the several cabins of a ship, with our heads within a foot of each other, and the steady snoring of old Meggat in our ears as a lullaby.*

Yet I do firmly avouch and record it, that we thought not of love—at least, I did not—till one night I had a somewhat startling proof that others did it for us.

Joyce and I had been out all day on the hills, as was our wont at that time. To say that we thought no evil is a statement far within the bounds of our innocency.

The sweet and gracious time was good enough for us. From horizon to horizon the heather glowed red as wine on the lees. And over this, league beyond imperial league, the honey-bees trilled their low falsetto, while the orange-buttocked bumble-bees boomed a vigorous bass.

I do not remember what we had said to each other. I cannot report these day-long talks of ours. Indeed, it was not so much what we said as the pleasure we had in saying it—or still better, that of being silent at pleasure. For often our silences would explode into bursts of gay confidential talk—yet talk such as the whole world might have listened to, so purged was it of the ordinary common-places of love-making. I have often been told that I am a fool. It may be. I deny it not. Another in my place, and with Joyce Faa for a companion, might have done other and better. No matter. This is what I did.

And, more than that, the other man would have been dead long ago with a cairn over him for all memorial— that is, if he were fortunate. Otherwise the old Murder Hole of the Raider folk has not been fathomed yet, and lies but a mile or two, as the crow flies, westward from the Shiel of the Dungeon.'

But it's to escape that we now turn our minds. Paradise, after all, cannot last for ever. And while I am more reluctant than Maxwell Heron to leave the Shiel of the Dungeon, I know that you want to move on to more adventures.

MAKING AN ESCAPE

'You will help me to escape? I could have done it a thousand times before, but for my passed word to Joyce. I am under no promise now.'

While the gypsies in *'Silver Sand'* come in and out of the region with an enviable ease, for the rest of us, including Crockett's characters, the way out is fraught with danger and difficulty. You may feel we've faced difficulty enough getting into the Heart of the Dungeon, but I have to tell you that once there, and especially if being held against your will, getting out of it proves even more challenging.

The final part of our adventure then, is to escape from the Dungeon Hills. Though if you're anything like me, you'll be wanting to revisit them soon enough. Somehow I feel that though you can leave the Dungeon of Buchan, once you've experienced its charms, it never quite leaves you. Even though I've never been there, I know there's a part of the Shiel of the Dungeon of Buchan that will stay with me forever. That is the power of fiction.

We'll leave Maxwell and Joyce for a bit longer to enjoy each other's company, and return to an earlier pair of lovers, Patrick Heron and May Maxwell, as they make their escape from the House of Craignairny.

If you remember, we left them getting out of the window. Here's what happened next: *'We slid off the roof and found ourselves on the ground in a moment. Then hand in hand we stole out of the lee of Craignairny into the wild war of the elements. The wilder the better for us. I had meant to try the Wolf's Slock, but two things forbade me; first, the murderers knew that that was the way I had come; and, second, there was that terrible spout of broken stone which must be crossed.'*

Sensible Patrick knows to avoid revisiting the Wolf's Slock. We might learn from that. You will remember from earlier that: *'We stood towards the west along the margin of a loch that was lashing its waves on a rocky shore—a wild, tormented chaos of greyness. This I now know to have been Loch Enoch. Since then I have often and often followed our course that night with men of the hills who knew the ground, so that I am now able to give the names of the localities, which I had not been able to do then when the places were as new to me as the city of Solyman.'*

There's no time for reflection on the beauties of Loch Enoch now. Let's follow the young lovers. Watch your footing: *'May and I instantly set off running at the top of our speed, and by the guiding of Providence we managed to run a long way, keeping our feet somehow among those slippery screes that lie between Craignairny*

209

and Craig Neldricken.

It was indeed an uncanny night. The wind shrieked overhead, passing above us in a constant screaming yell, that sometimes sharpened into a whistle and anon dulled into a roar. There was no moon; but the storm-clouds had thinned, and anon the mist lifted. The wind scattered the thick, white clouds and threw a strange semi-darkness over the wild moorland.

Behind us we now heard that most terrible of sounds—the baying of bloodhounds on the trail of blood. May Maxwell ran steadily, with her hand in mine.

'I have another knife; carry you that too!' she said.

'But you may need it,' I urged.

'Indeed I may,' she said; 'but I want to carry my skirt.'

I thought I understood women. So do you. We are both in the wrong, my good sir—we know nothing about the matter.

Behind us on the uneven wind, high above its top note, rose the crying of the hounds.

'How many?' I said, with scanty breath.

'Two,' she said as briefly.

We came to the bed of a little burn that trickled down the steep sides of the Clints of Neldricken. I went first, feeling with my 'kent,' striking from side to side like a blind man because of the darkness.

Sometimes as we scrambled down I would catch her by the waist and run with her many yards before I set her down, then on again as though I had carried a feather. So we ran our wild race, and I think gained on our pursuers.

Lanterns began to dance on the slopes above us— that frowning many buttressed table-land, the outlaw's fortress, which we were leaving. Only the booming of the dogs came nearer. We ran on downwards and still down. We seemed to leave the ground beneath us. We passed a little tarn among the rocks which has for name Loch Arron, and then on again among the heather.

Suddenly in trying to lift May Maxwell I stumbled all my length on a heap of stones, dashing myself on the sharp corners till I felt the rough granite dint into my flesh.

I fell with my head on a stone, and knew no more.'

Patrick and May are rescued by Silver Sand and his dog Quharrie (remember him?) who help them down past the Murder Hole and towards the sheep ree above the Gairland Burn, where we encountered them much earlier in our adventures. Here they pick up horses and ride on. We leave them there: *'the morning broke as we rode through the shallow water of the Trool at Fordmouth... It was a wide, good road now, especially after we turned south at the House o' the Hill and rode towards Cree Bridge.'*

Patrick notes that: *'there were pleasant farmhouses*

211

about us.'

They may have escaped from Craignairny but their adventures are far from over, but you have to read *'The Raiders'* in its entirety to find out all that happens. There are many worse ways to while away a few hours in your armchair.

Meanwhile, let's return to our other set of lovers; Maxwell and Joyce as they attempt their own escape from the Dungeon. Patrick and May go west but Maxwell and Joyce's escape takes them in quite a different direction.

Let's join them back high on the Dungeon Range, where they fall in love – and fall over the precipice in more ways than one: *'I cannot tell what had come over us that night. But Joyce and I had to be called three times by Meggat Faa before we came in to the supper of sheep's kidneys and newly dug potatoes which she had prepared for us. Yet I can charge my memory with nothing that should have made us so forgetful - exactly the same turn of the path where on the night of my coming Joyce had met her father. The moon was rising red over Curlywee. The mist streamed like a snow-white torrent down the mountain slopes, we could just see the silver gleam of the Middle burn in its birchen hollow, peeping here and there through the ground mist as through a bridal veil. And the hoarse roar of its headlong progress from loch to loch came*

212

to us like the sough of the lowest notes of an Aeolian harp—we were so far away and the night so calm and clear.

I think, also, the perilous place from which we viewed all this beauty put something in our hearts that had not been there before.

We held each other's hands, because, as it appeared to me, the place where we stood was palpably unsafe. And so, indeed, in the event it proved.

'Joyce,' I began, and then forgot what I had set out to say, and fell silent again in the kindred silence of the hills and the moon's red beauty. Then I confessed to her that I had forgotten what I had begun to say. Whereat we both laughed—and I heard her heart beat!

At that moment something happened.

I know not whether she had ventured a trifle too near the precipice. Usually Joyce was as sure-footed as a goat; but certain it is that a part of the insecure rocky foundation of the path crumbled beneath us, and if it had not been that I caught her in my arms, she had fallen over the verge, a couple of hundred feet or so, on to a stone slide that tailed off steeply towards the ravine.

'Oh, Max!' she cried, for the first time using the shorter name; and, before either of us knew, her arm was about my neck, having come there in the effort to sustain herself, and—my lips were upon hers!

213

We did not kiss—that is, not in the ordinary sense; but these are the facts, unexpected, overwhelming, altogether revolutionary.

The pleasure of it? Well, I do not know. It was like fire in my veins.

We could not fall apart instantly. Even the shock could not effectuate that. The path was too narrow and perilous. So I kept my arm where it was, and her hand was still on my neck but we did not look at each other any more. The weight of a great embarrassment lay heavy on both of us.

We had not proceeded more than a score of the short steps that men and women take together before they grow accustomed when, at the corner of the path, just where it widens towards the Shiel of the Dungeon, a dark figure sprang past us, with a whirr and rattle of loose stones. Something long, sinewy, and snakelike distinguished the man's movements even in his haste and dim light. I could feel Joyce shrinking a little towards me. I remember the sensation distinctly, because it was the first time I had experienced it. The girl had always seemed infinitely stronger than I. Yet on this occasion, most undeniably she shrank towards me for protection. And for almost the first time in my life I had a sense of pride in myself as a man.

As I say, Joyce shrank against me. It was almost, on that narrow path, as if I had held her close against me

214

from knee to shoulder—a detail in the roll of conquest to a bold lover, but to me utterly subversive of all the feelings and resolves of a lifetime.

'Harry Polwart!' she exclaimed under her breath, with a kind of gasp.

'And who is Harry Polwart?' I asked, a new thing in my voice, and a new and wholesome anger in my heart. And then I first knew that I was as other men. A girl was afraid and I was not. An instinct of possession and protection surged upward in my heart.

And I kissed Joyce Faa for the first time—the other did not count.'

At this point escape seems to be the last thing on Maxwell's mind. There is no doubt that he loves Joyce, but his refusal to marry under duress leaves him with only one option. And it is unpalatable to both of them. Joyce realises that to prevent his death, she must break her word and help him escape. But they need to watch out. There is one who aims to hinder as greatly as Joyce aims to help. Here we go: *'So after waiting for the better part of an hour, till, indeed, the red of the peat ashes—the 'grieshoch,' as we say in Galloway—sank to the dull red of cooling iron, and finally grew scarcely distinguishable from the darkness about, I groped my way to my couch.*

Here I threw myself down without undressing and waited. It is difficult to wait in the dark with strained

215

attention and expectant ear, and I fancy I must have dozed a little.

For it seemed only a moment before I felt a hand on my arm, and a voice in my ear said, 'Hush.'

Within me my heart leaped, for I knew it was Joyce Faa.

'Else,' she said. 'You and I must escape for our lives! I have all things ready! Do not waste a moment!'

I did not answer, but, feeling her breath sweet on my cheek, I drew her to me. For a moment she resisted, and even somewhat indignantly tried to push me away. Then all at once I heard her whisper, 'Only this once! I deserve it!'

And I kissed Joyce Faa for the second time. But, though her lips were sweet, the fire was quite gone out of them. They were salt with tears, and she kissed me more like a mother who kisses her son whom she sends forth to the battle from which he will never return.'

They embark on a night journey. Maxwell quickly loses sense of direction, and so, if you're not careful, will you. Unless you know the peaks of these hills very well, there's no way you can follow the exact path, so I suggest the best we can do is give ourselves up to Maxwell's description in all its breathless, confusing glory: *'I shall try, and I know in vain, to describe that wonderful stint of night-travel upon which we now entered. We set out*

216

immediately, leaving the narrow shelf of the Dungeon Shieling, not by the way I had arrived, along the line of lochs, each deep-set in its own rock-basin, but by a track which led away to the east, a way narrow and difficult. Joyce it was who took my hand, and at the first I could just see her before me, a dark figure blotting out the stars.

Twice we heard the solitary whistle of the curlew, and twice it was answered with a significant variation—not by Joyce, as it appeared to me, but by some other person, who, though unseen, was of our company.

It occurred to me once or twice that after all I was being taken, as it were for facility of transport, upon my own legs to the Murder Hole. But instantly I put that thought from me. Joyce was there, and therefore nothing but good was intended towards me.'

Note that Maxwell is already confused. He is travelling east from the Dungeon but thinks he may end up at the Murder Hole which is clearly to the west. Fear and the darkness can easily cause such a confusion: *'Our route was swiftly downward, and then, turning to the right, I got a glimpse of steely grey waters sleeping far below, as if the very stones my feet stirred would drop with a splash into them. For the moment I could think of nothing but our precipitous road, and of the necessity I was under of keeping close to Joyce. For this was the first time I had made so long a journey since my wounding.*

Many times I tried to press her hand and to draw her nearer me; but she went ever the faster, murmuring only, 'Hush! Let be! We are not yet out of danger!'

And I tried to extract some comfort from the 'we,' but the yield was small when all was done, and of poor quality. I was always conscious of that other, our leader and guide, who now went on in front; and in spite of all Joyce's kindness there was a stand-off feeling in her touch which grated upon me. For I minded how differently a certain May Maxwell had acted when she fled in the dark down from these same mountains with one of my race.

But this at least was Joyce Faa's way, and it is her story I am telling.

Sometimes, on the less steep places, muirbirds would fly upward with a startling 'Brek-kek-kek,' and sometimes an old ram, rushed out of sound slumber, would break away with the rush of a war-horse into the deeper dark, a trail of stones and dirt rattling down after him. We heard the thunder of the torrent throwing itself over the steep, the white spouting of the 'jaws' (so the hill-folk call them), as if the mountains were venting their waste waters to feed the thirsty plains. Once an eagle or some other heavily flying bird passed across us, almost brushing our faces with his pinions. A raven cried 'Glonk-glonk' with a wearying iterance away to the left, perhaps encouraging us to break our necks for his behoof. And I

218

noted all these things instinctively, like one in a dream.

What I really wanted was to find out whether Joyce Faa loved me, and whither she was taking me. Besides these questions there was one other.

Who was the unseen guide who had answered the sentries with his whistle, guided us down the wild mountain slides, and was now leading us across the trackless, plunging morasses by a path safe enough and practicable, if not particularly dry.

Presently we passed a stunted thorn-bush, from which I learned two things—first, that we had reached the upper limit of trees, which meant also of cultivation; and, secondly, that the night was growing slightly less dark than it had been.

I could now see the dark shape of Joyce going before, and, still more dimly, the shadow of our leader leaning forward, pole in hand, and striking this way and that among the morasses to test the way. There seemed something familiar about the figure, too, and I wondered where I had seen it before.

So, hour after hour, the three of us held upon our way. A cloud settled down over the east into which we were journeying. After the temporary illumination it grew darker again. The silhouettes of my companions dropped back into darkness and we all plunged blindly on, now through the deep hags of infinite morasses, anon crossing *by means of the leaping-pole some sluggish 'lane' or deep, black streak of oily water, in which I could dimly see the lilies set like white jewels when I could discern nothing else in heaven or on earth, not even my own feet.'*

Pause for a moment and ask yourself if you have any idea of where you are? Do any of the features seem familiar? Where are we headed? Have we been here before with Crockett, on another day, with another Heron?

On we go: *'A step or two farther and I was breaking my shins among an infinite wilderness of granite blocks and smooth-weathered stones, slipping upon the 'corklit' moss, and from time to time almost breaking my ankles in the 'traps' betwixt stones which abounded all over the dreary moorland. There was no slackening, no ceasing all that night. We kept at it as men run a long race—silently, determinedly—for a great prize, as, indeed, one among us was doing.*

It had been no more than the first breaking of the blackness—not dawn, but the false dawn that looks out of the windows of the east for a moment to see what kind of morning it is and then forthwith goes back to bed again.

Presently we came to a little farm-steading, or rather something as much smaller than that as my lady's spaniel is less than my lord's hound. The group of square-set buildings seemed to be castaway, deserted, left forlorn and derelict amid that world of heather. And yet it was evident that folk lived there, and folk, moreover, not ill-provided with the necessities of life. Within some stables close at hand we could hear the sound of horses shifting their iron-shod hoofs in the butt-end of the dwelling-house, and beyond that again cattle munching in their stalls. It all sounded to me good and friendly, and of the lowlands, though, indeed, we had descended upon the place out of the very heart of the wilds, and, as I afterwards found, the heather grew right up to the door on all sides.

The name of the place was Craigencailzie, and there was a well-marked track from it across the waste to the great Irish drove road which runs by the New Town of Galloway to Dumfries.'

Somehow, and perhaps appropriately in the dark, we've made our way back to relative safety east of the Dungeon of Buchan. But no doubt you have been asking yourself, as Maxwell did – who is the secret guide? Well, the path of true love is ever rocky and I can tell you that he is none other than Harry Polwart, himself in love with Joyce Faa.

We might all need guides to get us in and out of the Dungeon, but I suggest that Harry's price is far too high. For his services he demands that Joyce marry him. And as much as Maxwell is a man of his word, so Joyce is a woman of hers. But since Joyce and Harry's journey from the Dungeon of Buchan goes in the opposite direction, west towards Minnigaff, it's part of our final adventure and you will just have to wait to find out what happens next.

ADVENTURE THREE

ROMANCING THE STONE

7. GOD'S OUTLAWS

'I never saw a fairer place, for the heights about are good for sheep, and all the other hills distant and withdrawn.'

We're about to set off for our last adventure in the hills. And we'll be covering some ground. We'll start to the north of the Dungeon hills, in search of Covenanters and Caves. From Shalloch on Minnoch we'll go in search of Cove Macaterick, a hideout for men 'put to the horn' during the Killing Times; and the Aughty Cave, which is Crockett's fictional version of it. Then we'll head to the south and west of the Dungeon Range, taking in Craiglee, Clashdaan and Lamachan, Curleywee and Bennanbrack. Better stock up on provisions but be prepared to travel light.

We'll also be going back in time, travelling in the company of Covenanting cousins Will and Wat Gordon, along with our old friends Silver Sand, Patrick Heron, Marion Tamson, and Joyce Faa, as well as meeting some new characters. The weather, as ever, will be challenging. Wrap up warmly.

But first things first. To be fully prepared for this adventure there are a few things you need to know. I don't think it is too contentious to suggest that, in recent interpretations of Scottish history, the Covenanters, when they've been mentioned at all, have had a bad press. With Covenanters dismissed as a bunch of religious fanatics, if you are anything like me you'll have grown up with an unquestioning belief that the Jacobites cornered the market on romance in Scottish fiction.

Perhaps uniquely amongst Scottish writers, Crockett offers a view which, while it may be dismissed as partisan, goes a long way to exploring and explaining the complexities of the Covenanters. His work repeatedly illustrates the duality endemic in Scottish history, Scottish culture and the Scottish psyche. And in the case of his Covenanting novels Crockett manages to turn Covenanting history into a series of adventures as exciting and romantically dashing as Dumas' better known Musketeer stories. It's not going too far to suggest that in Will and Wat Gordon we have a home-grown version of such heroes. And in the process of these stories, Crockett breathes a whole new life into the period of history from the 1680's to the Act of Union, known as 'The Killing Times.'

Obviously you cannot write about Covenanting times without writing about religion, but Crockett's characters are not piously or overzealously religious; they are people caught up in larger historic events. They may be small amidst a bigger landscape, but if you've discovered anything in our adventures together, you'll

226

have learned that Crockett is expert at foregrounding the otherwise insignificant. This is as true for culture as it is for landscape. Crockett writes of religion, economics, politics and society. They may hide under the romance but they are there to be found like the blaeberries on Dungeon hill. So I contend that even if fiction isn't your bag, there is plenty to be learned from Crockett's interpretation of Scottish history. An interest in Scottish ecclesiastical history is not essential to enjoy Crockett's Covenanting novels; though you might find you develop one as you are drawn breakneck into the adventures which his heroes and heroines encounter.

But we can't put it off any longer. Let's set out with open minds and stout imaginations on our adventure to find the Covenanters and their kin, in their hiding places amongst the heather and caves of the Galloway Hills.

COVE MACATERICK

'It is a far cry to Loch Enoch, but how much farther to Loch Macaterick and Macaterick's Cove. Sound in wind and limb are those who can make the journey there and back in a single day.'

Outlaws (both gypsies and those of a religious persuasion) spent long periods of time out in the hills, so it stands to reason that they needed somewhere to stay. They had to stay in places in which it would be difficult to find them and from which they could move easily. Comfort was less of a concern. Thus caves became the obvious shelter of choice. There are caves aplenty in the Galloway hills. Some small rude shelters, others bigger – and some made bigger by the imagination!

In The Killing Times the accommodation in the hills was much rougher than that we've previously encountered. You'll remember the earliest version of the House of Craignairny? That would be a treat to your average Covenanter.

So let's go off in search of these elusive, hunted men. The best guide under these circumstances is, of course, Crockett. With his friend John McMillan, he travelled north in search of Cove Macaterick in 1894/5. They found it, and it features in *'The Men of the Moss*

Hags.' You'll remember in his preface to that book Crockett offered a tantalising tease as to the adventures the men experienced on their journey home.

While we'll never know exactly what happened to Crockett and McMillan, we can be reasonably certain that he took the events and fictionalised them in good measure in his novel.

I've noted before that writers are magpies; they take experiences; real and imaginary, good and bad; and recycle or in Crockett's case, often 'upcycle' them to add the romance and adventure. We should be grateful that he did. I agree with journalist Dan Kennedy in his *'Galloway Memories'* when he says that: *'we owe a sincere debt of gratitude to SRC for investing that rugged grey Galloway land with indelible colour and romance.'*

While lately Crockett has been as overlooked and misunderstood as the Covenanters themselves, interest in both was still strong in the 1920's and 30's. Our familiar guide McCormick's *Galloway* book shows a photograph of a group visiting Cove Macaterick during this time. But it's not a very impressive sight, however grandly the people stand in front of it.

You might look at the picture and wonder: is this the same cave Crockett and McMillan saw? Is it the same cave real or fictional Covenanters sheltered in? As so often with Crockett, I suggest the answer is yes and no.

229

We can follow the path Crockett and John McMillan took to Cove Macaterick in *'Raiderland'* travelling from the now familiar Glenhead. Once there, Crockett offers this candid and 'realistic' appraisal of which even McBain might approve: *'Indeed the cave itself is not worth going so far to see. One hole in the ground is much like another, and Macaterick's (at least in its present state), is the meanest of holes and the humblest of caverns.'*

But Crockett has vision. He has imagination. Crockett is always at last a romancer and continues: *'But it is quite likely that in two hundred years there may have been some subsidence, and that when Macaterick was a householder there, the cave of the bold cateran was somewhat more worthy of his reputation'*

Remember, Crockett was writing over a century before our time. He often wrote about times more than a century before his own life –so if you are looking for stark modern realism, you are looking in the wrong place. Crockett's realism is no more our realism than his romance is our romance. He works with the specific as well as with the universal. It is for us to meet him where he is.

To understand Crockett we must realise that times change both people and places – however eternal they may look to us. However unsettling this may be to our preconceptions, little in the Galloway hills remains as it was a century or two centuries ago. Even the features that seem to us the most permanent are subject to both natural and man-made interventions. The whole world around us is as uncertain as the scree under the feet of Crockett's characters as they navigate their way across the hills.

Remember also that our imagination is not an accessory but a vital part of our ability to connect with the landscape in anything other than the present moment. Fortunately, Crockett is the man to whip your imagination into shape in the Galloway hills. Of Cove Macaterick he continues: '*As in the days of the Covenant, however, the way to it is still by the side of a burn which they call the Eglin Lane, a long bare water, slow and peaty, but with some trout of size in it.*'

Crockett is well aware that other adventurers will want to find the caves, and he doesn't want to disappoint them. He wants to keep a sense of mystery and romance about the places he's described so well in his fiction. He says: '*I give no nearer direction to the famous Cove Macaterick for the plainest reasons, though it is there to this day, and the herds ken it well. But who knows how soon the times may grow troubleous again, and the Cove reassert its ancient safety. But all that I will say is, that if you want to find Cove Macaterick, William Howatson, the*'

231

herd of the Merrick, or douce, John McMillan that dwells at
Bongill in the Howe of Trool, can take you there—that is, if
your legs be able to carry you, and you can prove yourself
neither outlaw nor King's soldier.'

Here Crockett employs his trademark Scots humour. Fully appreciating the transitory nature of people and places he is surely telling us that we each have to find our own caves. And that our imagination will serve us as well as any guide.

As armchair adventurers we can take up the challenge and travel back from Crockett's own time to the 1680's where we'll find a similar journey made by Will and Wat Gordon in *'The Men of the Moss Hags.'* In their company we will not be disappointed. Will Gordon tells us: *'We kept wide of the rough and tumbled country about the lochs of Neldricken and Enoch; because, to our cost and detriment, we knew that place was already much frequented by the ill-contriving gipsy people thereabouts—rascals who thought no more of taking the life of a godly person, than of killing one of the long-woolled mountain sheep which are the staple of these parts. So there was no need to run into more danger. We were in plenty already without that.'*

Note that Silver Sand – John Faa in *'Silver Sand'* - is one of these 'ill-contriving gypsies' of whom Will speaks. Crockett likes to cross-reference characters and

232

places in his fiction. The more of it you read, the more familiar you become with both, and the more you feel a part of the whole story yourself. Crockett's characters become like friends and his places as familiar as the places you have known all your life. And this, even if you've never met the people or been to the places. Even if they don't exist and have never existed. That's the mark of a great writer.

Will Gordon's journey continues, taking us past another familiar landmark: *'After a long while we found ourselves under the front of the Dungeon Hill, which is the wildest and most precipitous in all that country. They say that when it thunders there, all the lightnings of heaven join together to play upon the rocks of the Dungeon. And, indeed, it looks like it; for most of the rocks there are rent and shattered, as though a giant had broken them and thrown them about in his play.*

Beneath this wild and rocky place we kept our way, till, across the rounded head of the Hill of the Star, we caught a glimpse of the dim country of hag and heather that lay beyond.

Then we held up the brae that is called the Gadlach, where is the best road over the burn of Palscaig, and so up into the great wide valley through which runs the Eglin Lane.

Wat and I had our precise information as to the cave

in which lay the Covenanter, Anton Lennox. So that, guiding ourselves by our marks, we held a straight course for the corner of the Back Hill of the Star in which the hiding place was.'

Will and Wat have been given the precise information Crockett himself withholds from us! Sometimes to find fact you have to resort to fiction. And for good measure, Will Gordon jumps out of history to offer us a piece of advice which in reality was a comment from John McMillan to Crockett himself – a piece of light-hearted banter in that context. With the words slightly altered but the sentiment the same, Will says: *'And this word also, I say, that in the process of your long journeying you will find out this, that though any bairn may write a history book, it takes a man to herd the Merrick.'*

That's as fine a piece of recycling (and Scots humour) as you'll ever find in fiction.

And so we arrive at Cove Macaterick in the company of the Gordon cousins: *'So in all good time we came to the place. It is half-way up a clint of high rocks overlooking Loch Macaterick, and the hillside is bosky all about with bushes, both birk and self-sown mountain ash. The mouth of the cavern is quite hidden in the summer by the leaves, and in the winter by the mat of interlacing branches and ferns. Above, there is a diamond-shaped*

234

rock, which ever threatens to come down and block the entrance to the cave. Which indeed it is bound to do some day...

...The hills were casting shadows upon each other towards the Dungeon and Loch Enoch, where, in the wildest and most rugged country, some of the folk of the wilderness were in hiding.

As I went I heard the grey crow croak and the muckle corbie cry 'Glonk,' somewhere over by the Slock of the Hooden. They had got a lamb to themselves or a dead sheep belike. But to me it sounded like the gloating of the dragoons over some captured company of the poor wandering Presbyters. It seemed a strange thing for me, when I came to think of it, that I, the son of the Laird of Earlstoun, my mother, that had long time been the lady thereof, and my brother Sandy, that was now Earlstoun himself, should all be skipping and hiding like thieves, with the dragoons at our tail...

...Thus we came to Cove Macaterick.'

With Crockett using his imagination to paper over the cracks of any disappointment of the reality, Will continues: 'Now the cove upon the hillside is not wet and chill as almost all sea caves are, where the water stands on the floor and drips from every crevice. But it was at least fairly dry, if not warm, and had been roughly laid with bog-wood dug from the flowes, not squared at all, but

235

only filled in with heather tops till the floor was elastic like the many-plied carpets of Whitehall.

There was, as I have said, an inner and an outer cave, one opening out of the other, each apartment being about sixteen feet every way, but much higher towards the roof. And so it remained till late years, when, as I hear from the herd of the Shalloch, the rocks of the gairy face have settled more down upon themselves, and so have contracted the space. But the cave remains to this day on the Back Hill of the Star over the waters of Loch Macaterick. And the place is still very lonely. Only the whaups, the ernes, and the mountain sheep cry there, even as they did in our hiding times.'

While considerably more substantial than the one McCormick photographs, do not be fooled into thinking it a wholly comfortable place. Will describes his first stay there and how after several days hiding out in the cave they begin to run short of food: *'After a day or two of this lack of food, it came suddenly to me what a dumbhead I was, to bide with an empty belly in a place where at least there must be plenty of fish near at hand. So I rose early from off my bed of heather tops, and betook me down to the river edge. It is nothing but a burn which they call the Eglin Lane, a long, bare water, slow and peaty, but with some trout of size in it. Also from the broads of Loch Macaterick, there came another burn with clearer sparkling water and much sand in the pools. There were trout in both, as one might see by stealing up to the edge of the brow and looking over quickly. But owing to the drought, there was water only in the pools of Eglin, and often but the smallest trickle beneath the stones.*

I had a beauty out in a few moments; for so eager was I that I leaped into the burn just as I was, without so much as waiting to take off any of my garments. So in the pool there was a-rushing and a-chasing till I had him out on the grass, his speckled sides glinting bonny on the heather as he tossed himself briskly from side to side. I followed the burn down to the fork of the water that flows from Loch Macaterick, and fished all the pools in this manner. By that time I had enough for three meals at the least; or perhaps, considering the poor state of our appetites, for more than that. I put those we should not want that day into a pretty little fish-pond, which makes a kind of backwater on one of the burns springing down from the side of the Rig of the Star. And this was the beginning of the fish-pond which continued to supply us with food all the time we abode there.'

Will and Wat Gordon discover that while the cave offers some refuge, leaving it is particularly dangerous in bad weather. They face the full force of Galloway as: *'we stepped out into the gloomy and threatening night. The wild-fire still flickered, and the thunder rolled continuously; but the rain held off...*

... It was an uncanny night, but in some fashion we stumbled along—now falling into moss-hags almost to the waist, and now scrambling out again, and so on without a word of complaining. Wat's attire was not now such as that he had donned to visit my Lady Wellwood. It was but of stout hodden grey and a checked plaid like the rest.

So we mounted shoulder after shoulder of heathery hillside, like vessels that labour over endless billows of the sea against a head wind. The thunder cloud which seemed to brood upon the outer circle of the hills, and arch over the country of Macaterick and the Star, now grumbled nearer and louder. Not seldom there came a fierce, white, wimpling flash, and the encompassing mountains seemed ready to burn up in the glare. Then ensued darkness blacker than ever, and the thunder shaking the world, as though it had been an ill-builded house-place with skillets and pans clattering on the wall.

We had been thus walking for some while, bearing breast to the brae all the time, and leaning forward even as a horse leans to its collar. We came in time near to the height of the pass. We could not see a yard before us. But suddenly we felt the ground begin to level in front; and lo! in a moment we were in the throat of the defile, with the hills black above us on either side. Suddenly there came a terrible white flash of lightning, brighter and longer

238

continued than any we had seen. The very air seemed to grow blue-black like indigo. The thunder tore the heavens, galloping without ceasing. Flash followed rending flash.'

There are dangers enough even in good weather. Will has left his girlfriend Maisie Lennox and her father sheltering in the cave and on his return: 'it was a bright morning when we clambered down the steep side of the hill that looks toward Macaterick. The feathery face of the rock above the levels of Macaterick, and the burn that flows from it by links and shallows into Loch Doon, glanced bright with the morning sun upon them. And there at last was the cave-mouth hidden under the boskage of the leaves. I ran on before Wat, outstripping him, albeit that for ordinary he was more supple than I—so great was my desire to see Maisie Lennox, and assure myself that all had gone well with her father. I had not a thought but that she would be sitting safely within, with the cave garnished with fresh leaves like a bower, and her father watching her at her knitting through his bushy eyebrows

Smiling, I lifted the curtain of birch leaves. Great God of Heaven! The cave was wholly empty, as I slid down into it. Maisie and her father had vanished!

I stood as one desperately amazed. There was no life or thought or soul left in me. I stood as one stands at the threshold of his home, before whom a gulf suddenly yawns fathomless.'

239

Crockett cannot be faulted for the romantic, evocative picture he builds of Cove Macaterick but remember a decade later in *'Raiderland'* he notes that the contemporary visitor will perhaps be less impressed: *'A wonderful wild place is Loch Macaterick, but the ernes have fled, and the cave has grown yet smaller, so that I would not desire to mislead the unwary.'*

It's a fair warning, but those of us who believe that a good sense of direction includes a good imagination, cannot be disappointed in the Galloway Hills any more than Crockett himself could be. He concludes: *'Still because of the wildness of the scenery, the strange shores of the loch, and also for the joy of having been in one of the loneliest places in Scotland, there is always a peculiar pleasure in looking back on the days we spent in that wilderness. Given length of days and strength of limb, I mean to go that way again before I die!'*

SHALLOCH ON MINNOCH

'Past the lonely copse at the Rowantree, by the hillside track from Straiton, up the little runlet banks where the heather was blushing purple.'

It's time to let our Covenanters out of their caves. Time to get out in the open and find other rocky places. We're headed for The Session Stone. We'll find it in the region of Shalloch on Minnoch. This is to the north of the area we've become familiar with.

McBain dedicates a chapter to Shalloch on Minnoch in his *Merrick* book. From him we find out about the farmhouse, the schoolhouse, the proximity to McBain's 'real' Murder Hole and the usual facts and figures about height.

Of the Session Stone he notes it is: *'said to be a relic of Covenanting times, in the shape of a flat slab of hard shale some several square yards in area, level with the surrounding turf on the edge of Shalloch Burn. The stone has the reputation of having been the natural pulpit from which some unknown Covenanting preacher addressed his flock.'*

McBain suggests it to be a *'bogus relic'* but then McBain is not the guide we'd take with us if looking for adventure romance is he?

241

McCormick places the stone a mile up the Shalloch Burn and describes it as a stone: *'on which is rudely carved the names or initials of people who have visited that lonely spot'*... he notes that: *'time and the weathering of the stone will, however, soon cause their names to perish,'* but suggests that *'the fine struggle for religion's sake made by the preachers and worshippers, nameless though these Covenanters be,'* is somehow everlasting.

That's a bit more like it. In the more recent *Galloway Highlands*, Dane Love refers to many different large stones (and their names) in this region. We have the Maiden's Bed and the Tailor's Stone – and of course everyone will be familiar with the plethora of Bruce's Stones which I might irreverently suggest litter the Galloway Hills. It's interesting (in passing) to note that Crockett never writes about Robert the Bruce. For my money there's enough written about him and I'm eternally grateful to Crockett that he focusses on other, less 'iconic' figures.

Crockett's interest lies in the hill folk and the ordinary people of Galloway, not in the big 'characters.' Real historical figures are rarely if ever given the foreground in Crockett's writing and he deliberately fictionalises well known families such as the Douglases – and in this adventure the Gordons - to show the impact history plays on the ordinary people. There's nothing

242

aspirational about Crockett. His perspective is firmly that of the ordinary.

And of course he is partisan in his descriptions. For Crockett, 'Bonnie Dundee' is 'Bluidy Clavers' who along with his side-kick Robert Grierson of Lag, provide us with a set of villains to do justice to any historical adventure romance. While James Graham of Claverhouse may have been 'Bonnie' to his Jacobite followers, the ordinary Gallovidian people suffered terribly at the hands of these larger than life historical figures. In fiction Crockett somewhat restores the balance by sticking up for the underdog.

And the Scottish duality theme comes to the fore again in *'The Men of the Moss Hags,'* which, along with its sequel *'Lochinvar'* charts the lives of fictional cousins Will and Wat Gordon. The two men are chalk and cheese on the surface. They stand together and they stand on opposing sides. They are both 'put to the horn' (outlawed) despite one being a Whig and one being a Jacobite. Will Gordon is always more comfortable in the Glenkens than in the hills. His cousin Wat Gordon of Lochinvar is more comfortable on horseback than on foot and most at ease with a sword in his hand, ready to fight.

As we've seen, times being what they are, this unlikely pair of cousins are forced, as many good men were, to take to the hills where they had to hide for

243

prolonged periods in caves like Cove Macaterick. The alternative (which the pair also experience) is exile in Holland. *'Lochinvar'* is largely set in Holland and the 'tamer' land of the Glenkens and so remains out of the scope of this book, but *'The Men of the Moss Hags',* while ranging from the Glenkens right across to Wigtown, gives us plenty of action set right here in the Galloway Hills.

Enough of that. Let's be on our way to find the Session Stone.

THE SESSION STONE

'A broad flat stone overhanging the little pourie burn that tinkles and lingers among the slaty rocks, now shining bone-white in the glare of the autumn sun. I never saw a fairer place, for the heights about are good for sheep, and all the other hills distant and withdrawn.'

Leaving doubters like McBain behind, we are best to go to the Session Stone in the company of the Gordon cousins. For them, a Conventicle (an outdoor religious service) which will draw the hill-folk from miles around, offers a brief escape from Cove Macaterick. It also offers the opportunity to spend some time with the family they left behind when, 'put to the horn,' they had to take to the heather clad hills. Will describes the journey: *'The catch of the autumn of the year was in the air, and it nipped shrewdly till the sun looked over the hills in the east. This was to be the great day of the Societies' general meeting, which had been summoned in the wilds of Shalloch-on-Minnoch. Though the morn had dawned caller, with a white rime of frost lying on the grass and for a little space making grey the leaves of the trees, the day of the great conventicle was one of great and lowering heat. My mother was set to go—and Kate McGhie also.'*

You'll note that Will is at least as much interested

245

in spending time with loved ones as he is in hearing a preacher. Will Gordon is no more a religious fanatic than any of us: *'For us who were used to making a herd's track across the hills, it was not a long step over the moors from Macaterick to the foot of the Craigfacie of Shalloch, where the General Meeting of the Societies was to take place. But it was a harder matter for my mother.*

She needed help over every little brink of a peat brow, and as we passed Tonskeen, where there is a herd's house in the wild, far from man and very quiet with God, I ran to get her a staff, which the shepherd's good wife gladly gave. For there was little that would be refused to a wanderer in these parts, when on his way to the Societies' Meeting.

Soon we left the strange, unsmiling face of Loch Macaterick behind, and took our way towards the rocky clint, up which we had to climb. We went by the rocks that are called the Rig of Carclach, where there is a pass less steep than in other places, up to the long wild moor of the Shalloch-on-Minnoch. It was a weary job getting my mother up the steep face of the gairy, for she had so many nick-nacks to carry, and so many observes to make.

But when we got to the broad plain top of the Shalloch Hill it was easier to go forward, though at first the ground was boggy, so that we took off our stockings and walked on the driest part. We left the burn of

246

Knocklach on our left—playing at keek-bogle among the heather and bent—now standing stagnant in pools, now rindling clear over slaty stones, and again disappearing altogether underground like a hunted Covenanter.'

It can be hard to imagine the Galloway hills, remote as they are, as anything other than isolated. But it was not always so. We're about to have plenty of company: *'As soon as we came over the brow of the hill, we could see the folk gathering. It was wonderful to watch them. Groups of little black dots moved across the green meadows in which the farmsteading of the Shalloch-on-Minnoch was set—a cheery little house, well thatched, and with a pew of blue smoke blowing from its chimney, telling of warm hearts within. Over the short brown heather of the tops the groups of wanderers came, even as we were doing ourselves—past the lonely copse at the Rowantree, by the hillside track from Straiton, up the little runlet banks where the heather was blushing purple, they wended their ways, all setting towards one place in the hollow. There already was gathered a black cloud of folk under the rickle of stones that runs slidingly down from the steep brow of Craigfacie.*

As we drew nearer we could see the notable Session Stone, a broad flat stone overhanging the little pourie burn that tinkles and lingers among the slaty rocks, now shining bone-white in the glare of the autumn sun. I never

247

saw a fairer place, for the heights about are good for sheep, and all the other hills distant and withdrawn. It has not, indeed, the eye-taking glorious beauty of the glen of Trool, but nevertheless it looked a very Sabbath land of benediction and peace that day of the great Societies' Meeting.

Upon the Session Stone the elders were already greeting one another, mostly white-headed men with dinted and furrowed faces, bowed and broken by long sojourning among the moss-hags and the caves.

When we came to the place we found the folk gathering for prayer, before the conference of the chosen delegates of the societies. The women sat on plaids that had been folded for comfort. Opposite the Session Stone was a wide heathery amphitheatre, where, as on tiers of seats, rows of men and women could sit and listen to the preachers. The burnie's voice filled up the breaks in the speech, as it ran small and black with the drought, under the hollow of the bank. For, as is usual upon our moors, the rain and storm of the night had not reached this side of the hill.

I sat down on a lichened stone and looked at the grave, well-armed men who gathered fast about the Session Stone, and on the delegates' side of the water. It was a fitting place for such a gathering, for only from the lonely brown hills above could the little cup of Conventicle

248

be seen, nestling in the lap of the hill. And on all the moor tops that looked every way, couching torpid and drowsed in the hot sun, were to be seen the sentinels—pacing the heather like watchmen going round and telling the towers of Zion, the sun flashing on their pikes and musket barrels as they turned sharply, like men well-disciplined.

The only opening was to the south-west, but even there nothing but the distant hills of Colmonell looked in, blue and serene. Down in the hollow there was a glint of melancholy Loch Moan, lying all abroad among its green wet heather and stretches of yellow bent.

What struck me as most surprising in this assembly was the entire absence of anything like concealment. From every quarter, up from the green meadows of the Minnoch Valley, over the scaurs of the Straiton hills, down past the craigs of Craigfacie, over from the deep howe of Carsphairn, streams of men came walking and riding. The sun glinted on their war-gear. Had there been a trooper within miles, upon any of the circle of the hills, the dimples of light could not have been missed. For they caught the sun and flecked the heather—as when one looks upon a sparkling sea, with the sun rising over it and each wave carrying its own glint of light with it upon its moving crest.'

The meeting itself is well described in *'The Men of the Moss Hags,'* and Crockett offers us much more with his romance than McBain can with his scientism.

249

Crockett peoples the event with a range of characters from Sandy 'the Bull' Gordon (Will's heroic brother) to Sir Richard Hamilton and a young, inspirational preacher called James Renwick. Crockett delivers Covenanter as hero. After the meeting, Will and Wat face the long journey back to Cove Macaterick: *'In the late evening we took my mother and Kate back again over the hill. My mother was very weary—so weary that at the house of Tonskeen we left her with the decent man and wife that abode there, with Kate to bear her company. She was not used to the life on the hills, and so for that time could flee no further. It was just grey day when we took the short way down the face of the gairy that lifts its brow over the desolate moor of Macaterick. Being unencumbered with women folk, Wat and I now came down the nearest way, that which leads by the strange rocky hollow, steep on every side, which is named the Maiden's Bed. So, fleet of foot, we fled westwards.*

As we looked, the sun began to rise over the Range of Kells and the tide of light flowed in upon us, gladdening our hearts. Wat was not so brisk as I, for he had left Kate behind; and though young men in times of danger have perforce to think of their skins first and of their maids after, yet it makes not the foot move so light when it must step out away from the beloved.'

We'll encounter Tonskeen (or Tunskeen) later in

our adventures. Don't forget the name.

Before we leave the Session Stone I should point out that Crockett writes other Covenanting novels which tend to range outwith the Galloway Hills, such as *'The Standard Bearer,'* and *'The Cherry Ribband,'* while his short, strange and allegorical story *'Mad Sir Uchtred of the Hills,'* an adventure we've yet to experience, gives Covenanting a sort of Gothic makeover.

And if you were paying attention, and not getting too distracted by the view, you'll remember that Will Gordon refers to 'ill contriving gypsies' of which Silver Sand is one.

'Silver Sand' has the dual distinction of being both Crockett's last Covenanting novel, and indeed his last novel (it was published on the day he died). In it he shows gypsies rubbing shoulders with Covenanters. The reader gets two adventures for the price of one. It's that duality again.

Crockett tends to use gypsies as a means of exploring loyalty, honesty and rule of law, often sadly at odds with the more orthodox examples of these in Scottish society. Crockett's gypsies come from an ancient lineage and, although wild, are quite different in character from 'tinklers'. And worlds away from our modern notion of what a gypsy represents.

As a young man, Silver Sand leads an itinerant

251

gypsy life. He has little interest in religion and Crockett describes him camping out in the hills, avoiding the grim reality of his times. But they cannot be ignored for ever: *'In the very midst of Silver Sand's dream of bliss there came a black sorrow to blight it, and to call him back again to the world.*

At the foot of Loch Moan, on the shore which looks toward the Shalloch-on-Minnoch they were camped, and the two asses which John Faa had bought for their lading beasts were wandering about seeking sound herbage, when there came a runner from the house by Loch Enoch. He had a foot wrapped in a handkerchief plucked from a washing green, and marks of haste were evident upon him.

'I am sent with this letter,' he gasped, 'the McKetterick and Jasper Stanley bade me find you, and give you this immediately. For it comes from Agnew, the Sheriff of Galloway, and has been following you many days.'

Silver Sand has been outlawed, which gives him some sympathy with others 'put to the horn.' So it is perhaps inevitable that he gets involved in helping Covenanters despite the dangers this brings to his own people: *'the bands of Lag and Windram were reaching ever farther and farther up into the hill country and driving the Wanderers deeper and deeper into the wilderness of*

252

the upper lochs from Enoch and McKitterick even to the old walls of Doon.'

Crockett often shows gypsies as having a more developed code of loyalty than the King's Men. Indeed in his fiction, gypsies like Silver Sand, and even Hector Faa, are closer to romantic heroes than the likes of the hated Robert Grier 'Lag' and his companions. This is quite a radical position for a writer to take. Crockett doesn't just write about gypsies as romantic characters, he uses them to explore social class and divisions within Scotland through history.

But let's get back to Silver Sand, helping his fellow man: *'The Glenkens men were now feeling the push so much that they were no longer safe among the lirks of green Cairsmuir or in the dens of Garpel and Garryhom. They set forth across the wilderness towards the central boss where, till now, the red of the King's coat and the trampling of his horses had never come.*

John Faa gave them help and shelter, and set the McKitterick's men who knew the wilds to construct them some shelters against the bitter season which must soon come over the uplands.

They were good men and loyal to their belief, but being of the Glenkens they brought with them a certain assertive hardness and even quarrelsomeness to which Mr. Dunning and the folk of Cree and Trool had not been

253

accustomed.

Silver Sand refused no man shelter. He sent none back to those dangerous glens where Lag's roysterers and Claverhouse's troopers were waiting for them, with musket primed and firing parties picked.'

Well, you'd expect nothing else from Silver Sand would you?

THE AUGHTY CAVE

'The Aughty was a commodious shelter, most part of which had been fashioned by the hand of man.'

I've pointed out (repeatedly) that there is more to Crockett's fiction than meets the eye. It stirs the heart while it challenges the imagination and encourages and rewards the adventurous spirit. All of this in the landscape of 'grey Galloway.' Like I said, there's nothing ordinary about Crockett's ordinary people or places. Not even the caves.

While Cove Macaterick might be disappointing to the modern man, the Aughty Cave is every bit as evocative as the Shiel of the Dungeon. And probably every bit as much a creation of the imagination. But *we* can still go there.

In the Aughty Cave Crockett transforms Cove Macaterick of *'The Men of the Moss Hags'* into a much larger place, much as he transforms the cave on 'Isle Rathan' in *'The Raiders.'* He also, in my opinion, relocates it.

Dane Love in *'The Galloway Highlands'* suggests that the two places are the same, but I beg to differ. McCormick also places both as on the north-east corner of Macaterick Hill. He even gives fairly explicit directions to it: *'to locate Cove Macaterick draw a line from the junction of the Black Garpel and the Eglin Lane to the top of Macaterick Hill, and about five hundred yards from the junction will be found the entrance to the cave, which is about the same distance from Loch Macaterick.'*

He gives the following warning: *'N.B. The entrance to Cove Macaterick has fallen in, and it is impossible to get into the cave now.'*

But this is McCormick's Cove Macaterick – the one photographed in his book. It is the one Crockett describes as disappointing. I contend the 'Aughty' is quite somewhere else. And this is why. McCormick's cave is described as at the 'Back hill of the Star,' which is Macaterick, and sited on its north-east face. Crockett describes the Aughty as: *'It was, in fact, set on the face of the hill that looked towards the Dungeon.'* This more likely places it on the eastern face of Mullwharchar, perhaps amongst the Tauchers. Mullwharcher is known as the Hill of the Star, which is distinct from the 'Back hill of the Star.' And Crockett says The Aughty Cave is: *'on the eastern face of the precipice of the Star which overlooks the Dungeon.'* It is stretching the imagination at least as much to suggest that Hill Macaterick overlooks the Dungeon as it is to suggest that there's a precipice overlooking the Dungeon on Mullwharchar.

I'm taking a risk here I know. But what is

256

adventure without risk? And my speculation is based on giving Crockett's descriptions precedence over other guides. Well, even if they are right in fact, as you could argue they are with the Murder Hole, it's Crockett's Aughty we are looking for and Crockett's Aughty that we may find if we look where he sites it. So bear with me. But feel free to make up your own mind and explore other options. I'm not one to pick a fight. It's just that as far as I'm aware the Aughty is Crockett's own imaginative creation and I'm going to look for it where I believe he sited it.

Before we go further I should point out that 'Aughty' is a Scots rendition of 'eighty' and presumably therefore a reference to the Killing Times of the 1680's. I don't know how far that is Crockett's invention.

So, if you want to come with me to find Crockett's Aughty Cave, we leave Cove Macaterick to its own devices on the north-east side of Macaterick and head south, towards the place which on current OS maps is called Mullwharchar, also known as the Hill of the Star.

Irrespective of where you place it, The Aughty Cave is where Patrick and Silver Sand stay during the legendary *'Sixteen Drifty Days.'* And it's in their company that we encounter it. Patrick describes their first arrival at the Cave: *'The air was chill and damp, but gusts of warmish wind blew at times, and in the south there was a*

257

luminous brightness. Just before I entered the cave I looked over the hip of the Merrick, and there, through a cleft of a cloud, I saw the stars and the flickering brightness of the northern lights. They shone with a strange green that I had never seen before.

'This,' said Silver Sand, 'is the Aughty of the Star. Ye have heard o' it, but few have seen it since the Killing Time. It is the best hiding-place in all broad Scotland.'

I looked about at the famous cave which had sheltered nearly all the wanderers, from Cargill to Renwick—which had been safe haven in many a storm, for which both Clavers and Lag sought in vain. My father had told me also how he and Patrick Walker the pedlar (he that scribes the stories of the sufferers and has had them printed), went to seek for the Aughty; but, though Patrick Walker had lain in it for four nights in the days of the Highland Host, he could never find it again.

'And how came you here, and what came you to do, Silver Sand?' I asked, as we stood in the flickering light of the wood fire.

'Will ye hae it bit by bit or a' at a meal?' said Silver Sand.

'I'll wait,' said I.

'An' that's best,' he answered, curtly.'

Crockett allows his characters a fair degree of comfort in what we might otherwise think of as a barren place. He's a man who sees a cave's full potential! 'The *Aughty was a commodious shelter, most part of which had been fashioned by the hand of man. It had a little platform before it, twelve feet wide, in the summer green with grass; but (save for this) from the very door the precipice, scarred and sheer, fell away both above and below. It was, in fact, set on the face of the hill that looked towards the Dungeon, and one turned into it by a sudden and unexpected twist among the rocks. Within it had been roughly floored with small logs, and arched above with the same, so that, though only about five feet in height in the highest part, it yet resembled the inside of a very small clay-bigging, or ordinary cottar's house, more than I had thought possible in a mere hill shelter. There was a fire at one end, the smoke of which found its way up through the matted heather in such a manner that but little of it appeared at the outside, seeking out unnoticed along the face of the cliff. It was the custom of the wanderers, however, to half-burn their wood at night, and then when cooking was needed during the day to make a clear fire of the charcoal —a very excellent plan, and one I should never have thought on myself.*

I had not been long in the Aughty before Silver Sand gave me something to eat and drink, which, indeed, stood ready in a goblet, only needing to be set on the grieshoch, —a kind of stew, very like that which Eggface had made on Craignairny, but richer.

*'Hoo hae ye keepit the secret o' this place sae lang?'
I asked of Silver Sand.*

*'Verra simple,' he said. 'I never telled a woman. But
it'll no keep lang noo, for ye'll tell yer May, as sure as
shootin'.'*

Silver Sand's caustic remark should serve to
remind us that some things are destined to remain
secrets. And I for one am happy for the Aughty Cave to
be one of them.

But now we've got here, don't put your feet up and
relax too long. Despite bad weather and the relative
comfort of the Aughty in the company of Silver Sand, it's
not long before they have to leave. Remember Marion
Tamson? Held captive at the House of Craignairny? We're
off to rescue her. Some things just won't wait any longer.
Listen to Patrick: *'Outside the storm burst at this moment
with exceeding fury. We had to draw nearer to hear
ourselves speaking above the roar of the elements.*

*'It's a peety that we didna think on't suner. We'll hae
an ill job noo, I doubt,' said Silver Sand.*

I asked where she was.

*'She's in the clay hoose o' Craignairny,' said Silver
Sand.*

*That I liked least of all—to turn from the Aughty
warm and safe, to face that terrible storm at the house of*

Black Murder, which I had such good cause to mind.

'An' the suner the better,' said Silver Sand, 'for lang afore the mornin' we shall be corked up as tight as if we were in a sealed bottle.'

Through the matted covering which formed a door I thrust my naked hand, and so close and fierce was the storm driving, that it seemed to me as if I had thrust my arm into a solid wreath of snow.

'Is there no other way of it?' I said, for indeed I had had enough.

'No,' said Silver Sand; 'the morning will be ower late. She's no wi' guid or provident folk, an' the Lord's arm reaches far.'

Which seemed to me at the time an inadequate way of putting the character of the inhabitants of the House of Craignairny.'

Silver Sand is determined. He knows the weather is only going to get worse. So putting our trust in Silver Sand as guide, let's go with him and Patrick, out into a fiercesome Galloway snow-storm. It doesn't matter how warm you wrap up, this is an extreme adventure! *'In a moment we were out facing it. In a step we had lost one another. We were blinded, deafened, blown away. I stood and shouted my loudest. When I got my eyes open I saw a fearsome sight. The darkness was white—above, around, beneath—all was a livid, solid, white darkness. So fierce*

261

were the flakes, driven by the wind, that neither the black of the earth nor the dun of the sky shone through. I shouted my best, standing with outstretched arms. My cry was shut in my mouth. It never reached my own ears. So standing, I was neither able to go back or forward. A hand came across me out of the white smother. Stooping low, Silver Sand and I went down the hill, Quharrie no doubt in front, though it was all impossible to see him. I heard afterwards that as soon as Silver Sand had stepped out he had fallen headlong into a great drift of snow which had risen like magic before the door in a few minutes.

We went blindly forward through the storm—yet with judgment, for after descending into the valley we saw, as through a partial break, the eastern end of Loch Enoch with the snowdrift hurtling across it. The black ice, swept clean by the fierce wind, showed dark in bars and streaks. We came to sleeked hollows which we crawled over on our faces, for we knew not how far down they went. We stumbled blindly into great wreaths, and rolled through them. In a little we were breasting the ridge of Craignairny.

'We're on it now,' yelled Silver Sand, putting hand to my ear.

I had set myself against a great heap of snow, and was cowering for the leap upon it when Silver Sand stopped me. We stood against the cot of Craignairny —the

House of Death itself. Eggface and all her crew lay within—under my hand, as it were.'

The rescue is underway. But don't you wish we'd taken her with us earlier when Patrick and May escaped? Patrick certainly regrets it: *'Leaving me where I was, Silver Sand went round the house to reconnoitre. I stood, rather sheltered in the snow, on the side at which the shieling was built against the rock. There was a swirl in the wind, the place was bieldy, and I had time to think. In a little while Silver Sand came back. He signed to me to give him a lift upon the roof. Up he went till he reached the window from which I had leapt that terrible night in the summer of the year. Above it was the skylight through which May had followed. We had come now for the little one who had been left behind—the thought of whom had lain heavy on my heart many a time.*

The skylight was barred with snow, but Silver Sand cautiously cleaned it away, pulled it open, and again came sliding down.

'If there's onybody sleepin' there, they'll think it's blawn open an' rise to shut it,' I could hear him say in my ear.

The window was not shut. We could hear the wind whistling on the iron edge of it, as though it were playing a tune.

Again Silver Sand mounted. This time he put a knife

263

between his teeth, and, raising himself on his hands, dropped lightly within. Then a few terrible minutes ensued in which I waited. The wind was so loud that had Silver Sand been murdered within I would not have heard a sound. I only leant against the end of the clay hut and thought what a fool I was and of how many various sorts.

In a little Silver Sand put his head out again and beckoned me up. I mounted upon the roof, my knee sinking among the waterlogged, evil-smelling thatch. When I reached the skylight Silver Sand suddenly thrust out something to me wrapped in a plaid. It was heavy, warm, and soft. The child, Marion Tamson herself, lay in my arm, but wasted and thin. She was no great weight for all her seven years. We were out and down in a trice. The skylight was again shut behind us, and the snowstorm blinding and shrieking about us. Quharrie I saw now. He had been sitting on the rigging of the house, looking into the skylight all the time that Silver Sand was within, a statue graven in the granite of the hills, his wild wolfish front shaggy with driven and frozen snow.

Down among the drifts we stumbled—up again over the hill, not a word spoken all the time, leading time about, the hindmost man carrying the little lamb that was too frightened to cry in the wild roar of the storm and the darkness of the plaid neuk. But loving arms held her, and I think she knew it.'

264

Silver Sand is a good guide, but let's not underestimate Quharrie's role in the adventure. Crockett knew the value of a good dog, and his fiction is riven through with the most excellent dog characters you'll come across. Most usually these are collies, sometimes terriers but our doggy hero tonight is Quharrie, the great wolfhound: *'Quharrie led us straight to the mouth of the Aughty. Without ceremony he shoved his sharp nose under the covering of matted heather and sprang in. Before we could cast a plaid, loose a button, or even take our little stolen lamb out of her bieldy nook, Quharrie had curled himself about upon the hearth and gone to sleep, as though it were a fine night and he had just come in from a friendly turn on the hill after the rabbits.'*

Exhausted from their endeavours, as the weather makes further travel impossible, Patrick, Silver Sand and Marion remain holed up in the Aughty Cave for what becomes known in legend as the *'Sixteen Drifty Days.'* Anyone who has spent a harsh winter in Galloway will not be asking if this is an historically accurate event! *'Without, the hurricane drove ever from the south. It was the first of the famous Sixteen Drifty Days which are yet remembered over all the face of the hill country, when of sheep and cattle the dead far outnumbered the living. The snow drove hissing round the corner of the Aughty and faced against the entrance in a forty foot wreath. Looking*

265

down in the breaks of the storm we could see only the wild whirl of drifting whiteness in the gulf of the Dungeon of Buchan.

But it was warm and pleasant within. The fire drew peacefully with a gentle draught up the side of the rock, and the heather couches on the floor were dry and pleasant. Even the House of Rathan had hardly been more homelike than the cave called the Aughty, on the eastern face of the precipice of the Star which overlooks the Dungeon.'

During their time holed up in the Aughty Cave, Silver Sand tells Patrick stories from his youth. They involve Patrick's father John – and go back to the times familiar to us as those lived by Wat and Will Gordon. You can read the whole saga in 'The Raiders.'

Of course even the fiercest storm doesn't last for ever and as Patrick recounts: 'On the morning of the seventeenth day, when we were becoming anxious for those whose anxiety for us we dared not think upon, we looked out, and lo! the great blast—the greatest of a century—had blown itself out. We gazed abroad on the face of the world, and the sight made us both fear and quake, and that exceedingly.

It was a clear, bright morning when we put aside the mat and looked out. The brightness was like the kingdom of heaven. There was a chill thin air blowing, and

266

the snow was already hard bound with frost. We looked down into the Dungeon of Buchan. Its mighty cauldron that had the three lochs at the bottom, was nearly full of snow. The lochs were not. The Wolf's Slock was not. The night before we had only seen a whirling chaos of hurrying flakes of infinite deepness. The morning showed us the great valley almost levelled up with snow, from Breesha and the Snibe to the Range of Kells.'

Did you notice? *'The Wolf's Slock was not.'* Snow has covered everything and I for one am slightly amused, if not grateful not to have to confront the Wolf's Slock again. We don't miss it as we take in the view: *'We stepped from the door upon the first wreath. It rose in a grand sweep which curved round the angle of the hill. We set foot on it, and it was strong enough to bear us. So closely had the particles been driven by the force of the wind, that as soon as the pressure was taken off, the frost bound the whole mass together firm as ice and smooth as ivory.*

Then as we stood on the top there was a wonderful sight to be seen. A wide world of wreathed snow. There was no Loch Enoch to be discerned. The dazzling curve of the blown snow ran clear up the side of the great Merrick Hill. There was no Loch-in-loch. There was no Outlaws' Island. The same frost-bound whiteness had covered all. The old world was drowned in snow and there was no

Bow of Promise to be seen. Perhaps because we had offered no sacrifice.'

Here we see a bright new world. A clean, white world in which all the places we've adventured to thus far are lost under the snow. I find some significance in that which eludes too much attempt at explanation. Maybe you'll feel it too.

The observant among you will also recall that among the victims of the Sixteen Drifty Days, was the House of Craignairny itself, demolished in the snow. But the house that never was, the Shiel of the Dungeon of Buchan, that's still out there to be found by anyone with a good enough imagination.

Even though with the snow, we might feel that the slate has been wiped clean of villains at least, we are not at the end of our adventures. All this has merely been preparation for you to step up your imagination one more gear. It's time to meet people and go places which no one can reduce to mere fact or history. Starting with *'Mad Sir Uchtred of the Hills,'* and not forgetting our old enemy Harry Polwart. Had you forgotten about him? Be afraid. Be very afraid.

8.LESSONS LEARNED

'It is morning over Glen Trool. The light has poured over from the east, flooding the valley. But there is a mist coming and going upon Curleywee. Lamachan hides his head. Only the 'taps' towards Loch Dee are clear.'

Leaving the Covenanters and their caves in the north-east, we're headed south west into the Lamachan Range, after a brief exploration around Craiglee which sits at the southern end of the Dungeon Range. As well as our guides we'll be in the company of a diverse range of Crockett's characters from Joyce Faa and Harry Polwart to Hal Grierson, The Minister of Education and the Tutor of Curleywee. But first we'll get taken on a weird and wonderful adventure in the company of Mad Sir Uchtred of the Hills.

Permit me to stop awhile on the path and reflect. My adventures with Crockett have not been confined to finding places in the Galloway hills. I range over all aspects of his work, sometimes as furiously as Mad Sir Uchtred roams the hills. And one thing that I have wondered about over the years is: which came first *'The Raiders,'* or *'Mad Sir Uchtred'?* It's a bit like the old chicken/egg dilemma.

I told you earlier that *'The Raiders'* was published

269

in March 1894. It was March 10th to be precise. The second edition was published just a week later. That's impressive by any stretch of the imagination. But of equal interest (to me at least) is that unusually amongst Crockett's fiction, *'The Raiders'* seems to have been published first and exclusively as a novel. I cannot find any evidence of it having been serialised. And while I will not stake my reputation on it being born fully formed like Athene, (any more than I will commit to the precise positioning of the Wolf's Slock or the Shiel of the Dungeon) I often wonder why this was. I like to speculate that T.Fisher Unwin offered Crockett a package deal. Here's my story, which may simply serve to illustrate the way fiction can be constructed out of fact. If so, I'm sure you'll forgive me that. We are in the realms of the past and for me that is the realm of fiction after all.

By 1894 Crockett had already served nearly a decade as a jobbing writer of short stories, including serial fiction and non-fiction in the periodical press. He had made some good connections, most notably William Robertson Nicholl (editor of The British Weekly) who acted as mentor and recommended him to T.Fisher Unwin, the foremost new writing publishing house of the day. Like most writers, Crockett wanted to be a novelist. (He'd given up being a poet as most writers do). Like most writers he had a day job. He had a family to feed after all. In 1894 he was working as a Free Church Minister in Penicuik. Retrospectively we might suggest that the pulpit was never going to be wide enough for Crockett's talents. I have been told that he wouldn't preach from the pulpit, but roamed around the congregation, waving his arms like windmills for emphasis.

Early on in his fiction writing he noted the dual nature of shepherding – the kirk and the hills - and I suggest he was always more comfortable in the hills of his imagination and always had more in common with the herds of the Merrick than with the ministers of the Kirk. He writes extensively about both and neither are above his sharp, observational humour. But I think he saw God as love, and found love more evident in nature than he ever did in the Kirk.

I have wandered from the path. Back to 1894. In their attempt to 'launch' the career of S.R.Crockett the novelist, (a thing they did extremely well by the way) T.Fisher Unwin published four of his works in rapid succession.

Fearful of turning into McBain for a minute, I'll counsel you never to think for a moment that publishing is anything other than a business. Crockett, as well as T.Fisher Unwin, and his agent A.P.Watt (the man who invented the concept of literary agent) all had a vested

271

interest in making his writing a success. Success is measured in sales. And sales rely on marketing. In plain terms, success means money. Money would get Crockett out of the pulpit into the world of the full time writer.

In 1894 Crockett was the newest and brightest talent, and being promoted extensively across the media of the time. The 1890's was a boom time in mass market publishing and quite sophisticated marketing strategies abounded. They could teach us a thing or two.

I suggest that the simple reason *'The Raiders'* is the book everyone knows is that as Crockett's 'breakthrough' novel it's the one that has been written and reviewed most over the years. 'By the author of *'The Raiders"* was a way to sell future works. That's the publishing business folks. While success can never be guaranteed, visibility is a great way to lessen the risk.

But what of the great deal? I like to think that Crockett was offered an interesting variation of the three for one price deal to 'launch' his career as a novelist. Here it is: He was to give them two short serials in the form of *'Mad Sir Uchtred,'* and *'The Great Preacher'* (serialised in *The Christian Leader* from September to November 1893) which became *'The Play Actress'* and *'The Lilac Sunbonnet,'* (serialised in *The Christian Leader* between January and September 1894 before being published in full in October) and they would also publish

272

'The Raiders' 'straight to novel' so to speak. For Crockett, who wanted to write novels, it would be an attractive proposition. While he found his niche (and excels) at writing episodic serial fiction, he confessed at times to finding it *'weariesome.'*

As I said, this is my speculation. The answer may well lie in correspondence between Crockett which I have not had access to to date. So I may be way off the mark.

However the actual deal was cut, it certainly paid off because Crockett finally became an overnight success, gave up the ministry the following year and earned a very comfortable living from writing until the day he died some twenty years later. That, as we say today, is a result. But Crockett was always aware that writing was a business, a job, a career, a way to keep money on the table. When he's looked down on (as sometimes he is) it is invariably because he was of the new breed of writer who earned a living from novels. This placed him (and others like him) as one spawned from journalism rather than as one of the elite literary gentlemen and women whose province novel writing had previously been. In one word? You've got it. Snobbery. Crockett wrote about ordinary people for ordinary people. And ordinary people loved it. Some of us still do. Is that not enough?

But I said I wondered which came first? I suppose in a way the answer is both. *'Mad Sir Uchtred'* was

273

serialised in the *St James Gazette* in March and April 1894 and published in its entirety later that year.

In the spring of 1894 you'd be hard pressed not to be reading one of Crockett's stories. The four published works illustrate the diversity of style which became Crockett's trademark (and for some literary critics, his downfall) throughout the next twenty years.

Some writers find a style and stick with it. Crockett's sixty-seven published works might be categorised into several types but each one has a uniqueness and variety which makes the primacy of *'The Raiders'* (wonderful novel that it is) sad if it merely serves to overshadows the others. You need look no further than *'Mad Sir Uchtred of the Hills'* to see that Crockett is not a one-trick pony and that in *'The Raiders'* he is not offering simply a version of either Stevenson or Hogg's stories. Far from being derivative he is quite an innovator.

There are many paths into the hills. Crockett can guide you on many adventures in Galloway (and not just in the hills) and the more you travel with him, the more you begin to understand him, the place, and perhaps your own relationship with fiction (and fact.)

But you are itching to find out more about Mad Sir Uchtred. I'll stop beating about the heather and get back on track. Crockett was interviewed extensively in 1894

274

and he reported that the story of *'Mad Sir Uchtred'* came to him in a dream (how very romantic - in a Coleridgean sense). He wrote: *'More almost than any imagined character of whom I have written, the vision of Mad Sir Uchtred, the Persecutor, the Beast-Man, possessed me. The public apparently does not agree with me, placing him at the bottom of my list of yearly sales.'*

Whether this in itself is a marketing fiction created by a man with romance in his very veins, I cannot say (but please note the trademark ironic humour regarding sales!) but we can be fairly sure that *'Mad Sir Uchtred'* was inspired during a sojourn at Glenhead, and set in the hills around Craiglee. So it's from Glenhead to Craiglee that we set off to find Sir Uchtred and learn about his madness.

CRAIGLEE

'Near the summit of Craiglee lies a little loch, high up among the crags—called the Dhu Loch; sombre, dark, and impressive.'

After having spent so much time in the Dungeon area, perhaps we need Crockett's description to 'place' us on Craiglee. In 1894 he writes: *'The way to the loch seems to be over the white granite bed of a burn that comes down from the rugged sides of Craiglee. Following it we reach the high and precipitous side of the hill, and follow the burn up to the 'lirk of the hill' where the streamlet takes its rise. This burn, which comes over the white rocks in sheets in wet weather, is named the Trostan. Near the summit of Craiglee lies a little loch, high up among the crags—called the Dhu Loch; sombre, dark, and impressive. From the jutting point of rock, called the Snibe, which looks towards the north, we see the great chasm of the Dungeon from the south. We can catch the glint of the Dungeon Lochs far to the north—all three of them—while nearer the Cooran Lane and other burns seek their ways through treacherous sands and 'wauchie wallees' to Loch Dee, which lies beneath us to the south. Seen from the Snibe, Loch Dee looks its best. It has indeed no such remarkable or distinctive character as the splendid series*

276

of lochs between Glenhead and Enoch. It would be but a wild sheet of water on a featureless moor, were it not that it derives dignity from the imminent sides of Craiglee and the Dungeon.'

He revisits Craiglee from his own armchair a decade later in 'Raiderland.' He, and it, have lost nothing of their evocative power: 'High up on the side of Craiglee, too, lies the Dhu Loch, a kind of weird, oblong, giant's bath, quite near the summit of the ridge—sullen and black, overhung by grey crags, and deep to the very edge— altogether one of the most impressive sights on all the face of the moorland. It seems a place where a murder might have been done, and the body disposed of (with a stone or so in the neuk of a plaid), without the least trouble.'

I cannot find any guide with any interesting thing to say about Craiglee, although I would note that we are talking here about Craiglee of Dee, not Craiglee of Doon. Dane Love makes that distinction and to keep us in the right place I felt I should mention it. But to find Mad Sir Uchtred we have to locate Clashdaan.

CLASHDAAN

'Once on a day I sat on Clashdaan and shuddered when I thought of him, and I hope some will ascend Clashdaan for the sake of 'the Man Hunted with Dogs.'

The guides seem remarkably quiet about it. I have found nothing from McBain or McCormick, nor Dick or Love about it. Maybe I'm getting tired and it's just not important enough to figure in indexes. It certainly doesn't feature on any map I've got. And even with modern Googling I can't pin it down. It's not because it's not there, so I can only assume that it's not generally considered important enough to merit being placed on a map, or talked about by guides. But by this stage I'm sure we're all experienced enough adventurers not to let that put us off!

If we're going to Clashdaan we've only got Crockett for company. That's good enough company for me. He tells us there is: *'a narrow cleft that leads downwards from the Snibe towards the loch. It is called the Clint of Clashdaan.'*

Hoping that *'Mad Sir Uchtred'* will inspire others into the hills, Crockett describes it as follows in *'Raiderland': Clashdaan lies immediately above Loch Dee, and forms the southernmost end of the wild Dungeon ridge which shuts in the country of the lochs. It should certainly be climbed, if not for the sake of 'Mad Sir Uchtred of the Hills,' at least for the sake of the magnificent view, and because it is the most thunder-battered of all the hills about, Craiglee, Craignaw, Curlywee, not even excepting the Dungeon itself. Any stray shepherd, if fairly spoken and with a little time on his hands, will show a traveller more of the effects of lightning on this single hill than an average geologist is apt to see in a lifetime.*

My friend, Mr. M'Millan of Glenhead, was present with me at one such scene, which I have done my best to describe elsewhere. It will be many years before that deeply scored record is erased from the side of Clashdaan where it looks out upon Loch Dee.'

Clashdaan clearly does exist – Crockett is encouraging others to go and look for it. Is it a local name perhaps? Or has he changed the name for some reason? There are adventurers, perhaps especially those who've been disappointed in their searches out in the Galloway Hills, who wonder why Crockett has such a habit of changing names and being 'flexible' with places. I can offer something of an explanation to that question.

Today we're quite used to historical fiction; that is to the fictionalising of history. In Crockett's day there was still something of a debate over whether it was quite 'right' to take from the past and turn it into fiction. And indeed in *'Mad Sir Uchtred of the Hills'* Crockett was subject to charges of plagiarism over his character. Critic Andrew Lang and reviewer William Wallace both sharpened their knives over the new writer's work, on charges of 'misappropriating' a real historic Covenanter and of fostering historical 'inaccuracies.'

So that you can judge for yourself, here's the history Crockett raided: *'Uchtred Macdowall, 10th of Garthland 1526-1593 was a combative kind of fellow. He was involved in a feud with Lochinvar following murder of Gilbert Macdowall of Barjarg and following a falling out with King James V1 in 1582 he took part in the Raid of Ruthven in which the Earl of Gowrie seized King James VI at Stirling.'*

Garthland, the ancestral home of the McDowall family no longer exists, but Crockett would have found plenty of sources for it. It is mentioned in the 1875 *'Handbook for Travellers in Scotland.'* *'Route 10: Dumfries to Portpatrick'* states that the road to the Mull of Galloway passed by *'Garthland Tower, once the seat of the M'Doualls, Lords of Galloway'*. It was also marked on *Bacon's New Survey Map of South Scotland* (1880). Suggestions are that it was a large tower, demolished in 1840. The site of it is the nearby Garthland Mains farm.

Crockett's crime, such as it was, was using his imagination. Which is what we expect from a novelist

280

these days. We don't like poorly researched fiction. But Crockett stood on a fault line in the history of literature. Even as he wrote about the past, he was doing something new. And the old always fears the new until the storm calms down and we learn to live in harmony with nature.

In *'Mad Sir Uchtred,'* Crockett was simply doing what romancers and fiction writers have done aplenty after him, and fictionalising. He was not accusing anyone of anything. He knew the facts. And he knew how to turn dry fact to exciting fiction. It might seems a storm in a teacup today, but you can imagine it might have been something of more thunderous force for a writer just starting out on his path to fame and fortune. However, he had to respond to the storm his writing had caused. And he did it with trademark good, if subtle, humour.

In response to the criticism, an 'advertisement' was issued in the front of the published work which states: *'He that tells the tale bears witness that the hereafter to be mentioned Sir Uchtred of Garthland is not the William MacDowall of Garthland in the parish of Stoney Kirk, who was a most constant and serious professor and defender of the Covenants National and Solemn League... The kindly reader will take carefully the advertisement, both for truth's sake, and still more, that the tale teller may dwell at peace in his own land, where men have long memories, and one may not speak hastily of another man's kin. So all shall be well.'*

Even as late as 1907, when a dinner was given for him in his honour at Dalbeattie, this early 'crime' was still a matter for debate, albeit now humorous. Sir Herbert Maxwell noted it in his toast, forgiving Crockett for insulting one of his relatives.

And what is the lesson we may learn from that? Maybe now you have a clearer understanding of why Crockett was more circumspect, or less 'fixed' in his naming of places and people in his subsequent writing. Nowhere is this more so than in his writing about his home town Castle Douglas. He refers to it as Cairn Edward, so that even today many local people are unaware that he was writing about their town.

But you're getting impatient to be on the move. Off we go in search of the fictional Sir Uchtred. His is a short but shocking story. Let's see if we can hunt him down: *'The indigo night, winking with stars, bent over Clashdaan. Uchtred the Beast-Man went back to his lair in the Hass of the Wolf's Slock, dancing along the fretted pinnacles of the granite as a withered leaf dances in the veering flaw of November. His familiar followed after, trailing a limb. To see them against the sky was to believe in devils; and that is sound and wholesome doctrine.'*

Oh – the Hass of the Wolf's Slock. That name comes up again. Where is it this time? Crockett tells us:

'Mad Sir Uchtred of Garthland sat in the place that is called the Hass of the Wolf's Slock. It lies on the hoary side of Clashdaan, when all the Dungeon of Buchan is seen to swim like blue beneath a blue cauldron shot with the silver threads of still and sleeping waters.'

You find that if you can: *'They had hunted him with dogs that day. He was no longer Sir Uchtred of Garthland, but only the beast-man of the hills, accursed of God, outcast of man, and the quarry of hunters.'*

I suppose if you really thought this was a description of your relative you'd feel justified in being a bit upset! Throughout the story Crockett shows the difference between the 'civilised' Italianate terraces of Garthland and the 'wildness' of the Galloway hills, but to interpret the story as simply setting one against the other does not do it full justice. At this point though, our interest lies up in the hills with Sir Uchtred, mad as he may be. The next time we find him he's gone to ground: *'The cave on Clashdaan was but a fox-earth between two stones; but it was overgrown with matted heather, and being set on a promontory it was a watch-tower looking three ways over the blue cauldron of the Dungeon of Buchan.'*

Amidst all the madness, (of which there is plenty) Crockett gives us a picture of the hills and the silence to be found there: *'Then the night came, a serene and*

283

austere coolness settled down on the hills. The world was full of sweet air to breathe. The bog-myrtle, which here men name 'gall,' gave forth a rare smell. It was very silent on Clashdaan. The hills that shut it in on the north glowed darkest amethyst, and the lakelet and tarns shone uncertainly in the hollows.

But on all the hills there was not a sound save of a stone that clattered down a slide of shale and slate.'

If it weren't for the madness, and the fact that Sir Uchtred is being hunted, it'd seem like an idyllic place, wouldn't it?

Morning comes: 'When Uchtred awoke the morning was breaking in the east. The red bars of cloud glowed like a furnace grate. The crest of the Dungeon bristled black against the fire. There was no sound, save a burn soughing somewhere in the hollows of the hills. But above the birds cried in the dewy chill of the sun-rising. Sir Uchtred came to himself and looked about him.'

I've already suggested that 'Mad Sir Uchtred' is a sort of Gothic Horror meets Covenanting story and I'd like to leave you to explore it for yourself. I'm sure you're ready to personalise your adventures by now. So we'll leave him out there on the hills, waiting for you. It may seem calm now, but a storm is brewing for him. You can read 'Mad Sir Uchtred' on a number of levels, both literal and analogous. It is about as far removed from 'The

284

Raiders' as you might hope to go – and yet there is something familiar in it too. I often wonder what contemporary readers made of the variety and range Crockett exhibited in his first year of fame. I suppose the answer is they were intrigued by it, because he stayed in the bestsellers list for most of the next decade.

But we've spent enough time pondering. And there are other storms on the way. Remember that Crockett described Clashdaan as: *'the most thunder-battered of all the hills about,'* and promised to fictionalise the experience he had during a storm with his friend John McMillan. And if you cast your mind back further you'll remember we left Harry Polwart up on the hills with Joyce Faa in *'The Dark o' the Moon.'*

Well, it's Harry and Joyce who endure the full force of Crockett's fictionalisation of the storm on Clashdaan as they make their way from the Dungeon to Minnigaff.

For those whose memories are struggling under the weight of our many adventures, I should remind you that Joyce Faa helped Maxwell Heron escape to the safety of Craigencailzie under the guidance of Harry Polwart. But the price Harry demands is that Joyce marry him. While Maxwell and Joyce love each other, he refuses on principle to marry her under duress, and she, loving him, promises to marry Harry, to save Maxwell's life. Nothing's ever simple in romance is it?

285

It's time to meet Harry and Joyce on their journey to Minnigaff where they intend to be married by the incumbent minister. Here they are in the face of a storm both literal and figurative: *'The morn had broken wild and uncertain, a drift of slaty blue clouds edged with white shouldering up from the south west, low across the landscape. There was not much wind, but the clouds drew down upon the mountains and far in the west there was the occasional growl of thunder like a ruffle of drums.*

Joyce heeded not, a physical callousness, the reaction after vehement emotion, taking for the time being complete possession of her. She followed as in a dream. The tall, hawk-faced young gypsy stepped out across the heather, keeping to the southward of the great valley of Glen Trool. He had his course accurately marked, and after passing Loch Dee, he bore away up the side of Curleywee, the peewits scattering and whinnying before him as he went. He followed a little stream which came down the mountain, dispersing its waters into spray a dozen times, again collecting them, apparently undiminished in volume, sending them to sleep in half a score of shallow lakelets and one deep unruffled tarn, and finally in one great white spout of foam, dropping itself into the valley far below.

Without a word spoken on either side, Joyce and her companion took this goat's track up the mountain-side.

286

They were just on the border lands of Lamachan and Curlywee. Above them the blue thunder-clouds streamed eastward at a uniform height along the side of the huge precipitous ridge of Bennanbrack. Up, up they went, Joyce scarce wondering whither they were going, but blindly obeying, and in a certain sick and weary-hearted way glad to obey, if only to do anything, and to keep on doing it.

Harry Polwart did not slacken his speed till the stagnant airs of the valley began to give place to an occasional puff of icy wind blown downward from above. He was marching right upward into the thunder-cloud. Joyce felt more than once the sting of hail in her face. Suddenly a whitish-grey tongue of cloud came rushing towards them, at sight of which the gypsy uttered a warning cry, and Joyce caught at a projecting corner of rock which gave under her hand.

In a moment the gypsy had sprung to her side, and pulled her down behind a huge boulder, which, after sliding thus far, had remained perilously poised on the mountain-side. He put his arm about Joyce and forced her into the most interior crevice of the rock, standing in front of her. The threatening arm reached out as if to snatch them from their refuge. As it came nearer, Joyce saw a funnel-shaped cloud, its point spinning like a top along the mountain-side. It rushed upon them. The next moment,

287

with a tremendous explosion of sound and a blinding pale-blue light, the world seemed to end, and the heart of Joyce Faa gave a bound of thankfulness. God had surely heard her prayer. The end was come! The thunderbolt had smitten them both!'

In saving Joyce, Harry Polwart has paid a terrible price as we are about to discover: *'He could not even see the ripples of fire that played level all about them, running from scarlet and lavender upon the leonine haunches of Curlywee to blinding and burning opal as the flame ran along the ragged cloud edges beneath the ridge of Bennanbrack.*

A constant rattle of falling stones accompanied the storm as the thunderbolts shot every way along the mountain-side. Every moment's safety seemed to Joyce a miracle; and Harry Polwart, like a child in fear of the dark, caught at her hand and nursed it to his side, saying, over and over, 'You will not leave me now, Joyce! You will keep your promise?'

'I will keep my promise,' she answered; and he heard her even amid the loudest roaring of the storm, yet was not satisfied.

'Promise me, Joyce! I am blind! I cannot see you, or follow you! But you will keep your word to Harry the Gypsy, who dared death and kept his word to you?'

'I have said it,' answered Joyce Faa.'

The devastating effect of the storm has been to render Harry Polwart blind. But don't confuse him with the Blind Harry of Scottish literature. It's just Crockett playing fast and loose with names again. By the time *'The Dark o' the Moon'* was published in 1902 he no longer worried about charges of plagiarism. Times, it seems, change men – but equally, men change with the times. Either way: *'The thunder-storm was a long one, and did not move with the wind. It seemed rather to hang heavily between the hills about the head of the great glens, venting itself after a while, not in short, sharp, frequent explosions, but rather in long brooding silences, which were followed by tremendous outbursts of sound and flame.'*

Of course it would now be easy for Joyce to leave Harry, but it is not so much his extended avowal of love that keeps her beside him as the fact that: *'I have told you that I would keep my promise,' said Joyce Faa, still letting him hold her hand.*

'Then you will take me to the Manse of Minnigaff, and there the minister will marry us. For not otherwise will I be wed to you, Joyce Faa, but even as was your own choice when your father would have given you to the young laird's son!'

The storm passed away as it had come with scattering peals, a dying flicker of lightning far away to the east, and gusts of cold wet wind that rumbled about the rock clefts and soughed eerily through the deep glens on the flanks of Cairnsmuir.

All about them there was the glimmering haze, which is the rain driven into spray as it danced off the boulders and was exhaled from the soaked and sodden heather.

In this fashion, hand in hand, Joyce Faa and the blind gypsy took their way towards the Manse of Minnigaff, where that very day another bridegroom was to have stood up beside her.'

We'll leave them there – as you can imagine, their story is far from over. But we still have a few more lessons to learn before we turn homeward, and the place to learn them is Curleywee.

CURLEYWEE

'Curleywee. The name is surely one which is given to its whaup-haunted solitudes.'

Curleywee is high up and remote, but it is a place we can meet up with our guides again. McCormick makes it a feature of his story *'A Galloway Fox Hunt',* which might be fiction, might be biography. You see how times have changed from the 1890's to the 1930's. No one minds if McCormick waxes fictional in the middle of his guidebook. And we don't care do we? It's the story we're after.

McCormick tells us of Sandy, the Caldons herd: *'In an hour or two he must start to climb the mountains in order to be on the top of Curleywee by daybreak.'* There is to be a gathering of the herds with dogs. But this time they are not hunting a man but a fox.

Factual as ever, McBain tells us: *'The head and shoulders of Curleywee are very rugged, and though one can walk on grass, to the top, the upper slopes are cut up into precipitous scaurs with their usual appendage of fan-shaped talus screes descending into the valleys. The explorer need not climb Curleywee on his way to Lamachan, for there is a sort of track round the shoulder by the saddle between this and the dominant hill. It will,*

291

however, repay the trouble of an ascent when the day is clear. Indeed there is no better summit in the whole region where so much detailed foreground can be seen as from this isolated peak.'

But Crockett reminds us that in Galloway, a clear day is far from a given: *'It had been our thought that from Curleywee it might be possible to obtain a general view of the country of the Granite Lochs, but the persistent downward sweep of the mist makes this impossible. Yet by persevering along the verge we have some very striking glimpses down into the deep glen of Trool, at the upper end of which lie cosily enough the farmhouses of Buchan and Glenhead.'*

As we've seen, Crockett revels in the very name: *'Curleywee. The name is surely one which is given to its whaup-haunted solitudes, because of that most characteristic of moorland sounds—the wailing pipe of the curlew. 'Curleywee—Curleywee—Curleywee.' That is exactly what the whaups say in their airy moorland diminuendo, as with a curve like their own Roman noses they sink downward into the bogs.'*

And he gives us two more very good reasons to visit Curleywee in the form of his short stories *'The Last of the Smugglers'* and *'The Tutor of Curleywee.'* These can be found in *'The Bloom o' the Heather'* and *'The Stickit Minister'* respectively.

We first ascend Curleywee in the company of one Hal Grierson. Here is his story: *'It was now the middle of December, and so late as the month before here was a letter dated from the 'Cothouse of Curlywee.' It ran as follows:—*

'Dear Son, —Herewith I enclose bank-bill for twenty-five pound. We have had a good back-end and are well. Please acknowledge receipt.—Your afft. father, John Arrol.'

I laughed aloud when I came upon the letter. It seemed to me that it was rather late to add a live grandfather to my family connection. Then the 'we' puzzled me. Had I a grandmother too—or several uncles? At any rate, my curiosity was highly excited...

...I discovered, however, that fifteen years before Walter Arrol had bought a little moorland property in Galloway which had then come into the market. He paid what, with my knowledge of English prices, seemed to me a ridiculously inadequate price for the five or six thousand acres it was stated to comprise.

The title-deeds were there, all in due order, and the receipts for taxation stamps, and lawyers' charges. There was also the memorandum of a loan of a thousand pounds to 'John Arrol, my father, to stock the farm of Curlywee with black-faced sheep,' together with notes of payment of 4 per cent, for the first five years. After that I

293

could trace no further receipts on that account.

It was just the day before Christmas that I set out from a midland town where I had had some business, resolved to find out all that I did not know about my Galloway relatives. I might easily have written, indeed, either to 'John Arrol' himself, who from his style of correspondence would have been the very man to give me exact information, or to the firm of lawyers in Cairn Edward whose name was upon the deeds and parchments.

But, though it would have ruined me from a business point of view had it been known in Highgate, I have always had a romantic strain in my blood, and the little adventure pleased me.

I would take a little climb, I told myself, into the branches of my family tree. I would go in person to the Cothouse of Curlywee, and make the acquaintance of my grandfather. I wondered if 'John Arrol' would turn out to be as ignorant of my existence as I had been of his. At any rate, he was clearly not a person to waste words or squander his sentiment broadcast. Had I been content to prove my title to my uncle's property, he would have continued to sign himself 'John Arrol,' to enclose his half-yearly rent, and to require a receipt therefor to the end of the chapter without making the least effort to cultivate my acquaintance.'

He has no idea of how steep his 'climb' will be. His journey takes him to *the little wayside station of Dornal.'* You'll note he mentioned Cairn Edward (Castle Douglas) and the likelihood is that Dornal station is New Galloway Station (which confusingly was sited in Mossdale.) Crockett uses 'Dornal' often in his works set in the Glenkens. But those are other stories for another time.

I hope we've spent enough time and gained a good enough knowledge of the area ourselves now for you to appreciate that Mossdale is some distance by foot from Curleywee! Hal is about to find that out for himself: *'It was a grim and greyish winter afternoon, and I had occupied myself in speculating, as the train slowly struggled up the incline, how long this rough bouldery desolation was to continue, and at what point it would issue forth upon the level strath and kindly hamlets of men, where I had pictured to myself my venerable relative residing in patriarchal dignity.'*

Crockett has previously made us laugh with his description of whaups thus: *'High up on the side of Curleywee, where the whaup are crying the name of the mountain, like porters at a railway station'* and he now introduces us to the real station porters. One is as strange as the other to city dweller Hal Grierson: *'Can you show me the way to the village of Curlywee?' I said to the stationmaster, who came out of his office to take my*

295

ticket. He made a dash at me almost like a terrier at a rat.

'The what?' he said sharply, dropping his official manner in his surprise.

'The village of Curlywee!'

The stationmaster laughed a short, quick laugh, almost as one would expect the aforesaid terrier to do in mirthful mood. He turned about on the pivot of one heel.

'Rob!' he cried sharply. 'Come ye here!'

'I canna come! I'm at the lamps— foul fa' them! The oil they hae sent us this time will no' burn ony mair than as muckle spring water!'

'Come here, I tell ye, Rob, or I'll report ye!'

'Report awa'—an' be!' Something that I did not catch.

The stationmaster did not further attempt to bring his official dignity to bear upon his recalcitrant subordinate. He tried another tack.

'There's a man out here wants to ken the road to the village of Curlywee!'

And as he spoke the little wiry stationmaster glanced quizzically up at me, as much as to say, 'That will fetch him!'

I failed to see the humour— then.

Immediately I heard a bouncing sound. Heavy feet trampled in the unseen lamp-room, a stool was knocked over, and a great broad, jovial-faced man came out still

296

rubbing a lamp globe with a most unclean piece of waste.

'The village o' Curlywee?' he inquired, smiling broadly at me, as it were from head to foot. 'Did I understand ye to say the village o' Curlywee?'

I nodded. I was growing vexed.

'I never heard tell o't!' he continued slowly, still smiling and shaking his head.

'Is there not a conveyance— an omnibus, or a trap of any kind which I can hire to take me there?'

I was getting more than a little angry by this time. It seemed past belief that I should have come so far to be laughed at by a couple of boors in the middle of a Galloway morass.

'Ow ay, there's a conveyance,' said the porter, 'a pair o' them!'

'Then,' said I tartly, 'be good enough to put my bag in one of them and let me get off!'

The big man continued to rub and grin. The stationmaster watched me quizzically with his grey birse of a head at the side.

Then, with the piece of dirty waste in his hand, 'Rob' pointed to my knickerbockered legs and brown leather shoes.

'Thae's the only conveyance ye'll get to Curlywee if ye wait a month at the Dornal!'

'What!' I cried, 'is there no road? There surely must

297

be some kind of a highway.'

Again the waste rag pointed. It was waved like a banner across the bleak moorish wilderness upon which the twilight was settling grey.

'Road?' he cried gleefully, 'highway? Ay, there's the hillside—juist the plain hillside!'

He waved me an introduction to it like a master of ceremonies.

'Enough of this,' I said tartly. 'I have come from London.'

'So I see by your ticket—it's a fine big place London!' interjected the stationmaster, with the air of one about to begin an interesting conversation.

'To see a gentleman in the neighbourhood of the name of John Arrol who lives at Curlywee. I would be obliged if you would point out to me the best and quickest way of reaching his house!'

The two men looked at each other. There was nothing like a broad grin on the big man's face now. The stationmaster also had lost his alert and amused air and had become suddenly thoughtful.

As neither of the two spoke, I added still more sharply, 'Do you know the gentleman?'

'Ow ay,' said Rob, 'we ken the man!'

'Well, be good enough to put me on the road to his house!'

298

Rob of the lamp and rag turned slowly as one of my own cranes turns with a heavy load of stone. His arm pointed out over the thin bars of shining steel of the railroad track.

'Yonder,' he said. 'Keep straucht up the gully till ye come to yon nick in the hill. Then turn to the left for three or four mile through the Dead Man's Hollow. Syne ye will come to a water, and if ye can get across, haud up the face o' the gairy, and gin ye dinna break your neck by faain' intil the Dungeon o' Buchan or droon ye in the Cooran Lane, ye will see the Cothouse o' Curlywee richt afore your nose!'

It was not an appetising description, but anything was better than stashing there to be laughed at, so I thanked the man, asked him to put my bag in the left luggage office, and proffered him a shilling.

The big man looked at the coin in my fingers.

'What's this for?' he said.

'To pay the ticket for the left luggage,' I said, 'and the rest for yourself!'

Slowly he shook his head.

'There's no' sic a thing nearer than Cairn Edward as a left luggage office,' he said; 'but I'll put the bit bag in the lamp-room. It'll be there if ever ye want it again!'

'What do you mean?' I cried furiously. 'Do you know that I am?'

'I mean,' said Rob deliberately, 'that ye are like to hae a saft walk and to need a' your daylicht before ye get to Curlywee this nicht. A guid journey to ye!'

Hal, intrepid adventurer that he is, strikes off into the hills. And in case you feel we've been travelling too slowly in our trips across the hills, here's the opportunity to go east to west in one long tramp with Hal for your companion. I wish you good luck: *'Upon the details of that weary and terrible journey I need not linger; though, when at first I threw my leg over the wire fencing of the railway and stepped out on the moor, the instinct of the heather seemed to come back to me. I lost my way at least half a dozen times. Indeed, if the moon had not been shining about half full in behind the grey sky, I must have wandered all night without remedy and most likely been frozen to death. My London-made single-soled shoes were soon completely sodden, and the uppers began to part company with the welt. I was wet to the waist or above it by falling into deep moss holes, where the black peaty water oozed through the softest of verdurous green.*

I was bruised by constant stumbles over unseen boulders, and scratched as to my hands by slipping on icy rock. A thousand times I cursed myself for leaving my comfortable rooms which looked over to Hampstead Heath. I might have been reading a volume of Rob Roy with my feet one on each side of the mantelpiece. And— at that very moment my foot plunged through the heather into a deep crevasse between two boulders, and I wrenched my ankle sideways with a stound of pain keen as a knife.

By this time I had been six or seven hours out on the moor. I had, to the best of my ability, endeavoured to steer the course set for me by the big-boned genius of the lamp. I possessed a little compass at my watch-chain, and my profession had made me accustomed enough to using it. But in the grey uncertain light the glens seemed to turn all the wrong way, and what 'the face of the gairy' might be I had not the least idea. I only knew that at the moment when I sprained my ankle I had been descending a hillside as lonely as an African desert and apparently as remote from anywhere as the North Pole.

I managed, however, by an effort to get it out of the trap into which I had fallen, and sat down upon a rock, half dazed with the shock. I remember that I moaned a little with the pain and started at the sound, not realising that I had been making it myself.

When I came round a little I was looking down into a kind of misty valley. The ground appeared to fall away on every side, and I could see shadowy and ghost-like forms of boulders all about me, some standing erect like menhirs, pointing stony fingers to the grey winter sky; some with noses sharpened took the exact shape of Polar *bears scenting a prey as you may see them in the plates of my favourite Dr. Kane.*

Gradually it dawned upon me that there was some sort of a light beneath me in the valley. It seemed most like a red pulsing glow, as if a nearly extinct fire were being blown up with bellows. A sense of eeriness came over me. I had been educated by my uncle in a severe school of practicality. To be a contracting builder in the better-class suburbs of London is destructive of romance. But I have the Pictish blood in me for all that. Aboriginal terrors prickle in my blood as I pass a graveyard at midnight, and never when I can help it do I go under one of my own ladders. But now, for the first time in my life, I felt a kind of stiffening of the hair of my scalp.

But this did not last long. My foot and ankle recalled me to myself. I could not, I thought, be worse off than I was— wet, miserable, hurt. If that light beneath me betokened a human habitation in the wild, I was saved. If not— well, I was no worse than I had been.

So, with a certain amount of confidence, I made shift to limp downward towards the strange pulsing, undulating glow. But though the sweat ran from me like rain, I could only go a few yards at a time. Nevertheless, the ruddy eye grew ever plainer as I descended, winking slowly and irregularly, waxing and waning like a fire permitted to go low and then again replenished.

302

At last I was near enough to see that the light proceeded from beneath a great face of rock which sprang upwards into the sky so high that it faded ghost-like into the milky glow of the choked moonlight. Just then my injured foot jarred painfully upon a stone which gave beneath its thrust. The loose boulder thundered away down the declivity, and with a cry I sank upon my hands and knees.

When I came to myself I could not speak. Something had been thrust into my mouth, something that gagged and almost choked me. My hands also were tied behind me. The red pulsing glow had vanished, but between me and the faintly lit grey sky I could see a tall dark figure which moved purposefully about. Presently I found myself dragged to my feet and thrust rudely forward. I tried to make my captor understand that I could not walk; but as I could not speak, I could only do this by lying down and utterly refusing to proceed. Then my captor drew a lantern from behind a heather bush and flashed it upon my face.

As he did so I held up my foot and endeavoured by signs to show where and how it was hurt. I was utterly unprepared for what my captor did next. He took me by the arms and laid me over his shoulders, pulling the plaid which he wore about my body as a kind of supporting belt. Then, with slow steady strides, he began to descend the hill. I suffered agonies lest we should both fall, and my *ankle pained me till I nearly wept with sheer agony.*

At last, with a fling of his foot my captor threw aside a door, stepped down a step, and I found myself stretched upon some straw.

Then a candle was lit, and the flame, sinking to nothing and then rising again, illuminated a little barn half-filled with sheaves and fodder. Upon a heap of the latter I was lying with my head away from the door.

'So,' said he who had brought me, 'I hae catched ye, sirrah!'

It's not quite the reception Hal was expecting. And if you want to find out what happens next, you'll have to take your own adventure by reading the rest of the story. We have other lessons to learn.

While Hal Grierson finds Curleywee a remote and somewhat barbaric place, in *'The Tutor of Curleywee'* Crockett reminds us that when it comes to place, perspective is everything. He offers another humorous tale which also gives insight into rural education. But if you thought it was a chance to get your breath back while he tells us the story, think again. We're about to take off east to west again in the company of John Bradfield also known as The Minister of Education. Are you up for that trip again so soon? Here goes: *'The Minister of Education started to walk across the great moors of the Kells Range so early in the morning that for*

304

the first time for twenty years he saw the sun rise. Strong, stalwart, unkempt, John Bradfield, Right Honourable and Minister of the Queen, strode over the Galloway heather in his rough homespun. 'Ursa Major' they called him in the House.'

You'll notice that while he takes much the same route as Hal Grierson before him, he doesn't see things quite the same way, or make quite such heavy weather of the trip: *'When he started on a thirty-mile walk over the moors, along the dark purple precipitous slopes above Loch Trool, the glory of summer was melting into the more Scottish splendours of a fast-coming autumn, for the frost had held off long, and then in one night had bitten snell and keen. The birches wept sunshine, and the rowan trees burned red fire.*

The Minister of Education loved the great spaces of the Southern uplands, at once wider and eerier than those of the Highlands. There they lie waiting for their laureate. No one has sung of them nor written in authentic rhyme the strange weird names which the mountain tops bandy about among each other, appellations hardly pronounceable to the southron. John Bradfield, however, had enough experience of the dialect of the 'Tykes' of Yorkshire to master the intricacies of the nomenclature of the Galloway uplands. He even understood and could pronounce the famous quatrain: 'The Slock, Milquharker, and Craignine, The Breeshie and Craignaw; Are the five best hills for corklit, That e'er the Star wife saw."

Note 'The Slock.' And the pride with which John Bradfield thinks he's mastered *'the nomenclature of the Galloway uplands.'* Forgive me if I laugh just a little. The phrase 'pride comes before a fall' springs to mind. Finally The Minister of Education arrives at Curleywee. As we now do: *'About midday he came upon a shepherd's hut which lay in his track. He went briskly up to the door, passing the little pocket-handkerchief of kailyaird which the shepherd had carved out of the ambient heather. The purple bells grew right up to the wall of grey stone dyke which had been built to keep out the deer, or mayhap occasionally to keep them in, when the land was locked with snow, and venison was toothsome.*

'Good day to you, mistress,' said the Minister of Education, who prided himself on speaking to every woman in her own tongue.

'And good day to you, sir,' heartily returned the sonsy, rosy-cheeked goodwife, who came to the door, 'an' blithe I am to see ye. It's no that aften that I see a body at the Back Hoose o' Curlywee.'

John Bradfield soon found himself well entertained— farles of cake, crisp and toothsome, milk from the cow, with golden butter in a lordly dish, cheese from a little round kebbuck, which the mistress of the

306

Back House of Curlywee kept covered up with a napkin to keep it moist.

The goodwife looked her guest all over.

'Ye'll not be an Ayrshireman nae, I'm thinkin'. Ye kind o' favour them in the features, but ye hae the tongue o' the English.'

'My name is John Bradfield, and I come from Yorkshire,' was the reply.

'An' my name's Mistress Glencairn, an' my man Tammas is herd on Curlywee. But he's awa' ower by the Wolf's Slock the day lookin' for some forwandered yowes.''

We cannot escape the Wolf's Slock can we? I'm not going back that way, not even to look for lost references. I'm staying at Curleywee with the Minister of Education and I suggest you do too. While resting here he comes across the children of the family. He's about to learn something – and so are we: *'What a pity,' said the Minister of Education, 'that such bright little fellows should grow up in this lonely spot without an education.'*

He was thinking aloud more than speaking to his hostess. The herd's wife of Curlywee looked him over with a kind of pity mingled with contempt.

'Edicated! did ye say? My certes, but my bairns are as weel edicated as onybody's bairns. Juist e'en try them, gin it be your wull, sir, an' aiblins ye'll fin' them no' that far ahint yer ain!'

307

Going to the door she raised her voice to the telephonic pitch of the Swiss jodel and the Australian 'coo — ee, Jee-mie, Aa-leck, Aa-nie, come ye a' here this meenit!'

The long Galloway vowels lingered on the still air, even after Mistress Glencairn came her ways back again into the house. There was a minute of a great silence outside. Then a scuffle of naked feet, the sough of subdued whispering, a chuckle of interior laughter, and a prolonged scuffling just outside the window.

'Gin ye dinna come ben the hoose an' be douce, you Jeemie, an' Rob, an' Alick, I'll come till ye wi' a stick! Mind ye, your faither 'ill no be lang frae hame the day.'

A file of youngsters entered, hanging their heads, and treading on each other's bare toes to escape being seated next to the formidable visitor.

'Wull it please ye, sir, to try the bairns' learning for yoursel'?'

A Bible was produced, and the three boys and their sister read round in a clear and definite manner, lengthening the vowels it is true, but giving them their proper sound, and clanging their consonants like hammers ringing on anvils.

'Very good!' said John Bradfield, who knew good reading when he heard it.

From reading they went on to spelling...'

Much to his surprise, the children acquit themselves remarkably in all the tests the Minister sets them. Curleywee, and its inhabitants are not what he expected and certainly give him pause for thought. After some time reflecting on the charming remoteness of the place he: *'remembered his letters and telegrams even now entering in a steady stream into his London office and overflowing his ministerial tables, waiting his return—a solemnising thought. He resolved to build a house on the Back Hill of Curlywee, and have his letters brought by way of the kirk and the Lamachan herd's lass that lived three miles from the post-office.'*

But he wants an answer to the mystery of the children's knowledge. He wants to know how children can be so well taught in such a remote location: *'How far are you from a school?'*

'Weel, we're sixteen mile frae Newton Stewart, where there's a schule but no road, an' eleven frae the Clatterin' Shaws, where there's a road but no schule.'

'How do you manage then?' The Minister was anxious to have the mystery solved.

'WE KEEP A TUTOR!' said the herd's wife of Curlywee, as calmly as though she had been a duchess.'

This was the last thing he (and we?) expected to hear. I told you there is a lot to be learned in the detail of Crockett's fiction. It's time for a lesson from the wife of

309

the cot house of Curleywee: *'Ye see, sir, it's this way,'* she said, *seating herself opposite to him on a clean-scoured, white wooden chair: 'there's mair hooses in this neighbourhood than ye wad think. There's the farm hoose o' the Black Craig o' Dee, there's the herd's hoose o' Garrary, the onstead o' Neldricken, the Dungeon o' Buchan—an' a wheen mair that, gin I telled ye the names o', ye wadna be a bit the wiser. Weel, in the simmer time, whan the colleges gang doon, we get yin o' the college lads to come to this quarter. There's some o' them fell fond to come. An' they pit up for three or fower weeks here, an' for three or fower weeks at the Garrary ower by, an' the bairns travels ower to whaur the student lad is bidin', an' gets their learnin'. Then when it's time for the laddie to be gaun his ways back to college, we send him awa' weel buskit wi' muirland claith, an' weel providit wi' butter an' eggs, oatmeal an' cheese, for the comfort o' the wame o' him. Forbye we gather up among oorsels an' bid him guid speed wi' a maitter o' maybe ten or twal' poun' in his pooch. An' that's the way we keep a tutor!'*

If we've learned one lesson from our adventures in the hills of Galloway I hope it's that nothing is ever quite what it seems. The lonely, isolated places we may stand in today, where the boulders strewn around may as likely be ruined homes as natural features, have plenty to teach us if we are only willing to learn.

And for the final stage of our adventure in the hills, we're going to let imagination of these lost places come to the fore, without paying too much attention to the grid reference. We're in search of places that are going, going, and in some cases, long gone.

9.GOING, GOING, GONE

'They tell you that nobody is really alive to the beauty of their birthplace. Well, perhaps not for some time after. But in the long run it depends on the person. For me, Rose Gordon of the Dungeon in the uplands of Galloway, from my earliest years I was glad of the large freshness of every breath I drew.'

This final stage of our adventure offers the biggest challenge to the imagination yet. But that's because we're approaching the final summit, so to speak.

In Galloway (as all across rural Scotland) rural dwellings from the past have been lost at an alarming rate and continue to disappear. In Galloway there are any number of bothies which no longer exist, and other rural dwellings which teeter in the balance. While we may like to think of the enduring nature of the wild landscape, the Galloway hills today is a quite different place from what it was a hundred or even fifty years ago. What now seems desolate and empty was once a vibrant (if small) network of communities, stretched out from the Kells in the East right to the Mull of Galloway.

We've been travelling from the comfort of our armchairs, but until relatively recently a network of bothies was maintained for walkers in the Galloway Hills,

313

most notably, Caldons, Tunskeen, Culsharg, White Laggan and Back Hill o' Bush. The situation changes but currently I understand that Tunskeen and White Laggan are maintained by the Mountain Bothies Association, while Back Hill o' the Bush is maintained by the Forestry Commission. Caldons campsite was closed down in 2006 and Culsharg remains open but basic.

In Crockett's day, as the wife of the cot house of Curleywee notes, there were many more people living and making a living on the hills than we can even imagine today. Herds' houses and bothies existed in number if not in proliferation but most are impossible to place or find these days.

Many are now only fixed in fiction and once something is gone it can be hard to know if it ever existed. In my armchair adventures there are two places I have grown particularly fond of. One is Glenhead of Trool and the other the Shiel of the Dungeon of Buchan.

I don't know if The Shiel ever existed. I do know that the fate of Glenhead is uncertain. A tenanted farm until some fifteen years ago, having fallen into disrepair, the Farmhouse and two acres was recently put up for sale on the open market. How and whether it can be 'saved' I don't know, but the McMillans' Glenhead, is already in one sense now as much of a fiction as The Shiel of the Dungeon. I find this sad. I know I have said

314

more than once about how things change in the hills and how we have to accept that, but I also think we should have enough respect for our shared heritage not to just let it vanish into fiction for lack of care.

If nothing else, I'd advise that if you want to have a real experience of the bothies and hill-farms of Galloway, you visit them sooner rather than later. Or join a campaign to have them restored and maintained as part of our natural and cultural heritage. Crockett has fixed them for us in fiction. But how great would it be if we could maintain them in fact as well. We still, just, have the chance to maintain a real link between past and present. But it's vanishing like the winter snow.

My daring suggestion for this last stage of our adventure is that we go in search of places which we cannot find, and link them to places which still in most cases just about exist. In the process I'm throwing down the challenge for those who can leave the armchair, to go out in the spirit of imagination and adventure, into the Galloway hills, to the places which are fast disappearing. Take imagination and vision with you. Instead of looking at them as they are today, use Crockett's descriptions and fix them in your mind. Fiction may be the only way we can hold onto bothies and hill-farms in Galloway in the all too near future because, while ruined castles retain their charm for tourists, far fewer people think, or care, about the humbler dwellings; those places lived in by ordinary folk. Through his writing Crockett has done what he can to keep the places alive. Now it's up to us to realise that they have a value even in a modern world.

As I've said, various places still cling to the scree of existence across the whole range of the Galloway hills. The ones we're going to find in the last stage of our adventure include Tunskeen and Caldons, both mentioned in *'Men of the Moss Hags,'*

The Back Hill o' the Bush bears a striking resemblance to the description of the Gordon farm in *'Rose of the Wilderness.'* And our final stop will be with the fictional Anton McMillan at Bennangour.

Let's set out for the last time, with our imaginations refreshed and our spirits high. Even if the reality is grim, we carry with us the spirit of the romance adventurer, which will allow us see the places and meet the people of a time now faded into history and fiction. Some of us still feel a vital connection to the past. For some of us it's a bond of love.

'Tonskeen, where there is a herd's house in the wild, far from man and very quiet with God.'

Tunskeen features in *'Men of the Moss Hags'* as Tonskeen. If you remember our earlier adventure, to The Session Stone, you'll recall that Kate McGhie and Will Gordon's Mother stay briefly at *'the little house of Tonskeen in the howe of the hills.'* It provides a place of refuge and safety for the women and Will Gordon notes: *'The good folk of Tonskeen were very willing to let my mother and the maids abide with them.'* They also provided refuge for Thomas Wilson, brother of the Wigtown martyr Margaret Wilson.

But it is also mentioned as a place where people starve in bad weather as Gash Gibbie says: *'Preserve us!'* *he cried. 'This is as fearsome as that year there was nae meat in the hoose, and Gash Gibbie brocht some back, and aye brocht it, and brocht it even as it was needed. And Kate o' the Corp-licht, she readied it and asked nae quastions. But only tearin' belly-hunger gied us strength to eat that awesome meat. An' a' the neighbours died o' starvation at Tonskeen and the Star an' the bonny Hill o' the Buss—a' but Gib an' his mither, their leevin' lanes. But yae nicht Yon sent Gibbie's sin to find him oot; or maybe*

317

the Black Thing in the Hole gat lowse, because it was his hour.'

We do not want to question too closely what the *'awesome'* meat was – I'll just suggest you remember Eggface and Sawney Bean and leave it at that. There's no one here to feed you at the bothy today but it is still there, managed by the Mountain Bothies Association. Visit their website and take guidance from them on Bothy etiquette before you attempt a visit.

'The farm sits four square on a knowe-tap, compact with office-houses and mailings. There are the little three-cornered wickets in the walls.'

Caldon's campsite was closed some years ago, but those who hold it in their memory probably remember it as a place of giant midges. However, it has an even darker and more unpleasant history. For those of us who want to stay in our armchairs and thus avoid the ravages of the giant midge, Toskrie Tam's tale in *'Men of the Moss Hags'* paints a picture of it in 'The Killing Times': *'Somewhat after the following manner Tam told his tale, a trifle unwillingly at first, but warming with the recollection as he proceeded.*

'Aweel, Sir William, gin ye insist. No that I like to be speakin' aboot thae days; but as ye inform me that it is a' to be written doon, I'll tell ye it word for word. Weel, after the Conventiclers had outfaced us at the Shalloch-on-Minnoch, Clavers and Douglas rode south to the Minnoch Brig that looks to Loch Trool.

'There's a dour pack o' Whigs up that glen,' says Clavers. 'Think ye we will take a turn and steer them?'

'They will just be hiving hame frae the conventicle. We shall catch them as they run,' Douglas made answer.

319

So without a word more, slack rein and go-as-you-please, we rode up Glen Trool. It was a bonny nicht and at a' times a bonny place, but the track was ill to keep, and we rode loose and scattering. Douglas was fair foaming with the affront of the Shalloch, and vowed, as he had often vowed before, that he would never more spare hilt or hair of the accursed breed.

At the Caldons, a bit farmhouse set on a rig among trees at the foot of Loch Trool, Gib Macaterick and I were riding on ahead down by the water side by the loch, when suddenly, without warning, we came on a little cloud of men all on their knees praying behind a dyke back. They were so busy with the supplications that they did not notice us. And we that looked for promotion over the head of the business, covered them with our muskets and called to them to surrender for traitors and rebels. But in a trice they were over the dyke and at us like wild-cats, gripping our horses and tumbling us off. They got Gib down, but I that was suppler, managed to jook among the young oak-trees and run what I was fit back to the troop.

Douglas was in command, for Clavers had ridden on. He was a wild man when I told him that the rebels had taken Gib Macaterick.

'Curse you and him both!' Douglas cried. 'Do I command a set of porridge-stuffed, baggy knaves that fall off their horses whenever they see a Whig tyke skartin' for

320

fleas? I'll tan Gib's hide for him and yours too, my man, when we come to the post. Ye shall ride the timber horse with a bit musket at your heels to learn ye how siccarly to sit your beast.'

Whereat he cried to wheel, and we went twos about down the Caldons road. The farm sits four square on a knowe-tap, compact with office-houses and mailings. There are the little three-cornered wickets in the walls. As we came to the foot of the brae we found Gib Macaterick stelled up against the dyke, with his hands bound and a paper in his teeth—a printed copy of the Covenant. He was quite safe and sound. But when we loosed him, he could do nothing but curse and splutter.

'Thou foul-mouthed Whig,' cried Douglas, 'hast thou also been taking the Covenant? Have him out and shoot him!'

But Gib rose and made an end of the Covenant, by setting his foot upon it and crushing it into the sod. Then we moved forward, carelessly, thinking that the enemy would never stand against a troop, but that they would at once scatter to the hill which rises steep and black at the gavel end of the house.

However, when we came within sight of the steading, half a dozen muskets cracked, and one of our company cried out with the pain of being hit. Indeed, the second volley tumbled more than one trooper from his

321

saddle, and caused their horses to break ranks and run back, jingling accoutrements.

So Colonel Douglas dismounted half his men, and sent the better part of a troop, under the Cornet of the same name, round to the high side of the farm to take the Conventiclers in flank. Which with all success they did, and came down at the charge upon the steadings, capturing half a dozen, mostly young lads, that were there with muskets in their hands. But there was one that threw himself into the lake and swam under water for it. And though our soldiers shot off a power of powder after him, we could get no satisfaction that he had been hit. We heard, however, that he was a Carsphairn man and that the name of him was Roger Dunn.

So Douglas ordered a dismounted file to lead the young lads out into a dell a quarter of a mile from the house, where the noise of the shootings would not annoy him at his refreshment. So the Cornet took them out, well-pleased. For it was a job that suited him better than fighting, and there, in a little green hollow, he speedily laid the six featly in a row.

'So perish all his Majesty's rebels!' said Colonel Douglas as he rode past, bung full of brandy and good mutton ham.

'That's as bonny a kill o' Whigs as we hae gotten for mony a day. Rothes will be pleased with this day's work!'

322

said the Cornet.

It was growing dark by the time that we drew up from the loch and it was ill getting a guide. No one of us had ever been in the country, and there is no wilder in all the south, as I have cause to know. But we had not got to any conclusion, when one came running with the news that he saw a light. So we spurred on as briskly as we dared, not knowing but that we might again hear the whistle of musket balls about our ears.'

Surely this story provides explanation enough as to why the Galloway folk hated Claverhouse and his henchman Robert 'Lag' Grierson. Once again we see that places which (midges aside) can seem so remote and peaceful today, have a bloody history attached to them.

So if you're getting the taste for bothy life, we'll move on to a more substantial dwelling, set to the east of the Galloway hills, in the lee of the Dungeon Range, to visit with a character we've met before, one Rose Gordon. We should probably take something with us, as we'll be staying quite a while.

*'The Back Hill is fairly safe... But on the Dungeon itsel'
and up by the Clints, likewise by the Head o' Dee, there's
nae sayin' what may not happen by the mornin' licht!'*

Our modern guide Paddy Dillon describes Back Hill o' the
Bush in his 1995 *'Walking the Galloway Hills'* as:
*'formerly a shepherd's dwelling, in the days before forests
were planted across the broad flats of the Rhinns of Kells.'*
He suggests that at that time the bothy was well
maintained – sadly this is no longer the case: *'There are
two rooms downstairs, one with a stove and one with a
fireplace, plus a small room under the stairs. The stairs
lead up to a long room under the roof.'*

Most recently Dane Love is informative about Back
Hill and other Galloway Bothies. His book includes some
pictures and details of a plane crash near Back Hill.
McCormick describes flying over the hills in the 1930's
and revels in the new perspective this adventure gave
him.

McBain notes the: *'exasperating series of [moss]
hags on the direct route between Back Hill of the Bush
and the Lochs of the Dungeon.'* He also talks of Back
Garrary, which is: *'the nearest house to the lonely shieling
known locally as Back Hill of Bush, about three miles*

distant.' He notes that beyond Back Garrary: *'there is no road. At any rate there is no vehicular road past Mid Garrary marked on the one-inch Ordnance Survey map. The Mid Garrary no longer exists, at any rate under that name,'* which serves to remind us of the constantly changing nature of things in the hills.

A century ago we find the deserted Galloway landscape quite a different place. Among the hill-folk (McKittericks excepted of course) there was a tradition of hospitality for travellers. In his 1916 book, C.H.Dick suggests that you stay with the shepherd at Back Hill if you're going to spend time up in the Dungeon hills, as it's too long a trek for one day.

Into the 1930's, McBain confirms that this tradition still holds, suggesting that anyone who takes to the hills: *'has many a weary tramp before him and is often glad to find rest at some shepherd's cottage at the end of the day's fight with the rugged conditions he encounters.'*

Dan Kennedy tells us in his preface to the 1967 *'Galloway Memories':* *'Back on the wings of memory comes a picture of a remote herd's dwelling, now derelict and deserted among the moss-hags. To the southward the black cliffs of the Dungeon rise sheer from the valley, grim and menacing - a treacherous bottomless bog to trap the unwary, lying in between... Yet there was a day – not so far distant – when to call at Back Bush on a round of*

325

travel and salute the shepherd was the very spice of mild adventure. Was it not reckoned the loneliest outpost in the wilds of Galloway? Old times have changed, old friends have gone, yet remembrance still holds the door of happy memories.'

The shadow of the Dungeon Range is undoubtedly a remote part of the country, but today you can visit it either by track going south from Loch Dee, or going north using the forest track from Craigcaillie. Those amongst you who have been particularly observant will recall it's on the way to Cooran Lane and the Silver Flowe.

Previously maintained by the Mountain Bothies Association, Back Hill of the Bush is now 'managed' by the Forestry Commission. Sadly, what should be a refuge for walkers suffers regularly from vandalism. For those who want to see the reality of Galloway rural dwellings, you may need to go and visit sooner rather than later to get any sense of what is being and has been lost. And you already need to turn to writers to give you perspective. If you want to have a last glance at the real life of the Galloway hill-folk, you could do worse than track down Dan Kennedy's writing.

We of course will take Crockett for our guide. And mix fact with fiction, as is our want.

I am not suggesting that Rose Gordon's family lived at Back Hill o' the Bush, but in order to get a sense of

326

place in *'Rose of the Wilderness'* I suggest we use The Back Hill o' the Bush as our template for the Gordon farm. We can best imagine her there and if you do visit the bothy, I'd recommend you take a copy of the book with you.

The rest of us will have to rely solely on Crockett. He sets up the loneliness of the place from the start. The novel opens with the seventeen year old Rose Gordon reporting that she has never seen a lighted street: *'Four times I had been at Newton Stewart, twice at Dalry, and once at Dumfries, which has thousands of people and pavements that go right across the street. My name is Rose Gordon, and silly folk call me 'The Rose of the Wilderness'—though not in the hearing of my father.*

He is Henry Gordon of the Dungeon. The Dungeon is a farm—a little sheep farm with heathery hills thronging about it as far as the eye can see. Many gleaming little lochans separate these, and in the flat places between there are slow blackish 'lanes' of water turning and twisting among the black peat hags.

The nearest school is at the Rowan Tree, but it is a long, rough road, so my father mostly taught me himself. He is a well-learned man, my father, even for a Galloway herd, and in his younger days, before he wedded my mother for good and all, he had many strange and terrible adventures.

327

But he settled down well enough, only for the sake of peace very far from his fellow men. He had plenty of books—more than could be brought to the Dungeon on the backs of four strong horses. For when he came here there was not even a cart-track over the moss-hags and the heather grew to one's armpits.

Of course, also, up in that solitude there was great dearth of nutriment for everything—that is, except black-faced sheep, whaups, and all the wild things of the moorland. My poor mother died when I was three days old, and my father brought me up.'

We previously saw the difficulties Rose's father had keeping her in milk after her mother died; how he went to the McMillans at Bongill – a good ten miles away, until he went lame. He also *'carried tins of preserved milk on his back, a dozen at a time, all the way from Dalry, coming over the smooth green mountain called Corscrine in order to do it, his lame leg trailing wearily behind him.'*

The observant among you will note that this would take him over much the same route as Patrick Heron takes in *'The Raiders'* before he goes up The Nick of the Dungeon into the Wolf's Slock.

The journey from Mossdale to The Dungeon Hills can be wet, dangerous and difficult, as more than Patrick Heron find out. But for Rose it's just the road home: *'I set out for New Galloway Station, on the Portpatrick line, from which a neighbour's gig would take me to Craigencailzie, a lonely little farm (but one highly to be desired) set gallantly, like a forepost of civilisation, in a wilderness of heather. From thence I must push my way alone to the Dungeon.*

There was no time to send messages. If there had been, who was there to carry them? The penny post had not yet reached the Dungeon, or, save at intervals the herd's house—our nearest neighbour— on the Back Hill of the Buss. My mission was accomplished. My father was delivered, yet in a way I was wae, and the tears were ready to flow, save only out of respect for the jet beads on my aunt's bonnet. These kept all taut.

I had met a good man who had done much for me. Never should I forget him; and now he was going back to meet, perhaps bodily harm, certainly ill-will, for our sakes. It was on my tongue-tip to ask him to be sure and come up to see us at the Dungeon.'

Rose mentions their nearest neighbour as being at Back Hill of the Buss. So of course the bothy that stands there still cannot be her house. Perhaps the Fore Hill of the Bush was? Dan Kennedy writes about it. Or it could have been McBain's Back Garrary. For us it doesn't matter. We know more or less where we are. If you have the stamina to get to Back Hill o' the Bush, you'll surely have the imagination to see it from Rose's eyes thanks to

329

Crockett's description.

Rose reminds us that isolation is really only a state of mind and that with solitude can go peace. And Rose loves her home. She tells us how: *'morning dawned with a great peace, a peace so great that it positively awoke me. I thought I was in heaven, and that it was the eternal Sabbath there, so clean and high and gay was the air, and in all that world no sound. Even at the Dungeon we were too far away to hear our neighbour's dog bark or his cock crow.*

The peace was like the peace of God (as Absalom Kenmore often said afterwards). It passed understanding. Yet it was gladsome, too, and at the first call of dawn upon the mountains I ran to my father's room, so glad that I think I should have awaked him, if he had not already been lying watching the peaks of the Star and the Dungeon grow rosy, while between them and him a buzzard wheeled in widening circles in the kindling blue.'

Much has changed since Rose's day. But change is life's one constant and she herself faces many changes through her life. Perhaps there is a message to us in her reflection: *'Even in Galloway things change. The old was passing away and we were in the new and less kindly time.'*

Rose and Henry Gordon's story is not a new one, nor a particularly unusual one in their day, when tenant

330

farmers held seventeen or nineteen year leases and could be turfed out of their farms on the whim of an unscrupulous landowner, even if they weren't in rent arrears. The Gordons have such a writ served on them. But Galloway folk don't give up without a fight. Especially not the likes of Muckle Tamson, whom we've met before.

Among other things, Muckle Tamson is the Gordon's herd. He is determined they will not be put from their home: *'while we were still waiting for the minister to arrive, the man with the warning—a writ to serve, I think they call it, came to the moorlands seeking Henry Gordon and the Dungeon. It chanced that Muckle Tamson was down at the Clatteringshaws that day, for we were in instant expectation of the minister of Riddlings.*

The sheriff's officer was a little man, who wore a rusty black suit as if he had bought it off a kirk beadle after it had grown too shabby for weekly pulpit use. His arms swung low by his sides, and he looked anxiously at the threatening array of peaks which barred the road to the Dungeon.

'Henry Gordon?' said Muckle Tamson, scratching his head as if in great bewilderment, 'I believe I hae heard tell o' sic a man! And the Dungeon? That's a prison, is it no? That will be mair in your way I'm guessin' by the look of ye!'

331

'But I am advised that this is the most direct road to the House of the Dungeon,' said Guidsakes Gill. He was called 'Guidsakes' because of his favourite exclamation of surprise.

'Guidsakes! What a place—I never thocht to see the like in the Queen's dominions!'

'This is no the Queen's dominions, my lad, as ye will soon ken,' said Muckle Tamson, darkly. 'Nae writ rins ayont the Water o' Dee—not till ye hae passed the Moss o' Cree. And the sooner ye do the like, the better it will be for your health. There are some desperate characters up this way!'

Muckle Tamson takes the writ server on a merry dance in an attempt to prevent the Gordons being served notice to quit. We're familiar enough with the lie of this land now to appreciate how its wildness works to his advantage: 'Muckle Tamson smiled, as from the hedge he produced an extra long leaping pole, such as is used all over the Cooran and Dungeon country for crossing the dull black stagnant 'lanes' of water which lie summer and winter upon the face of the moorland, criss-crossing each other like fortune-telling lines on the palm of the hand.'

Remember Patrick found such a pole at Cooran Lane. If you're going to go near this part of the country, you might be well advised to fashion yourself one.

Weather plays a central part in 'Rose of the

Wilderness,' and Crockett's description of the snows in *'Rose of the Wilderness'* at least matches that of The Sixteen Drifty Days we experienced in *'The Raiders'.*

Sheep have to be protected in such weather as Muckle Tamson points out: *"It's a baad nicht!' he said in Henry Gordon's ear.*

My father assented with a sound that was almost a moan. I knew what he was thinking of—a little narrow grave, which had hardly yet had time to grow green. The snow would be falling thick on it, away there to the north.

Muckle Tamson tried again, leaning down and moistening his lips apologetically.

'The yowes!' he said, 'they should be lookit to! The Back Hill is fairly safe—me and That Craitur,' he pointed to 'Stoor,' now playing with the collies and pretending to let them eat his head in turns, 'we drave them ahint the 'bunkers.' But on the Dungeon itsel' and up by the Clints, likewise by the Head o' Dee, there's nae sayin' what may not happen by the mornin' licht!"

Thus Muckle Tamson, Stoor and Henry Gordon go up into the hills in the worst of weathers: *'It was almost morning before any news came from the wild hills behind which two men and a boy wandered, storm-battered. And then through the deepening drifts of snow I ploughed my way to the outer 'yett' of the farm-steading and set it open. I do not know to this day why I did this, save that our house of the Dungeon stood with its back to the hill, and I could see a great drift gathering behind, which my father and the rest would need to turn before they could reach the courtyard and the open door.'*

From Lila's funeral at the start of the novel, to Rose's marriage part way through, *'Rose of the Wilderness'* shows the reader the full spectrum of Galloway weather in all seasons. The harshness of the life is not ignored, but ultimately it simply serves to remind us that real people lived real lives up in these hills. And loved their homes despite the hardships.

Despite its remoteness, once Rose is away from the Dungeon both she and her husband miss it: *'My husband told me he even liked the smell of the wet shepherds' plaids on rainy days, but that, though hill born, I admit to be a cultivated taste.*

In fine, he yearned for the Dungeon, and, save for the libraries, Edinburgh was to him a weariness.'

Rose travels a long way from the Dungeon Hills. But she always misses it and always wants news from home. At one point while she is in Edinburgh: *'My husband brought news of the Dungeon which made my heart ache to be back again—sometimes a sprig of white heather, hardly touched by winter, just browned a little in its dry shelter under the 'brow o' some bunker.' Once he fetched a whole peat in his bag, which caused me to weep*

334

because I could not start back immediately. Nan said that he should have had more sense, but I could not help it. I laid the peat reverently in my room and smelt it every day. When I went, I would take it back where it belonged. Its aromatic fumes should not be lost in any foul Edinburgh chimney. They would 'pew' out sweetly from the old kitchen hearth, and what part of them was not dispersed among the hams and smoked puddings on the rafters, would be wafted back to where they belonged, trailing over the bog-myrtle, and losing themselves little by little across the miles of Dungeon heather, the reddest and the most long-lived in all the country.'

While we may experience the Dungeon Hills as being a place of danger and adventure, as Patrick and Maxwell Heron do, we can also see them, as Rose and others do, as a place of peaceful isolation. For them it is simply home.

Now it's time for us to turn our thoughts homeward, which for this adventure means a return to Glenhead. Where I'd like to introduce you the last of our companions, Anton MacMillan, the Herd of Bennangour.

THE HERD OF BENNANGOUR

'For a time I could discern the great hill of Bennanbrack between me and the sky, which made a friendly sort of landmark for me.'

Just as we cannot firmly place *'Rose of the Wilderness'* at Back Hill o' the Bush, so it's impossible to confidently place Anton MacMillan. He is at least partly fictional of course. But that suggests he's also partly fact. Because of that I am placing him at Glenhead, even though I know that is an imaginative leap. And I know what follows is speculation. But in my imagination that's where I place him. You can do differently if you wish. We could site him at White Laggan Bothy, (which still exists) or Black Laggan Bothy, which doesn't. Or somewhere else entirely.

All I know of Bennangour is that it's in the lee of Bennanbrack, which is some way to the south of Glenhead, but when I think of Anton MacMillan, 'The Herd of Bennangour,' I think of John McMillan and so I'm placing him here.

Anton MacMillan features in *'The Banner of Blue'* which is set in the 1840's and is ostensibly a novel about 'The Disruption.' But don't dismiss Crockett's skill and hidden depths. You can be totally disinterested in

336

Scottish ecclesiastical history and still enjoy the novel.

The hill of Bennanbrack is to the south of the Dungeon Range in the Minnigaff Hills and is overlooked by Curleywee Hill. To find Anton MacMillan's house you go: *'up the burnside towards the herd's house of Bennangour,'* where the house rests, in the leeside of Bennanbrack and where: *'The house shone out white and bonny.'*

I believe Bennangour is a fictional construction. The main settings of the novel are the fictionalised Gatehouse of Fleet (as Kilgour), and Cardoness Castle (as Castle Gower). Crockett may have taken the name from the nearby Killiegower woods. This is all some distance away from Bennanbrack but in the novel the Laird of Glendower, one Gregory Glendonwyn owns a large estate stretching, it seems, all the way from his home at Castle Gower to Bennanbrack and possibly beyond.

While setting Anton MacMillan at Glenhead is possibly pushing the bounds of credibility for proximity to Bennangour, as a description of a place, both real and emotional, the herd's house at Bennangour does offer some resemblance to that of the home inhabited by the McMillans at Glenhead.

Add to that the fact that Crockett's friend John McMillan not only had a brother called Anthony, but that his father (alive in the 1840's) was also called Anthony and you can perhaps speculate on the origins of the character Anton MacMillan, herd of Bennangour. Remember McMillan's quip: *'ony cuif can write a book but it takes a man to herd the Merrick.'* If Anton MacMillan is drawn from John McMillan, I'd say Crockett was paying his friend a compliment. And of course he was 'raiding' from his own observations and experience and mixing them up with his imaginative powers to complete the picture.

If you are still curious about Crockett's use of duality in his fiction, *'The Banner of Blue'* is the book for you. Duality is central to the story and offers an analogy for the state of the Kirk in Scotland at the time of the Disruption. Gour and Gower are used interchangeably, and the two central families are the rich Glendonwyns and the poor Glendinnings, whom we have to believe come from the same root stock.

And for me, lest you think that I am too much enamoured of Hector Faa, I will nail my colours to the mast and say that if I could meet just one of Crockett's characters, I'm not sure if I could choose between the charismatic but deeply flawed gypsy Hector Faa and his complete opposite, Anton MacMillan.

These are the games we adventurers of the imagination can choose to play from our armchairs. From the page we can meet them all. So now, let me introduce you to Anton MacMillan. He's at home with his dogs. And what dogs they are. I'd like to meet them too:

'Grim, grey, dour, fell the early December twilight upon the seaboard parish of Gower— the outward and visible sign, a stranger might well suppose, of a similar grim humour among its inhabitants. But up on the side of Bennangour Anton McMillan, the herd, drew his checked plaid more closely about him and hummed a cheerful psalm. The sheep were 'a' weel.' There was yet no sign of the shepherd's chief winter terror, an onfall of snow. So the 124th psalm in the Scottish version was Anton's vesper. For he agreed with the wise man who said: 'Whoso is merry of heart, let him sing psalms.'

'Now Israel may say, and that truly, If that the Lord had not our cause maintained; If that the Lord had not our right sustained,'

At this point Anton stopped abruptly, and shading his eyes as if the summer sun had been shining in them, made an impromptu night-glass of his palms and exclaimed, 'Davert!'

Now when a west-country herd, born in the purple of the Kirk of the Covenants, valiant in defence of Headship and joyously confident of Total Depravity and the Eternity of Punishment stops on his hillside and says 'Davert,' it may be taken for granted that he sees more than a ewe fallen 'aval' in a hollow, or a slap in the dyke through which his flock had streamed away to the Promised Land of another man's pastures.

So Anton McMillan, rugged champion of the Way, stood a long minute fixed, his faithful dogs sniffing and whining beside him with eagerness to share their master's knowledge as they had already shared his wonderment. Yet that which struck the shepherd stiff and astonished as he looked down from the rugged side of Bennangour was but little apparently to be astonished at—chiefly indeed the gloaming, dusking down more grimly over the cottage-fringed shores of the bay of Gower, and a darkly straining silhouette of horses and ploughmen on a neighbouring ridge, the man stretched over his plough-stilts almost fiercely, like a helmsman over a wheel in stormy weather.'

From the dog's perspective we see how Anton looks down from on high (and he generally holds the moral high ground as well as the physical in this novel): *'it was to a spot far down the slope of Bennangour that the keen grey eyes of their lord were directed. Beyond the village, beyond the kirk and the manse, set on the opposite braeface and backed by the sea as by a pearl-coloured curtain hung across the valley, Anton McMillan saw the dark and solemn towers of Castle Gower, and, strung across them like a fairy necklace, certain bright points which told of lighted chambers and festal cheer.'*

He says: *'Forty year hae I herded Bennangour, clear*

340

day and mirk nicht, but never hae I seen the great Hoose
o' Castle Gower shining as if auld Gregory Glendonwyn
had herded the stars o' heaven into his windows, as Tyke
and Tod there micht drive a wheen silly sheep into a
bucht!'

It's not his religiosity that makes him appeal to me.
It's the very fact that his belief is just a part of who he is,
amongst people for whom religious belief has become
corrupted. Like a light to welcome you home in the
darkness of *'The Banner of Blue,'* Anton MacMillan the
herd is a simple man, a good man, a man of integrity. He
offers a place of refuge to John Glendonwyn when cast
out by his father – despite their religious differences and
without regard to the consequences this might have for
his own tenantship.

We've already seen how easy it was for landowners
to throw off their tenants. And Gregory Glendonwyn is a
man without any integrity: *'He denied his son the use of*
any cottage upon his estates of Gower. He sent Factor
Halliday to warn all who should frequent schismatic
meetings that by so doing they would not only forfeit their
landlord's favour, but in all cases of yearly lease, their
holdings also. A still severer penalty was to befall all who
should entertain, encourage, or support the new
dissenting minister, the only one indeed who had ever
dared to set foot within the virginly Erastian parish of

341

Gower.'

Anton is brave enough to stand up for what he believes in. And gives us an insight into the nature of Cameronians into the bargain. Like bothies, Cameronians have all but disappeared from Galloway:

'It's like the auld Covenants times,' said Anton MacMillan, Cameronian herd upon Bennangour.

'Aye,—but—withoot poother and ball,' retorted another, less favourably impressed with the new system of things. Anton eyed the speaker severely.

'What kens a bletherin' mender o' the laird's flunkies' breeks aboot poother an' ball?' he inquired with bitter irony (the critic being on his way to Castle Gower at that moment for the purpose thus pithily put by Anton), 'Maybes if ye were the laird's son ye micht think that ye were gettin' poother an' ball eneuch, to miss a' that braw lairdship and Castle Gower itsel', to leave ahint ye the heartsome manse an' no hae where to set your fit or lay your heid in a' the pairish that was as guid as your ain— maybe, ye wad think that nocht? Weel, gin ye think sae, come up for yae winter season to Bennangour wi' Auld Anton, and ye will learn different—you and your het guise irons and 'whuppin' the cat' frae ferm-toon to ferm-toon!'

And so Anton takes in John Glendonwyn regardless of the consequences: *'John Glendonwyn went to bide in the herd's house of Anton MacMillan, the*

Cameronian shepherd of Bennangour. And on the following Sabbath day, judge ye with what strange feelings John Glendonwyn arose, and donning his clothes hastily upon him, went out to meditate upon the side of the mountain.

It was still early. The mists went slowly trailing up the great swelling buttresses of the hills, dipping into brackeny corries and bridging with dim white arches the chasms from which came the roar of many waters, as the Black burn threw itself down the linn (in which of old the Hill Folk had oft sequestered themselves).

Far beneath John looked down upon the green fields, the springing cornlands of the valley with the broad Gower Water running through them, and there—on a little eminence, the Kirk of Gower with the white tombs of the dead about it. Farm and cothouse and farm steading lay in that marvellous unbroken Sabbath quiet. The peculiar brooding silence, the hush and awe of that day affected John Glendonwyn keenly. His was the only foot, save those of the black-faced sheep, which that day had trod the great solitudes his eye wandered over, or scattered the morning dew upon these purpling ridges.'

Once again we see the peace and solitude triumph over isolation. *'The Banner of Blue'* certainly works well as an analogy for the state of Scottish religion in the mid 19th century, and it is a cracking romance story too, but as with all Crockett's novels, as reader there are a number of views to pick from the full panorama of the text. My personal favourite is the relationship between Anton MacMillan and his collies.

Crockett often includes dogs in his narrative and Tyke and Tod in *'The Banner of Blue'* are amongst his finest creations. A keen observer of nature and human nature, Crockett is just as keen an observer of man's best friend.

Here he describes the dogs' thought processes: *'And so whistling on his dogs Auld Anton of Bennangour rebuked them for behaviour unbecoming responsible collies on their own hillside, and strode away up over the heather at his invariable pace of three miles and a quarter in the hour, up hill and down dale.*

But when Anton had looked his sheep, taken supper in his lonely herd's house under the solemn lee of Bennanbrack, he indulged in an operation which considerably astonished his observant dogs.

One night in the week the tenor of their life was altered. At five of the clock they were all put out— no mercy or aegrotat allowed—no place under table or beneath beds for any one of them. The yard was their portion while Anton 'cleaned himself up.' He could not be 'tagled wi' messan dowgs gurr-wurrin' aboot his feet' when engaged in such an occupation, the next thing to a

344

religious function. Anton was by no means uncleanly in his person and washed his face (strictly so called) every day more or less. But on Saturday night, he 'cleaned himsel up' —-which was quite another thing. And so experienced collies, well-informed as to the course of events, and careful of their personal dignity, rose as soon as the razor and big strop were produced. It is a favourite practical joke with these bushy-tailed wags to leave a novice sleeping on the hearth (where indeed none but young foolish dogs would lie at any rate, to be trodden on, 'goldered' at, spilt water upon and so forth) and then, voluntarily and timeously expatriating themselves, to sit on their 'hunkers' in the yard to await the event. The sober historian cannot aver as matter of fact that they laughed, but that they smiled seems indubitable.

Then from within would come a sharp short word, a rush, a bumping of foolish flesh in too great a hurry to hit the open-half of the outer door, a bunched heap of yelps and tightly in-drawn tail, and (for a moment only visible) the practical end of a large hob-nailed boot.

This was the time when the veterans Tyke and Tod are reported to have lain down and laughed—yes, even rolled over and over till they could laugh no more. But a corruption in the text is supposed since it is a minister of the gospel who makes the assertion in clear script over his own signature. He says he has seen and heard these

345

things.

At any rate on this particular evening the dogs withdrew promptly at the production of the strop and razor with a dim idea that if Clean-up-Saturday-Nights were to occur at such short intervals, life would hardly be worth living upon Bennangour. They must seek another service and a master of more fixed habits as to personal cleanliness.

But though this was not Saturday night Anton 'cleaned up' with more than usual fervour, so that a pink flush like scraped pork began to overspread all his visible flesh, and even appeared to invade the grey tangle of his locks.

For Anton MacMillan, herd on Bennangour, Cameronian and practical Christian had a work on hand which must be done, ere he could rest sound in his bed.

When Anton appeared in the little yard where were his thatched byre and the tiny 'office houses' which his own hands had built out of the granite boulders of Bennangour there in the midst were his collies Tod and Tyke—with Messan the novice aforesaid, now grown wiser and vacuating the hearth of his own proper initiative without application of the force majeure.

Is he going to the kirk or is he not going to the kirk? Tyke and Tod cocked their wise heads and thought. You can easily see a good collie think. No professor does it

346

more obviously when asked a question in class. He has no Bible, for there is no hump in his tail coat pocket. So much against. On the other hand—he has taken his red handkerchief out of his Sabbath hat and wiped his brow. That means Kirk all the world over. In a moment more they would know, and in this way. There is a little gate where, on Sundays, he always turns round and shakes his stick at them. This means that they are not to follow him but to stay and look after the steading of Bennangour faithfully and well during his absence. If he takes no notice, they will be after him in a moment, tumbling over each other and barking, scouring the hillside like the wind for sheer joy of living, erected tails, cocked ears, and playfully snapping jaws—all because it is not yet the precise and playless Sabbath day of their native land.

Wicked dogs! Unnatural collies! Slink back there! It is the Sabbath and after the strictest sort. To your kennels in hay and peatshed! Read 'Early Piety' and 'The Course of Time' with vague hopes that they will do you good! Sleep and wait. For this night of all nights your master has paused at the gate and shaken his stick at you.'

It's time to take our leave of Anton MacMillan. I sense that we've reached the end of our adventure, and have come full circle, returning home with Crockett at the end of the day to the homely hearth of Glenhead after a long day out in the hills with our imaginations.

347

What better way for Crockett to leave us than with a final description of the pleasure of coming home to Glenhead at the end of the day: *'As soon as we leave the ridge above, it is downhill steeply all the way till we come to hospitable Glenhead, where by the burn the warm-hearted master is working quietly among the sheaves...'*

'... It is dusking into dark as we master the final slope, and to the barking of dogs, and the cheerful voices of kindly folk, we overpass the last hill dyke, and enter the sheltering homestead of Glenhead, which looks so charmingly out over its little crofts down to the precipice-circled depths of Loch Trool.'

So much of what we have seen has to remain in our imagination. But surely we can agree with Crockett that: *'It does one good in the turmoil of the world to think that there are kind souls living so quietly and happily thus remote from the world, with the Merrick and the Dungeon lifting their heads up into the clouds above them, and over all Loch Enoch looking up to God, with a face sternly sweet, only less lonely than Himself.'*

A warm hearth, good company, and the friendly barking of dogs. What more is there to wish for at the end of a long adventure?

CONCLUSION

We have come to the end of our adventures in the Galloway Hills. Some may feel that an obvious high point has been overlooked. Today, if you mention the Galloway Hills most people will instantly think of The Merrick. After all, The Merrick is the highest point in Galloway, probably the best known and certainly the most frequently climbed by the modern adventurer and indeed to our eyes it might be said to dominate the Galloway hills. And yet, Merrick doesn't seem to feature in Crockett's fiction that prominently. Why might this be so?

MERRICK

'Giant Merrick on one side, the weird Dungeon on the other, and beyond only the grey wilderness stretching mysteriously out into the twilight of the north.'

For Crockett, biggest is not always best. Most important is not always most interesting. He is the champion of the ordinary after all. And indeed Crockett doesn't ignore The Merrick, you'll have found it mentioned numerous times in our armchair adventures. But he does not privilege it. Crockett bows down in front of no man and no thing, not even the Merrick. It is never the prize, never the goal and when he does include it in his narrative it usually sits as the backdrop to the real action.

In *'Raiderland,'* he writes: *'The Merrick soars away above in two great precipices, whereon Thomas Grierson, writing in 1846, tells us that he found marks showing that the Ordnance surveyors had occupied their hours of leisure in hurling great boulders down into the loch. There were fewer sheep on the Merrick side in those days, or else the tenant of that farm might with reason have objected. It seems, however, something of a jest to suppose that this heathery desolation is really a farm, for the possession of which actual money is paid. Yet our guide tells of an old shepherd, many a year the herd of the Merrick, who, when removed by his master to the care of an easier and lower hill, grew positively homesick for the stern majesty of the monarch of South Country mountains, and related tales of the Brocken spectres he had often seen when the sun was at his back and the great chasm of Enoch lay beneath him swimming with mist.'*

Our other guides give much more prominence to The Merrick than Crockett does. McBain announces that *'The Merrick is the monarch of the Southern Highlands, though it does not conspicuously lord it over its neighbours.'* And if you want to know more about Merrick itself, I recommend reading his guide *'The Merrick and the Neighbouring Hills.'*

McCormick also starts his Galloway guide with a chapter on The Merrick entitled *'The Merrick and how best to climb it.'* I suggest that we of the armchair adventure have little need of such detail, but it has its value and charm. More recently Dane Love's *'Galloway Highlands'* is peppered through with references to the Merrick and he states: *'the view from the Merrick is one of the finest in Scotland.'* I am not in a position to confirm or deny this – for my adventures I am happy to rely on Crockett to feed my eyes and my imagination with the best views in Galloway.

Because while all the fact based guides describe Merrick as majestic, like Crockett, my interest is in the ordinary, the natural and the overlooked. One of the strongest weapons in Crockett's literary armoury is the way he sites heroism in the ordinary man or woman. And he even makes heroism an ordinary thing. He puts his ordinary heroes (there's no such thing as a small or minor character in Crockett) in the foreground while the rich and the powerful (including monarchs) have to stand in the background. It's a deliberate statement and I like to think that there's a parallel in the way Merrick stands in the background of his fiction.

For Crockett, respect has to be earned and beauty is to be found as plainly in the bog-myrtle and the winter snow as anywhere else. That, at least, is my explanation as to why The Merrick has not been a real part of our adventures in the Galloway Hills. The Merrick has had attention enough elsewhere. We have taken paths less travelled, routes less known. And had some very good adventures out of it too.

For Crockett, the Merrick is often seen as no more than a stage on a journey, and most often seen in the context of Crockett's beloved Loch Enoch. From there he gives it its place: *'Beyond to the west, the massive buttresses of the Merrick.'*

He next contextualises it as part of a panorama encompassing the entirety of what was in his day known as the Dungeon of Buchan: *'The Merrick begins to tower above us with its solemn head as we thread our way upward towards the plateau on which Loch Enoch lies. We are so high now that we can see backward over the whole region of Trool and the Loch Valley basin. Behind us, on the extreme south, connected with the ridge of the Merrick, is Buchan Hill, the farmhouse of which lies low down by the side of Loch Trool. Across a wilderness of tangled ridge-boulder and morass is the Long Hill of the Dungeon, depressed to the south into the 'Wolf's Slock'* —or throat. *Now our Loch Enoch fortress is almost stormed. Step by step we have been rising above the rugged desolations of the spurs of the Merrick.'*

352

As usual, we are left in no doubt that for Crockett Loch Enoch is the ultimate prize. But even about Enoch, he can be a humorous realist. He observes: *'Now at last the sun is dipping beyond the Merrick, and all the valley to the south, or rather the maze of valleys, grow dim in the shadow. Loch Enoch has turned from gleaming pearl to dusky lead, or, more accurately still, to the dull shimmer that one may see on so unpoetical a thing as cooling gravy. So great are the straits of comparison to which the conscientious artist in words is driven in the description of scenery.'*

It is surely proof that Crockett takes nothing, not the most magical of places, or indeed himself, too seriously. Who else would describe such a wonder as 'cooling gravy,' frequently as that most magical of places is seen in quite a different light.

Merrick also sits in the background of Mullwharchar, the Hill of the Star and the 'Aughty' of the Star as described in *'The Raiders'* by Patrick Heron: *'But this is what I saw, as clearly as the light permitted—a huge, conical hill in front, the Hill of the Star, glimmering snow-sprinkled, as it rose above the desolations of Loch Enoch and the depths of Buchan's Dungeon, To the right the great steeps of the Merrick, bounding upward to heaven like the lowest steps of Jacob's ladder. Loch Enoch beneath, very black, set in a grey whiteness of sparse*

353

snow and sheeted granite. Then I saw in the midst of all the Island of Outlaws, and on it, methought, a glimmering light...' he continues '... the air was chill and damp, but gusts of warmish wind blew at times, and in the south there was a luminous brightness. Just before I entered the cave I looked over the hip of the Merrick, and there, through a cleft of a cloud, I saw the stars and the flickering brightness of the northern lights. They shone with a strange green that I had never seen before.'

Crockett offers other perspectives on Merrick too. In 'The Dark o' the Moon,' Marion Tamson (the grown up version of the young girl abducted to the House of Craignairny) sits off Isle Rathan: 'she leaned a moment on her oars letting the water drip from the blades. She watched the distant blue mountains very faint on the horizon. There was the Merrick, yonder more tenderly blue, soft-bosomed Cairnsmuir, and though she could not see it for the lowering mass of the Black Craig of Dee, somewhere to the right lay the Dungeon of Buchan, of which she was thinking.'

She may be looking at the Merrick but she is thinking of the Dungeon of Buchan.

Far from being overlooked, the Merrick is mentioned in many of Crockett's stories. It is just never the hero of them. From time to time it plays the part of the villain however. In 'Mad Sir Uchtred,' the Merrick is

354

described as a place best avoided: *'This is the true story of the first vision that Sir Uchtred saw upon Clashdaan.*

Again the same night the madness came on Sir Uchtred and he fled along the shaggy tops of the lonely hills, till on the bare scalp of the Merrick, close under the lift with all the other mountains crouched and dwarfed beneath him, he had a vision. He saw himself like Lucifer, Star of the Morning, flash out of the blackness between the tingling points of light, for a moment curve in trailing fire across the firmament, and plunge into the lake of eternal fire in which burn for ever all the sins and despairs of the universe.

Sir Uchtred sprang to his feet, and there, pinnacled on Merrick, he raised his hands to heaven and cried out in a terrible voice which only God heard:

'A fallen star! a fallen star!'

And this was the second vision of Mad Sir Uchtred of the Hills'.

It is perhaps not surprising that Crockett's other 'man of the hills,' Silver Sand seems to 'know' the Merrick best: *'Silver Sand piloted his company into the heart of the wilderness, till he came to the bottom of the great precipice which is called the Spear of the Merrick. Then he led them behind a fallen rock where was a den of clean-laid sand and heather, wholly cleared of boulders. The hanging brows of the rock sheltered it.'*

Sir Andrew Agnew notes: *'If I am driven from the Gled's Nest, I must even go farther afield—perhaps up into your Faa's shelter among the hills at the back of the Merrick. That would be a strange turn-about of fortune — that the Sheriff should bide and hide with broken men and outlaw gipsies! Eh, man, what think ye o' that?'*

What indeed? Far from the tourist destination it is today, in times past the Merrick, along with the whole of the Galloway Hills, was seen as the province of gypsies and outcasts. And far from offering the best view in the region as we are told today, Crockett's Merrick generally illustrates harshness, especially in comparison to the beauty of Enoch.

The Merrick, however, is the place in which most frequently in Crockett's stories, the sun sets. So it's appropriate our adventures should end here too: *'But we must turn homeward. The Merrick itself is dusking.'*

THE HERD OF THE MERRICK

'Any cuif can write a history book, but it takes a man to herd the Merrick.'

Crockett writes beautifully and powerfully about nature and the natural world. But it is when he adds character that the magic really happens. And while the Merrick itself doesn't get much of a look in, Crockett's respect for herds perhaps meets its zenith when describing the men who herd the Merrick. But even as he respects them, he does not revere them unnecessarily. Crockett is never averse to poking fun at his characters (or indeed himself.)

'The Herd of the Merrick' is a case in point. The story is to be found in *'The Bloom o' the Heather.'* Here Crockett gives a herd his head. The herd in question, old Willie Mabie, is a man who may be respected, but is also a figure of fun. Note Crockett's description of the Merrick itself: *'Dowgs—dowgs!' said old Willie Mabie, the herd of the Merrick (which is a void mountain, the crown of Galloway and the highest south of the Grampians on the mainland of Scotland), 'dowgs! There is never a collie nowadays worth his brose and the bacon-rind he steals at the kitchen 'backet.' But in my young days there were dowgs wiser than mony humans. Eh, lad, but the tales I could tell ye. And true tales— ye needna look!'*

357

Throughout what might best be described as a 'shaggy dog' story, Willie Mabie tells of the struggles and trials of his youth, particularly as relates to love. On the way he speaks of his particular struggle with the demon drink: *'The minister strove hard to persuade me that the Deil was in my ain heart, and that I must sign and be a sober man from that day. And a sober man I have been. Only a sober man can herd the Merrick for near on to fifty year without a day off!'*

And now we are really at the end. It seems only fitting therefore, to give the last word to Crockett's last hero. First and last, Silver Sand, more than any other character, is bound most tightly to his creator. As he offers us a final word, I cannot help but see Crockett beside him, merging his own thoughts with those of his character. Living and dreaming together. I may simply have been taken in by the charms of a great romancer. I hope in some small way, you have too. Because then we will have shared a truly great adventure out in the Galloway Hills. And I too, can wish for nothing better: *'He smiled his patient smile—not an old man's smile, though he must have been nigh on to seventy. Silver Sand did not look any particular age. One might have guessed him anywhere between forty-five and sixty, for no look or action suggested old age.*

'Ah!' he answered, 'I was born on the hills. I shall die, as I hope, on the hills. The clean-strae death of the house-dweller is not for Silver Sand.''

FURTHER READING

The Guides who came with us and how to find them:

C.H.Dick: *'Highways & Byways in Galloway & Carrick,'* 1916 Special Memorial edition published G.C.Book Publishers Ltd, 2001 www.gcbooks.co.uk

Paddy Dillon: *'Walking the Galloway Hills'* Cicerone Press 1995 http://www.paddydillon.co.uk/guidebook/walking-the-galloway-hills/

Dan Kennedy: *'Galloway Memories,'* The Ayrshire Post 1967; *'Tales of the Galloway Hills,'* The Ayrshire Post 1972. There are numerous editions and you can track him down via abebooks, amazon or other second hand booksellers

Dane Love: *'The Galloway Highlands,'* Carn Publishing, 2014. www.dane-love.co.uk

J.McBain: *'The Merrick and the Neighbouring Hills,'* 1929 Reprinted Jackson and Sproat Publishing 1980. Best tracked down via second hand and online book retailers Abebooks, Amazon, Book Despository etc.

A.McCormick: *'Galloway: The Spell of its Hills and Glens,'* 1932. Various editions (1947 edition has map and illustrations). Best tracked down via second hand and online book retailers.

The books we took with us:

(All available as The Galloway Collection in ebook and paperback formats)

'The Raiders,' GC Volume 7 (1894)

'The Dark o' the Moon,' GC Volume 8 (1902)

'Silver Sand,' GC Volume 9 (1914)

'Rose of the Wilderness,' GC Volume 28 (1909)

'Men of the Moss Hags,' GC Volume 3 (1895)

'Mad Sir Uchtred of the Hills,' GC Volume 30 (1894)

'The Banner of Blue,' GC Volume 12 (1903)

'Raiderland,' GC Volume 32 (1904)

Stories: 'The Tutor of Curleywee,' from *'The Stickit Minister,'* GC Volume 13 (1893)

'The Last Smuggler' and 'The Herd of the Merrick' from *'The Bloom o' the Heather,'* GC Volume 31 (1908)

Crockett biographies:

M.McL Harper: *'Crockett and Grey Galloway,'* Hodder & Stoughton, 1908

I.M.Donaldson *'The Life and Work of Samuel Rutherford Crockett'* AUP, 1989

Both available through second hand booksellers online. New editions forthcoming from Ayton Publishing Ltd.

People and places who offered helpful direction:

Websites

http://www.walkscotland.plus.com/ Duncan Devlin's site has good reports of walks in Galloway and pictures galore.

http://www.walkhighlands.co.uk/ Doesn't seem the obvious place, but I made some good friends with local knowledge of the Galloway Hills here who were happy to share stories and pictures

http://www.gallowaymrt.org.uk/ A good place to look for things to remember if you're about to hit the hills for real.

http://www.newtonstewartwalkfest.co.uk/ Run a festival of walks every year and lots of information. Thanks especially to Joan Mitchell for hosting the launch of this book at the 2015 festival.

https://www.google.co.uk/maps/ if you want to get right into the action from every angle on your computer.

Maps:

OS LandRanger 77

OS Explorer Maps 318,319 Galloway Forest Park (North and South)

Samuel Rutherford Crockett

Born in Balmaghie on September 24th 1859, Samuel Crocket was the illegitimate son of dairy maid Annie Crocket. He was brought up on the farm of Little Duchrae by his strict Cameronian maternal grandparents, and the family moved to Castle Douglas in 1867. He gained a Galloway bursary to Edinburgh University in 1876. His writing career began as a way to support himself through his studies. He had articles and short stories/sketches published in a wide range of contemporary magazines. He travelled abroad extensively and became a Free Church minister in 1886. He married Ruth Milner in 1887 and they had four children. His writing became successful following the publication in 1893 of *'The Stickit Minister'* and he gave up the ministry to concentrate on his writing in 1895. His popular, episodic and serialised style of writing ensured him bestseller status in his day and despite prolonged ill health he published on average two novels a year throughout his long career. He died on April 16th 1914 in France.

Cally Phillips

Brought up and educated in Dundee and Edinburgh, Cally is a graduate of St Andrews University and worked professionally as a screenwriter and playwright for twenty years before shifting focus towards creative advocacy. Cally was first introduced to the work of S.R.Crockett when she moved to Galloway in 1995, where she was Writer in Residence for three years (2002-2004). Over the past decade she has set up and run a variety of innovative creative projects. She now lives in North East Scotland where, as well as being series editor for Ayton Publishing, she also reviews, edits and writes fiction and non fiction. In 2014 she founded The Galloway Raiders.

Other forthcoming books in this series:

Discovering Crockett's Galloway (Volume 2)
Island and Inland Adventures (2015)
Discovering Crockett's Galloway (Volume 3)
Towns and Villages (due 2016)
Discovering Crockett's Edinburgh (due 2016)
Discovering Crockett's London (due 2017)
Discovering Crockett's Europe (due 2017)

Crockett's books available from Ayton Publishing Ltd as books and ebooks at www.aytonpublishing.co.uk and from the Galloway Raiders online store at www.gallowayraiders.co.uk

If you want more history, adventure and romance in your life, why not join The Galloway Raiders. It's the hub for all things S.R.Crockett and is free to join. www.gallowayraiders.co.uk

Republished to commemorate the 100th Anniversary of the Death of S.R.Crockett on April 16th 1914 and available in paperback and ebook format, The Collection is listed below with dates of first novel publication.

Volume 1 The Black Douglas (1899)
Volume 2 Maid Margaret (1905)
Volume 3 Men of the Moss Hags (1895)
Volume 4 Lochinvar (1897)
Volume 5 The Standard Bearer (1898)
Volume 6 The Cherry Ribband (1905)
Volume 7 The Raiders (1894)
Volume 8 The Dark o' the Moon (1902)
Volume 9 Silver Sand (1914)
Volume 10 The Moss Troopers (1912)
Volume 11 The Smugglers (1911)
Volume 12 The Banner of Blue (1903)
Volume 13 The Stickit Minister (1893)
Volume 14 Lilac Sunbonnet (1894)
Volume 15 Bog Myrtle (1895)
Volume 16 A Galloway Herd (1895)
Volume 17 Lad's Loves (1897)
Volume 18 The Stickit Ministers Wooing (1900)
Volume 19 Love Idylls (1901)
Volume 20 Cleg Kelly (1896)
Volume 21 Kid McGhie (1906)
Volume 22 Kit Kennedy (1899)
Volume 23 Strong Mac (1904)
Volume 24 The Dew of Their Youth (1909)
Volume 25 Cinderella (1901)
Volume 26 The Loves of Miss Anne (1904)
Volume 27 Vida (1907)
Volume 28 Rose of the Wilderness (1909)
Volume 29 Sandy's Love (1913)
Volume 30 Mad Sir Uchtred of the Hills (1894)
           And The Play Actress (1894)
Volume 31 The Bloom o' the Heather (1908)
Volume 32 Raiderland (1904)